Sailor's Mail
S.W.A.K.

© 2014 Marsha Norris Knudsen
All rights reserved. No part of this book may be reproduced or transmitted in any form or by any means, electronic or mechanical or by any information or storage and retrieval system without permission in writing from the author or publisher.

Cover photographs from the Norris family archives:
Ruth Yancey Norris 1943, Seaman Homer Norris

ISBN 978-1-936688-68-5

Published by Compass Flower Press
an imprint of AKA-Publishing

Sailor's Mail
S.W.A.K.

A World War II Love Story

Marsha Norris Knudsen

Dedication

This book is dedicated as a loving remembrance
to the two best parents a girl ever had.
As long as we remember, they're never really gone.

Acknowledgments

Thank You...

To my wonderful husband, Ron, for his encouragement and patience while I crawled into my woman cave to write and revise, and revise some more. He makes me happy—every day.

To my memoir writing group who listened while I honed my writing skills. They convinced me that this story spoke to people of many age groups, not just the World War II generation. Without their initial interest there would be no book.

To Pat Holt who shared the journey and helped me believe I could write a book. Her computer expertise made a dramatic difference in the photographs.

To my son-in-law, Randy who enthusiastically followed my progress and continued to remind me that he wanted a signed copy. Randy, the first signed copy is yours.

To friends who read book drafts and offered editing suggestions.

To Yola who gave me permission to exercise my narrative license. Her editorial expertise and creative insights were invaluable.

To my brother, Howard, who trusted me to share our family history with the world. I am strengthened by his unconditional love. He always has my back.

Finally, I would like to pay tribute to my parents who taught me life lessons that shaped the woman I am today. They encouraged me to always give my best effort, and believe anything is possible.

Table of Contents

Dedication	(i)
Acknowledgments	(iii)
Table of Contents	(iv)
Editing Notes	(vii)
A Note to Set the Record Straight	(ix)
Introduction	(xi)

Part 1: Love and War

First Came Love	1
Then Came Marriage	5
Then Came War	7
I'll Be Seeing You	11

Part 2: Boot Camp

The Middle of Nowhere	19
30,000 Sailors!	24
On the Home Front	27
Smile, Boys, Smile	29
Service School	32
Making Money	38
Mail Call	40
First Liberty	43
A Lovely Sailor's Wife	46
The Navy Way	49
Graduation	58

Part 3: Ship's Company

Base Electrician	63
A Place for Ruth to Stay	68
Wanted!!! A Wife AT Once.	73
Summer in Sandpoint	76
Furlough	82

Part 4: Preparing for Sea Duty

Ridin' the Rails	87
Sun Shiny California	90
ACORN 16	94
Riding the Emotional Roller Coaster	98
Orders to Ship Out	104

Part 5: Anchors Aweigh

Remember Pearl Harbor	109
Operation Galvanic	122

Part 6: Journey Into War

The SS *Robin Wentley*	127
Operation Boxcloth	130

Part 7: Apamama

(DECEMBER) Norris Code	137
(JANUARY) Un-Happy New Year	147
(FEBRUARY) Rear Base	159
(MARCH) Pecking Order	164
(APRIL) At Ease	171
(MAY) Native Friends	176
(JUNE) Island Adventures	184
(JULY) Sick	190
(AUGUST) Tropical Heat Wave	195
(SEPTEMBER) Settling Debts	201
(OCTOBER) Goodbyes	207

Part 8: Island Hopping

Kwajalein	213
Guam	218
Captain's Mast	224
Boys From Home	228
The Countdown	233
The Battle For Iwo Jima	239
A Little Misfortune	245
Post Script—Iwo Jima	247

Part 9: Homeward Bound

Last Letters	251
Letters From Mom and Dad Norris	254
Letters From Ruth	258
Western Union [STOP]	261
Furlough	266

Part 10: Stateside Duty

Atlantic Adventures	271
New Orders!	277
Demobilization	280

Part 11: Home, Sweet Home

Coming Home	287
The Final Chapter	290

Epilogue

Everyday Heroes	295
Endnotes	296
Works Cited	300
About The Author	303

Editing Notes

In order to retain as much authenticity as possible, great care was taken to allow Homer and Ruth to speak for themselves. Any editorial changes are respectfully faithful to the spirit of their letters and diaries.

Homer's letters home were written to communicate his thoughts and feelings to his wife and parents. Much of his writing was stream-of-consciousness with little attention to detail. These letters appear as written—with spelling, punctuation, and grammatical mistakes to suggest the circumstances under which they were written. Some letters were penned while riding on a train or hunkered down in a fox hole with writing paper propped on his knee.

Homer tried to conserve paper, so he seldom broke for paragraphs. Extra spacing and paragraph indentations have been adjusted for the reader's convenience and to indicate breaks in flow. Most letters included the date and time of day they were written, but where letters have been combined for brevity, a few dates have been added for consistency. Every effort was made to keep a low editorial profile, so only a few bracketed notes have been included for clarity.

In 1942 World War II reached the heartland of the United States, and became very personal to Homer and Ruth's families in Ralls County, Missouri, near the small rural town of Perry. The State of Missouri is located in the middle of the United States. Ralls County is located in northeast Missouri, and the town of Perry is in the southwest corner of Ralls County.

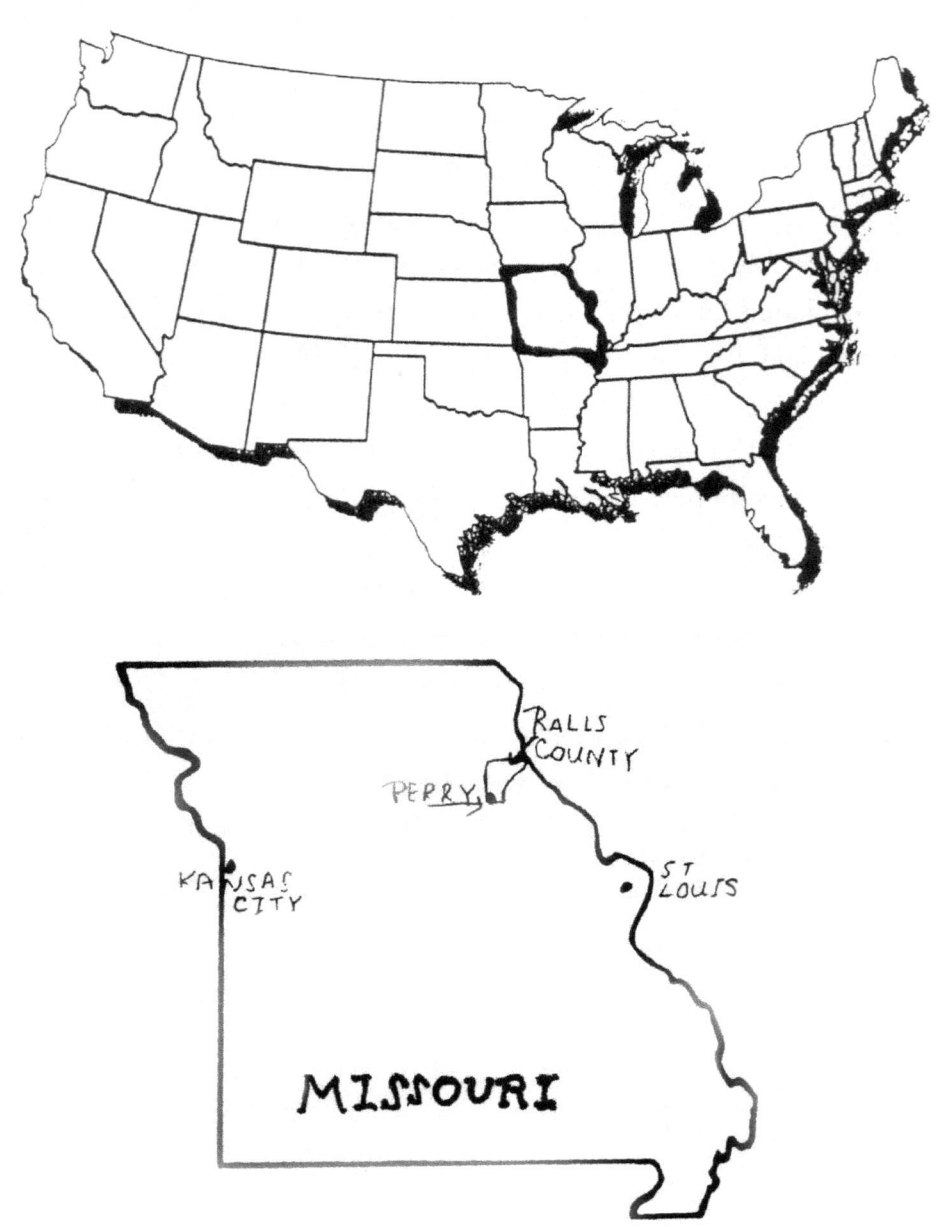

A Note to Set the Record Straight

I apologize to the 350,000 women who served in the United States Armed Forces during World War II. This book makes no mention of their contribution to the war effort because Homer did not talk about them in his letters. Men and women were mostly segregated during their military training and deployment. Women had their own branches of services. The following figures are for women serving with the American military during World War II:

Army - 140,000
Navy - 100,000
Marines - 23,000
Coast Guard - 13,000
Air Force - 1,000
Army and Navy Nurse Corps - 74,000[1]

Women were not permitted to participate in armed conflict; however they served in combat zones, on ships, and participated in dangerous work in direct support of military efforts. Some worked as part of the medical corps, others took traditional men's jobs in non-combat work, to free more men for combat.

In order to relate Homer's military experience the way he told it, women have been left out of this story. To set the record straight it must be noted that our victories in World War II were only possible because of a total war effort by men and women who served our country in the military and in civilian roles.

Introduction

I never thought of my parents as extraordinary, but they were. My father never thought of himself as a hero, but he was. He was a hero because he did the right thing. During World War II when the country called for men to serve, he volunteered for the Navy. My father didn't want to leave his wife and go to war, but he did. My mother didn't want to move into a tiny apartment and work at a store, but she did. I never realized how much my parents sacrificed during the war, but they did.

For many years I took my father's military service for granted, probably because he took it for granted. Like many veterans he never spoke of the war. Then one year when I was searching for Christmas decorations I ran across a zippered bag that hung in the attic. Inside was my father's Navy uniform and a woman's dress.

"Mother, is this your dress?" I asked as I held up a petite navy blue dress with a delicate white ruffled collar.

"Well yes, dear," she explained matter-of-factly, "that's my wedding dress." I couldn't believe I had never before seen my mother's wedding dress.

That was the day I realized it was time to let my eighty-year-old parents reminisce while I listened. They talked about their courtship and wedding day. They spoke of using ration coupons and riding trains.

Homer's Navy uniform   Ruth's wedding dress

When I asked about the war, Mother went to her cedar chest and pulled out Daddy's Navy Service Record Book.

She handed it to me without further explanation, because she never spoke of the war either. As far as my parents were concerned, World War II was an awful time of their lives and when it was over they put it behind them and never looked back.

A few years later my parents passed from this earthly life and I became the keeper of their war-time memories when an old trunk came into my possession.

For over fifty years their steamer trunk had been stored in the attic. Mother always said it contained stuff from the war. Over the years I had peeked inside, but never really looked at the contents—until that day.

The drawers in the trunk were filled with memorabilia from the 1940's, photograph albums, diaries, scrapbooks, train tickets, newspaper clippings, ration books, and old letters. Two canvas bags with "Homer L. Norris" stamped on them hung on one side.

One box attracted my attention. The lid was covered with quilted satin, aqua blue in color. The box sides were wrapped in wallpaper, brightly colored, in a pattern of red roses.

Steamer trunk of memories

I opened the box to reveal a divided one-inch deep tray. The sections held various trinkets: a ring and a gold locket, a little black book, a red military patch, a pocket knife, seashell necklace, a little bow and some note cards.

Under the tray were dozens of old letters. One envelope was postmarked U.S. Navy March 15, 1943, and had the words "Sealed for Victory" neatly printed on the flap.

The letter inside was written on plain stationery in the unmistakable handwriting of my father.

Trunk contents

Saturday night
March 13 Six thirty

My Darling

I received your package of candy about thirty minutes ago   sure is good, couldn't be better   I'm not passing it around like I did the cake   it didn't last five minutes but this is going to last longer. I just received three pictures, I'm sending two of them home and sending a couple of jokes, too.

I have got to study so may not get to write for a day or two   we have a test over 13 chapters in our blue jackets' manual Friday.

We only had one hour off all day and we filled out pay receipts then. This morning we washed our sea bags   they are about the size of a timothy seed sack and water proofed. There has been about 500 new men came in this camp in the last two days. So I expect they will get us out just as quick as they can.

An admiral was here inspecting today so everything had to be in ship shape, and then he never came in our barracks so we had to do all the cleaning for nothing. *Ha Ha*

I think we go to the lake tomorrow to learn how to row boats the Navy way. There are three ways to do anything   right way, wrong way, and the Navy way.

I have got to wash clothes tonight so I think I'll write Mother & Dad a few lines now   its a good time. Darling if I don't write to you, you know I don't have time because I love to write to my wife, know fooling. I'll have to close now.

Lots of love & kisses
OXXOXOXOXOXOOOXOXOXOXXOXXOXO
I love you, I love you, I love you, I love you, I LOVE you

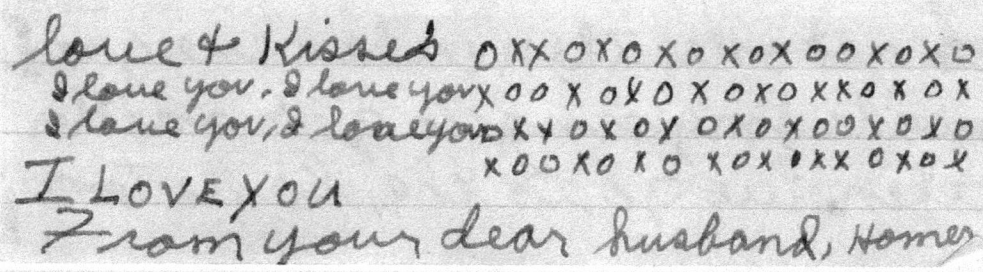

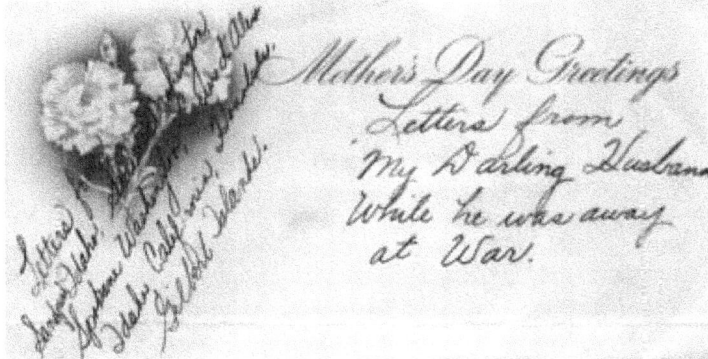

In the bottom of the letter box was a piece of USO stationery with a note written by my Mother. It read, "Letters from My Darling Husband, while he was away at War."

Suddenly I realized that these were my father's **letters home!**

I will be forever grateful that Mother saved all the war memorabilia. It has little monetary value. However, to me it is priceless because it introduced me to my mother and father when they were in their twenties—and I was only a twinkle in their eyes. The sense of humor and strong work ethic I admired in my parents were also present in this young sailor and his newlywed wife.

It has taken me as long to write this book as it took the Allies to win the war. However, I was in no hurry to finish because while I compiled page after page I also grieved for my parents. Every time I held one of Daddy's letters or Mother's diary it was like having a visit from them.

My parents were changed by the war, and by reliving their experience I, too, am forever changed. Their trunk of memories allowed us to have one more glorious adventure together. By sharing their memories I have fallen in love with my parents all over again.

Marsha Norris Knudsen,
Keeper of Memories

Part 1: Love and War

First Came Love

"<u>May 25, 1941</u> Homer is simply wild about me. I imagine we will be married right away. We look forward to seeing each other all the time."
—Diary entry by Ruth Yancey (age 18)

Ruth, age 16

Homer, age 19

Once upon a time in Ralls County, Missouri "a most attractive and charming young lady" named Ruth Marie Yancey met Homer Lee Norris, "an industrious and likeable young man."[2]

The year was 1936 and Homer was a sophomore and Ruth a freshman at the Perry High School. She played saxophone in the school band and ran track; he raised prize winning hogs in vocational agriculture classes.

It may not have been love at first sight, but for the next five years Ruth and Homer were either happily together or using some poor unsuspecting dupe to make the other one jealous.

Homer graduated from high school at the age of nineteen and that same month he asked Ruth to be his wife. They planned to be married once she was out of high school.

After graduation Homer continued to live at home to help his parents on the farm. He got a job at the Farber Brick Plant and took electrician's classes at night.

Dating in high school (1938)

Ruth dressed for work (1940)

The next year Ruth graduated and received a scholarship to Gem City Business College in Quincy. But Quincy was too far away from Homer, so she gave up her scholarship and became a clerk at the local variety store. Her starting salary was $6.50 every two weeks. It wasn't much income, but they were miserly with their money—saving to get married and set up housekeeping.

While she worked at the variety store Ruth continued to live at home with her parents. However, Dad Yancey (Ruth's father) wanted her to go to college and was not happy that Ruth and Homer were talking about marriage. Sometimes Dad Yancey drank too much and was short-tempered with Ruth and her mother. Living at home was often tense, but when Ruth was with Homer—life was good. However, their lives would soon be affected by overseas political events.

Since 1939 war had raged in Europe. First Germany was at war with France, and then the Soviet Union invaded Poland and Finland.

The American people were adamantly opposed to going to war, and the United States still maintained a position of neutrality when Congress established the first peacetime military draft in U.S. history. The Selective Service set up local draft boards in each county and sent postcard notices to report for active duty. During the next five years over fifty million registered, including Homer Norris.

News of the draft spread quickly, and everyone took notice. Eighteen-year-old Ruth Marie wrote in her diary on September 18, 1940: *"The Draft Bill passed. Boys from 21-35 have to go to camps."* The camps Ruth referred to were boot camps—the first stage of military training.

When President Franklin D. Roosevelt ran for re-election in 1940 he promised that American boys would not be sent into any foreign wars. The nation hoped for peace, but prepared for war. It was a tense time for everyone.

Homer and Ruth used Christmas as an excuse to forget about the war, at least for awhile. Ruth's diary mentions that for Christmas Homer gave her a beautiful cedar chest—the best he could buy. She gave him a leather jacket.

Ruth's Diary

Going to President's Dance (1941)

By January of 1941 war continued to engulf more of Europe, but Homer and Ruth were so much in love all they thought about was each other.

Ruth's diary tells their love story:

1941 Jan 5 Homer and I went to the show and drank a soda after the show.

Jan 8 Homer came in town   we played some cards and we won. We parked down by the bridge.

Jan 22 I went out to Homer's house for oyster supper. We had a good time.

Jan 30 Homer and I went to the President dance.

Feb 5 Homer and I went to see a Golden Glove boxing match. Our tickets cost 84 cents apiece. It was my first boxing match. I really had a swell time.

Feb 14 Homer gave me a box of candy for Valentines.

Apr 9 Homer and I are going down home tonight to make ice cream.

May 11 We were driving by Nolan's filling station and Homer asked if I would wear his diamond. I told him I would.

May 14 Homer's birthday was today. He was 21. I gave him a little gold knife with initials on it. $1.25. He kissed me when I gave it to him. I went out to his house for supper.

May 23 Homer stopped by the store, and brought the ring sizes in for me to try. Size 6

May 25 Homer is simply wild about me. I imagine we will be married right away. We look forward to seeing each other all the time.

June 23 This was the most important birthday in my life. I got my diamond ring!

Homer's pocket knife

<u>July 10</u> Mother and I went to Hannibal after my wedding dress.

<u>July 12</u> Homer and I went to town and bought his wedding suit, also our kitchen and living room furniture. We had so much fun. . . . I will never forget when we bought our furniture

<u>July 15</u> Homer and I rented an apartment in town from Mrs. Cole.

<u>July 18</u> Mr & Mrs Norris gave us our silverware named 'First Love.'

<u>July 21</u> The beauty pageant man asked me to enter the pageant.

<u>July 27</u> Mother and I got my gold formal out. . . . We girls practiced down at the Strand. We are suppose to 'put on the dog.'

<u>July 30</u> I won the title of 'Miss Perry' tonight at the Strand theater. Received a bouquet of white lilies.

<u>Aug 2</u> Worked until late. Homer took me home and I couldn't realize that tomorrow was to be my wedding day. I couldn't sleep *Ha Ha*

<u>Aug 3</u>

Ruth's Beauty Pageant Formal

1941 "My Wedding Day" Married 9:45 o'clock at Rev. John Goldenie Went to the Ozarks on our wedding trip. Stopped at Mary's. Homer went to have a party

Then Came Marriage

<u>Aug 4, 1941</u> Homer said, 'I love you my wife.' I like the sound of that."
—Ruth's diary entry

On August 7, 1941 the following article appeared on the front page of *The Perry Enterprise* newspaper:

Popular Young Couple Married[3]

Miss Ruth Marie Yancey and Homer Lee Norris, two of Perry's popular young people, were united in marriage by Rev. John W. Golden . . . in his home in Hannibal at 8:45 o'clock Sunday morning, August 3rd.

The bride wore a navy blue dress with white accessories . . . Mrs. Norris is the only daughter of Mr. and Mrs. Claude Yancey. She is a most attractive and charming young lady and just last Wednesday evening was honored by being named Miss Perry in the Merchants Beauty Parade. . . .

Mr. Norris is the only son of Mr. and Mrs. Harry Norris . . . . He assists his father on the farm and is employed at the North American Refractories in Farber. He is an industrious and likeable young man . . . .

After a honeymoon trip to the Ozarks, they will be at home in the Cole apartments in south Perry. *The Enterprise* extends congratulations and best wishes.

Wedding Day, August 3, 1941

Homer and Ruth on Honeymoon

According to Ruth's diary, married life agreed with the newlyweds:

Aug 9 My first week of married life. I am doing fine.

Aug 17 Mr & Mrs Norris ate their first Sunday dinner with us. I didn't realize I could cook so good.

Aug 24 Went to box supper. I got a box of candy for being the most popular young Lady. Homer got a bank for being the strongest man.

Aug 26 Mother and Daddy got me my wedding present a lovely automatic electric iron. It was very nice. Grandma got me everyday dishes.

One month after their wedding, Homer received a postcard from the Selective Service. He was classified as II-A because of his occupational status of farming and deferred from serving until further notice.

For the next several months Homer and Ruth were blissfully happy. Under normal circumstances, their lives probably would have continued along the course they had planned—but 1941 was not a normal year.

On November 28 Ruth's diary mentions that she and Homer went to have their picture taken for Christmas presents. One week later her diary entry says, *"Churchill, prime minister of Great Britian has been to the White House. They are asking for volunteers for the army-navy."*

Christmas photo

Churchill's visit to the white house confirmed that this was indeed a world war, but the United States still hoped the war would stay "over there."

Then Came War

"<u>Sun, Dec 7, 1941</u> JAPAN DECLARED WAR TODAY on Pearl Harbor and on the U.S.A. So now we are in a Bombing War with the Japs or 'saps.'"

—Ruth's diary entry

The U.S. position of neutrality went up in smoke on Sunday morning, December 7, 1941 when 350 Japanese planes attacked Pearl Harbor, Hawaii. The attack killed an estimated 2400 Americans and destroyed 347 planes and 21 ships anchored in the harbor.[4] Within hours Japan, Germany, and Italy declared war on the United States.

The bombs that struck Pearl Harbor sent a shock wave through every home in the United States. The following day the U.S. declared war on Japan and Germany. Homer knew this would eventually concern him, but his exemption was still in effect so he took one day at a time and tried not to think too far into the future.

According to Ruth's diary, they had a wonderful Christmas:

<u>December 24</u> *Homer and I opened our Christmas presents. My goodness I was excited. I got a clothes hamper, 2 dresses, hassock, end table, apron, bedspread, cookie jar, & card table. Homer gave me a utility cabinet.*

The year of 1942 started on a high note for Homer and Ruth. Their dream of starting their own farming operation came true when they rented a small house surrounded by farm land.

Ruth was unexpectedly sad when the time came for her to quit her job at the variety store.

Homer in feed lot (above) and with corn picker (right)

> *January 7, 1942 Time is drawing near for me to quit work. I don't want to quit but we are going to move to the Cox farm. I love Homer and want to quit because of him.*

Later that month Homer and Ruth bought a cultivator, harrow, binder, two Angus cows, paid $95 for a registered jersey cow, and $75 for a horse. They slaughtered hogs, ground sausage, and tagged their sheep.

After giving the old farmhouse a thorough cleaning, February 25, 1942 was moving day. Nothing got damaged and they had sausage and cake for dinner.

It was a cold season for baby lambs and at 4:30 in the morning Homer cut ice for the livestock before he went to work at the brick plant. Ruth painted woodwork, hung wall paper, churned butter and learned to use the cook stove. One day she ironed for four hours and still didn't get done. Keeping busy helped, but some days the war simply could not be ignored. On March 14 Homer had to appear before the local draft board for a hearing. The next week he got another postcard saying that his exemption would continue until September, so he could raise crops to help the war effort. The good news was that he would not be called into active duty for at least six months. The bad news was that with a farming exemption he was required to farm full time; if he also worked at the brick plant he would lose his exemption. So Homer reluctantly quit his job.

According to Ruth's diary, during the next six months the young couple got a true taste of farm life.

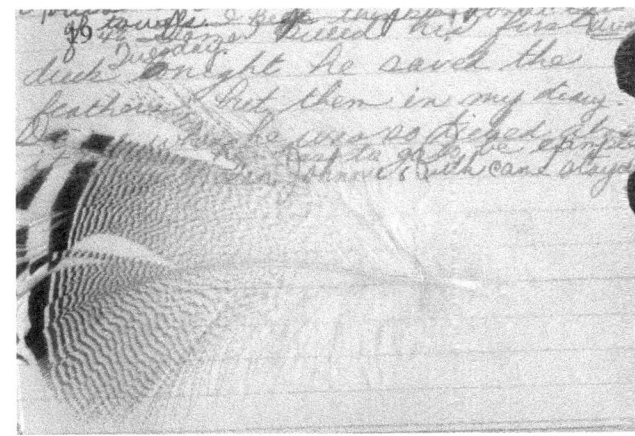

Duck feather in Ruth's diary

> *1942 March 10* Homer went after his oats, 65 cents a bushel... he signed his hog & corn contract... We hitched the young horse up for the first time.
>
> *March 19* Homer ran over an old hen, wonder how long it takes to cook an old hen? ^{Ha} Homer killed his first duck, he saved the feathers and I put them in my diary.
>
> *March 25* Ma & Pa Norris came over to help Homer sow oats. We have a new black calf
>
> *April 4* Made our "First Garden" We had a lot of fun
>
> *April 14* Stayed in the field with Homer all afternoon. We rode the tractor together. I sat on his lap, he sat on mine.^{Ha}
>
> *May 4* Registered for sugar this afternoon

This was the first time Ruth mentioned rationing in her diary.

* * * * *

Before they knew it the summer was over, and so was Homer's exemption. On September 10, 1942, Homer got a postcard notice to appear for a physical examination. On October 17 he received notice that his classification had been upgraded to Class I-A which meant he was available and fit for general military service. Homer immediately made an appeal to the draft board for another farming exemption.

For two months no news was good news. However, the day after Christmas Homer opened his mailbox and saw the dreaded postcard informing him that his appeal had been denied. World War II had just become personal.

Homer receives postcard draft notice from the Selective Service

With the postcard notice in his hand, he looked toward the house and realized the lane that led to their farmhouse wasn't nearly long enough to get his mind around this worst case scenario. Twenty-two year old Homer Norris would give up his dream of farming, and go to war.

I'll Be Seeing You

"We left the Federal Building yesterday morning at 10 A.M. for an unknown destination ... About 80 boys on a car. About fifteen cars to the train."

—Homer's first letter 2/11/43

From the minute Homer received his postcard "invitation to serve"—everything in their lives changed. He and Ruth immediately made plans to sell livestock and machinery and move from their farm.

On December 31 Homer's parents came over and helped write the sale bill. That night Ruth wrote in her diary, *"Made out Sale Bills. Oh that was awful but I didn't break down."*

The original sale bill is in Ruth's scrapbook:

PUBLIC SALE!

Having been called to the army, I will sell at Public Auction at the John Cox farm 8 miles Southeast of Perry, 2 miles West of Spencer Creek church, on gravel road, the following property, on

Monday, January 11, 1943

5 Work Horses
1 bay horse 4-years-old; 1 iron gray horse, 5-years-old; 1 black horse, 6-years-old; 1 iron gray mare 4-years-old; 1 bay mare 12 years old.

5 Head of Cattle
1 Angus cow 4-years-old, heavy springer; 1 Angus cow 6-years-old, calve in January; 1 Angus heifer calf weight 600 lbs; 1 Jersey cow 6-years-old, calf by side, extra good milker.

17 Head of Hogs
1 pure bred Chester White sow, had 2 litters, will farrow March 13; 6 gilts, farrow March 1st to April 1st; 6 shoats weight 125 lbs; 3 fat hogs weight 200 lbs; 1 pure bred Duroc male hog 9 months old. All hogs double treated.

14 Head of Sheep
6 ewes 2-years-old; 8 ewes 4 to 5-years-old, all native.

Farm Implements
1 John Deere disc harrow, 16 blades; 1 Jaynesville disc cultivator; 1 good 6 shovel cultivator; 1 smoothing harrow; 1 Black Hawk corn planter; 1 McCormick Deering binder, 8 ft., in running order; 1 high wheel wagon in good condition; 1 set leather harness and 2 collars; 1 good horn saddle and bridle; 1 Maytag motor and belt.

FEED—500 bushels good yellow corn; 200 bushels Columbia seed oats; 8 bales Alfalfa; 2 tons loose timothy hay; some bundle beans.

100 CHICKENS—12 White Rock year old hens. About 90 White Leghorn pullets.

HOME CURED MEAT—4 sides, 4 shoulders, 2 hams, 5 gallons of new lard.

HOUSEHOLD GOODS—1 Round Oak heating stove, 18 inch good condition; 3 Congoleum rugs 9x12 and some small rugs; 1 washing machine. Small articles too numerous to mention.

TERMS—Cash. SALE TO BEGIN AT 12:30 O'CLOCK

Homer Norris

COL. ED R. CALDWELL, Auct. J MAC FRY, Clerk

On sale day Mom and Dad Norris (Homer's parents) got there at sun up. In spite of twenty degree weather, a good number of buyers arrived and the adding machine tape shows itemized receipts that totaled $2377.65.

The next day Homer and Ruth stored their furniture and gave their dog (Perky) to Homer's parents. Then they waited for the military to decide their future.

The month of January was awful. Homer and Ruth were virtually homeless and spent nights with family. Each day brought uncertainty, dread, and life-changing decisions that must be made—decisions like which branch of the military to join.

There were differing opinions about what Homer should do, but for him the decision was easy. After seeing news reels that showed the big ships destroyed in the attack on Pearl Harbor, Homer decided that if he ever had to serve his country, he wanted to be a sailor. He jokingly said that he had spent his whole life in Missouri and wanted to see the ocean. So he volunteered for the Navy.

In the back of Ruth's diary is a section for Important Events. On that page she wrote, *"The most important thing in our lives. Homer's induction into the Navy, Wednesday, February 3rd at 3:30 P.M."* She was very proud that he passed without a red mark. Homer came home from the Navy induction ceremony with a letter ordering him into Active Duty.

The next day Homer's mother began sewing a money belt for him. Homer and Ruth went to town, deposited $120 worth of dimes into their savings account, and bought government bonds with the money from their sale. That night they played cards with Ruth's folks; Ruth and Homer won.

Saturday they went to several stores in the neighboring towns so Ruth could apply for jobs. Many women were looking for work, so finding a job would not be easy. A few businesses let her fill out an application, but couldn't promise anything.

Ruth's diary reveals that Sunday and Monday were miserable days for the whole family because Homer was scheduled to leave on Tuesday.

<u>Sun Feb 7</u> *Slept until 10:30 no breakfast. To Ma & Pa's* [Homer's parents] *for farewell dinner for Homer. "Old Hen"*

<u>Mon Feb 8</u> *Grandma had oyster supper for Homer. I cried when Mother & Dad* [Ruth's parents] *told Homer farewell.*

Instead of telling everyone "good-bye" Homer bid them "farewell." He said that farewell meant "I'll be seeing you" and he wanted everyone to know that he would be seeing them again.

The day finally came for Homer to leave. On Tuesday, February 9, Homer's Mother wrote in her diary, "Took Homer to Bus 5:30 PM."

Homer and Ruth's parents, and their friends Lecil and Laura Mae Ulry went with them to the bus station. Good-byes had already been said at home, so few words were exchanged while they waited for the other passengers to board the bus. Ruth kept a tight grip on Homer's arm in an effort to keep her emotions under control. She wanted be strong for him.

When it was time for Homer to leave, he leaned down and kissed Ruth. "I love you, my wife," he whispered.

Letting go of his arm, she whispered back, "I love you, too." And she pointed one finger as a warning to him and added, "You take good care of my husband."

"I will," he said with a smile. Then he turned and stepped onto the bus.

Her face suddenly felt flush and to keep from crying she bit her lip so hard she feared it might bleed. As soon as the bus pulled out of the station Ruth broke down and buried her face in both hands.

On the bus Homer fought back tears, took a deep breath, and clenched his strong Norris jaw. His heart ached, but his spirit was still intact. There was one thing the draft board and even the whole United States Navy didn't know about Homer Norris; and that was his spirit of determination. Sometimes Homer could be as stubborn as a Missouri mule; once he set his mind to something there was no changing it. Sitting on that bus full of Navy recruits, Homer was bound and determined to take care of himself and come back home.

February 9, 1943:

Homer spent his first night as a Navy Apprentice Seaman in St. Louis, but his heart was still back home with Ruth. He'd only been gone a few hours, but already he missed her, and regretted that he had to leave right before Valentine's Day. That's why there was a Valentine addressed to Mrs. Homer Norris in his suitcase. The next morning Homer would make sure it was in the mail.

February 10:

Ruth spent the night with Homer's parents. Wednesday morning she reluctantly crawled out of bed to assume her new role as a sailor's wife. She felt like the Navy controlled her life now. Somehow she had to find a way to take one day at a time and be strong until this nightmare was over.

Homer's troop train left Union Station at noon—destination unknown. As the train rolled northwest through Nebraska and South Dakota Homer took it all in, seeing these states for the first time, while he wrote his first letter home.

Seventy miles away Ruth sat in a dentist's chair. That night she wrote in her diary, *"had my first tooth pulled by a dentist. Wisdom tooth. Paid Dr Baize $4.00."* Mom Norris had a tooth pulled, too. Both recuperated at the Norris farm.

February 11:

Thursday morning Ruth got dressed and began day two without Homer. It was time to find a job. She already knew there were no jobs in Perry or Vandalia, so Dad Norris drove her thirty miles to the larger town of Hannibal located near the Mississippi River.

First she checked with Sonnenberg's Dept. Store, but it was a no-go there. So she went to the unemployment office and they sent her to the Kresge Dollar Store. The manager, Mr. Smith hired her on the spot; $12 a week for 48 hours of work. She was thrilled with her good luck, but the best part of Ruth's day was when she came home to discover a Valentine from Homer.

The manila envelope was postmarked from the Federal Building in St. Louis. Inside was a blue and white Valentine, with a heart-shaped doily tied to the front with a pink ribbon.

* * *

Homer's troop train was over six hundred miles from home before the recruits learned they were going to **Idaho**. The minute Homer heard their destination his goal was to let Ruth know.

On Friday morning recruits deboarded to eat breakfast in Helena, Montana. The Navy said no one was to mail anything until they reached Idaho, but before Homer got back on the train the following letter was on its way to Missouri.

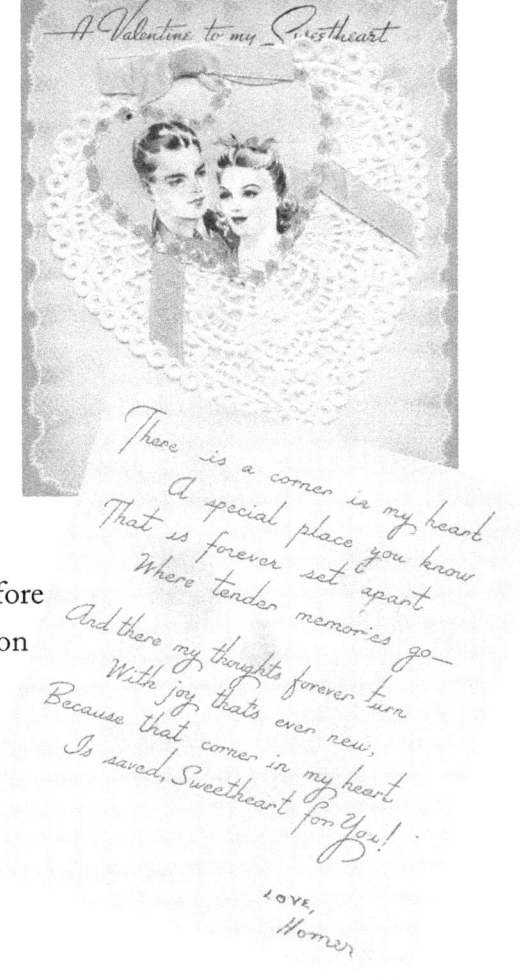

Thursday 11th, 2:00 pm
Hello Ruth, Mother & Dad
We left the Federal Building yesterday morning at 10 A.M. for an unknown destination we ate dinner at 11 at the Union Station boarded the Burlington Zephyr 1 west 12 oclock noon, and the first town we went through I knew was Martinsburg then Mexico to Kansas City, north through St.

15

Joseph about 10 last night   this morning at day light we went through Broken Bow Nebraska   now we'll soon be at Edgemont, South Dakota. All we see here in Neb. is big hills lots of good white face cattle   a house every 10-15 miles, towns 50-75 miles.

We have good eats and lots of it, but I never eat much you know. ^{Ha} *For supper last night on train chicken soup first then the chicken, gravey, mashed potatoes, green beans, ice cream & cookies, coffee & milk tomato juice & all the butter you want.*

Yesterday the captain told us that he wanted us to make ourselves at home, if we _____ on the floor at home do it on the train. About 80 boys on a car. About fifteen cars to the train. some of the boys are reading, playing poker, pitch, rumey, shooting dice, telling jokes, most everything you could think of. This letter won't be mailed until we get to Idaho. Its hard to write on the train it rocks around so much.

I wish you could be along. My arm is getting tired so I'll stop writing for a while   we are stopped in Edgemont South Dakota 3 oclock thursday after noon.

Friday we are going to eat breakfast in Helena Mont. I think mabe I can mail this letter   we're not suppose to until we get to Ido.

Lot of Love

Homer

Homer's letter set their minds at ease; oddly enough no one back home had ever heard of the Farragut Naval Training Station in Idaho, and neither had Homer.

Part 2: Boot Camp

The Middle of Nowhere

"We got in here at camp at 7 pm last night. Got chow at nine, went to bed about ten, got up this morning at 5:30 mopped deck or floor. This is hell!"

—Homer's first letter from boot camp 2/13/43

Note: Unless otherwise cited, material in this chapter is based on a booklet by Roger E. Glans, *Farragut Naval Training Station.*[5]

The Japanese attack on Pearl Harbor started a recruitment frenzy the likes of which the United States Navy had never seen. Within months all three Naval training stations in Illinois, California, and Rhode Island were filled to capacity. The Navy projected the need for additional training stations to be built in New York, Maryland, and Idaho. The Idaho site on the southern tip of Lake Pend O'Reille was selected because the lake was exceptionally deep and provided an inland ocean for training sailors.

In May, 1942 President Franklin D. Roosevelt named the Idaho Naval Station in honor of Admiral David Farragut, the first admiral in the U.S. Navy. Admiral Farragut's illustrious Naval career was highlighted during the Civil War. When his ship spotted torpedoes in the water, he yelled, "Damn the torpedoes, full speed ahead!" and proceeded with his flotilla to secure Mobile Bay.

The Farragut Naval Training Station (FNTS) rose almost overnight. After breaking ground in March 22,000 men worked around the clock. Six months later the base had a population of 55,000 making Farragut the second-largest

Naval training center in the world; second only to the Great Lakes. During the next thirty months the FNTS prepared 293,381 recruits for service to their country including Homer Norris from Missouri.

Homer's troop train left St. Louis at noon on Wednesday, February 10. Fifty-five hours later he got off the train on Friday evening, right in the middle of nowhere!

Homer was one of 1200 recruits who deboarded the Burlington Zephyr in Athol, Idaho and rode in cattle cars four miles from the train station to the Farragut Naval Receiving Station.

Homer didn't know much about where he was, but his hometown newspaper, *The Perry Enterprise* had an article about him on 11 February 1943, the day after he arrived. A copy of the article is glued to a page of Homer's mother's diary. The headline has been cut off, but the article reads:

Train tracks in Athol, Idaho

INDEX OF IMPORTANT
Joining the ever-expanding forces of the U. S. Navy, Homer Lee Norris, husband of Mrs. Ruth Marie Norris, of Perry, this week donned the smart, historic uniform of a bluejacket and began his training at the U. S. Naval Training Station at Farragut, Idaho, on the shores of Lake Pend Oreille. The next few weeks will be momentous ones in his life as he learns the fundamentals of seamanship and undergoes the rigors of the Navy physical hardening program. Shortly, however, he will have completed basic training and then will be sent to a Navy Service School or assigned directly to the U. S. fleet for combat duty against our axis foes.

Homer arrived during the night, slept in the receiving center, and had breakfast in the mess hall before beginning his first day of B.O.O.T. (Basic Organization & Operations Training) camp.

At the receiving station recruits were given detailed psychological and physical examinations including painful inoculations which caused fever and chills. Recruits endured three shots the first day and four more vaccinations during the three-week quarantine period when they were restricted to the base.

Co. No. _____ Pay No. _____	
Name & Rate _____	
C&SS REQUISITION – USNTS, FARRAGUT, IDAHO	Unit Price
Belt	.20
Blankets	7.00
Broom, whisk	.20
Brush, blacking & dauber	.50
Brush, scrubbing	.15
Buttons	.05
Buttons, bronze	.04
Cap Ribbons	.20
Caps, cloth, blue	1.85
Cap, cook's & baker's	.25
Cap, watch	.60
Clothes Stops	.10
Combs	.05
Covers, mattress	1.10
Covers, pillow	.25
Drawers, nainsook	.35
Gloves, woolen	.85
Handkerchiefs	.08
Hats, white	.60
Jackknife	.30
Jerseys	2.25
Jumpers, dress, blue	9.00
Jumpers, undress, blue	5.00
Jumpers, dungaree	1.10
Jumpers, undress, white	1.60
Leggings	1.00
Marks, all others	.05
Neckerchiefs	.65
Needles	.05
Overcoats	15.50
Overshoes	.90
Raincoats, enlisted men	7.50
Rating Badges, blue	.35
Rating Badges, white	.25
Service Stripes	.10
Shirts, chambray	.75
Shoes, gymnasium	1.00
Shoes, high, black	4.75
Shoes, low, black	4.25
Socks, cotton, black	.20
Socks, woolen, black	.35
Socks, woolen, natural	.35
Thread, cotton, white	.05
Thread, cotton, black	.10
Towels, large	.45
Towels, small	.30
Trousers, blue	7.00
Trousers, dungaree	1.10
Trousers, white	1.55
Trunks, bathing	1.00
Undershirts, cotton	.35
TOTAL............	
Division Off. _____	
Pay No. _____ USNTS, FARRAGUT, IDAHO	

After the physical examination, recruits placed their civilian clothes and toiletries in bags tagged for shipment home. Two hours later the new sailors were dressed in Navy-issued clothing that smelled of moth balls.

They were sporting G.I. haircuts and carrying $133 worth of clothes, personal items, a mattress and blanket. This initial issue of clothing was at no cost to them; however, there would be a replacement cost if any articles were lost or damaged. Homer's clothing requisition form listed fifty-one items and the replacement cost of each.

Upon leaving the store he boarded a bus that took him to his barracks. Homer was in Camp Ward named in honor of James R. Ward S1/C (Seaman first-class) who was killed at Pearl Harbor. Camp Ward had twenty-two barracks to house its 5000 boots-in-training. Each two-story barracks housed 240 recruits (two companies).

The sheer size of the FNTS was intimidating, to say the least. Farragut was comprised of six 5,000 man training camps. Each camp was designed to be self-sufficient, with its own mess hall, dispensaries, basketball courts, swimming pool, barracks, and

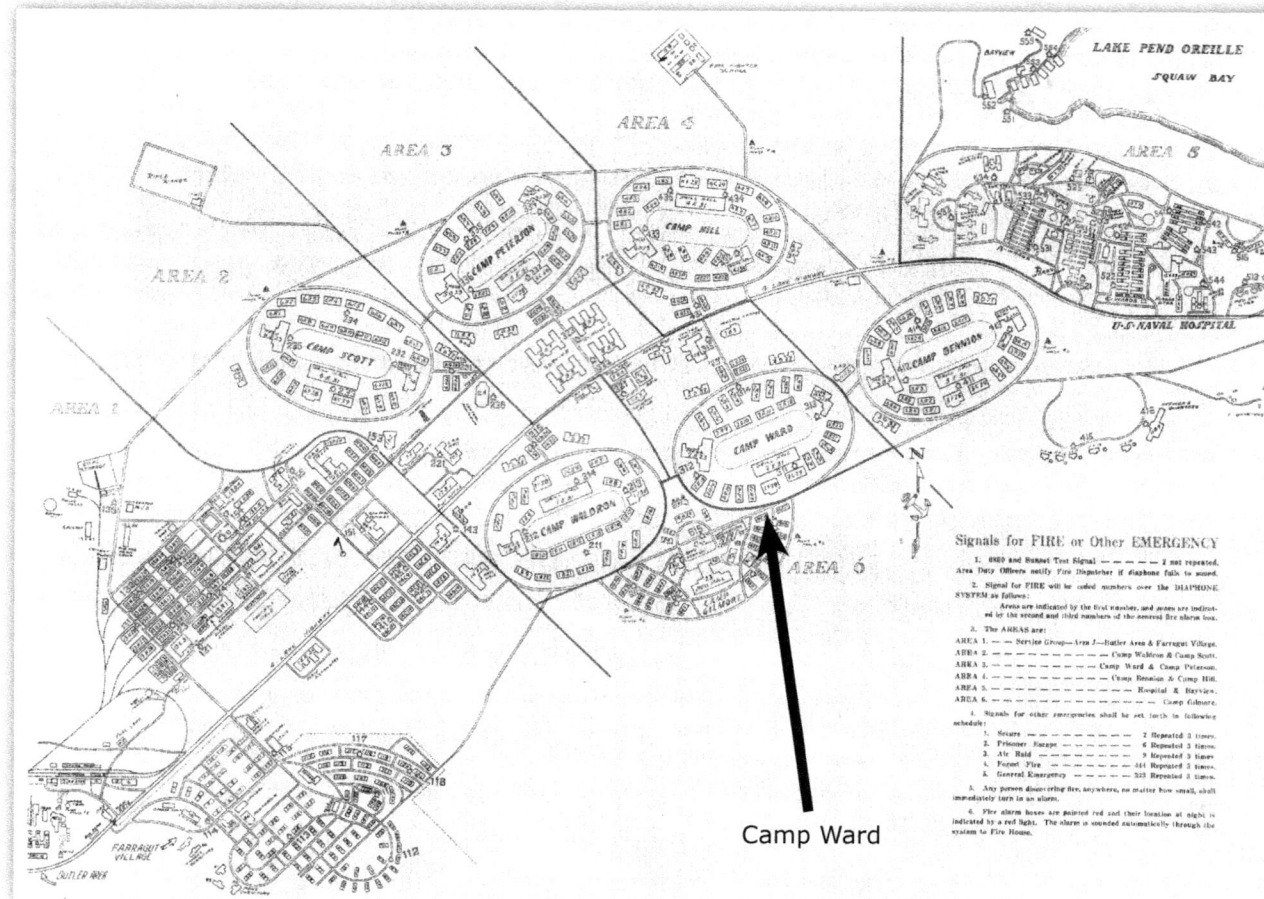

Camp Ward

rifle ranges. Camps were laid out in an oval configuration with a drill field in the center. The six drill fields were large enough to place eighteen football fields within them.

In addition to the six camps, the FNTS also had a hospital with fifteen hundred beds, low-cost housing for three hundred families, an auditorium for two thousand, a recreation building, officers' quarters, and two chapels—a total of 650 frame buildings . . . all painted a drab olive green. Surrounding the Naval base was seven miles of six-foot-high chain link fence topped with barbed wire to prevent sailors from leaving.

It would have been more cost effective to send recruits to the nearest training facility. However, the Navy deliberately sent recruits far from home to discourage them from trying to go back home. The Navy did not like sailors who went A.W.O.L. (absent without official leave).

The 4000-acre training station was an isolated city run with utmost efficiency according to Navy rules and regulations. In his first letter from boot camp, instead of writing 6:40 p.m., Homer wrote in "Navy time."

February 13, 1943
Sat, time 18:40

Hello, Honey

We got in here at camp at 7 pm last night. Got chow at nine, went to bed about ten, got up this morning at 5:30 mopped deck or floor. This is hell!

All Navy time is on 2400   there isn't such a thing as P.M. and A.M. The floor is deck, windows-port holes, front of room-bow, back of room-stern, the ceiling-overhead. We sleep in double bunks, I sleep on top. we had 3 shots today   smallpox, scarlet fever, and lock jaw   we have seven shots all togeather.

We got more clothes today than we know what to do with 5 prs pants, 5 shirts, two prs shoes, 12 handkercheifs, under wear, 3 caps & one pair of legons. [leggings]

This after noon we took out our insurance. I took out ten thousand dollars   they said you wouldn't get the insurance papers for five or six months because Washington D.C. was filled up.

My arms so sore I can't write any more, I'll write more the next time I get a chance. I'm sending my address so I can get some mail from home.

Homer Lee Norris A.S. [Apprentice Seaman]
Co. 85-43-B5 Camp Ward
U.S.N.T.S. Farragut, Idaho

GoodBye,
Your old Man

30,000 Sailors!

"There is a swell lot of men here from every state in the union."

—Homer's second letter from boot camp 2/14/43

When Homer arrived at Farragut to begin his boot training he was one man in a sea of 30,000 recruits. Homer might have been in the middle of nowhere, but one thing was for sure—he wasn't alone.

Feb. 14
Sunday Morning
Ten oclock

Dear Ruth,

It's 30,000 sailors here! There is 117 men in this deck of the barracks. Our Company is No 85.

My arm is a lot better this morning. Two boys past out yesterday when we got our shots. We got up at six today being Sunday morning   had oat meal, grape fruit, two slices of toast cup coffee. You wash your own dishes not dishes but tin trays.

I had to check the blankets this morning to see they were folded right and two thirds of them were wrong. When I get home I'll show you how a bed sould be made up.[Ha Ha] Shine shoes, shave every morning, bath at night, no smoking until after 11:A.M. on Sundays church 8 am to 11 a.m. but we couldn't go today.

We can go on a 14 hour leave in 21 days after we get out of quarenteen

> *Sunday night*
>
> *The boys are telling big stories around here about Arkansas and good old Missouri   I'm sure proud of Missouri now   I didnt know it was such a good state. There is a swell lot of men here from every state in the union.*
>
> *I'd like a picture of my wife to show the boys   some won't believe I'm married. I have been thinking of my dear wife wondering if you got a job or not.*
>
> *Ten minutes til lights out so I'll close for now.*
>
> *Lot of love & kisses*
>
> *Homer*

While Homer learned Navy rules and regulations, he also learned how to get along with the other 116 men in his company. Homer's Missouri buddies Harold Rhodes and Roscoe Gibbs were in the same barracks. It made the tough times easier with his buddies nearby. Part of the preparation for sea duty was training new recruits to work together. When each man did his job the whole company earned rewards like going to Ship's Service.

Each camp had its own recreation building called Ship's Service which included a soda fountain with 15¢ malts and sandwiches; a merchandise area that sold candy bars, hair oil, and toothpaste; two barber shops, an eight-lane bowling alley, and a library.[6] The men worked hard to earn the right to go to Ship's Service.

On the flip side, if one man shirked his responsibilities, the whole company suffered. There was a lot of pressure from the other men to do your best.

Monday night Homer wrote about his first day of training.

> *Feb 15th*
>
> *Monday 8 P.M.*
>
> *Hello, Honey!*
>
> *This life isn't so bad after we get over our sore arms   I had fever all day Sunday   didn't feel like eating dinner   Feel good today.*
>
> *Today we drilled two hours in the morning four hours afternoon   we*

ran about one mile all togeather and I don't know how far we walked. our captain told us a hundred & one things to remember   tonight after chow got to go over to the ship service or canteen   I had a malt and was it good, a big one for a dime, very few men get to go to ship service as soon as we did. At ship service you can bowl, play pool, table tennis and most any game a person would want. It cost twenty cents for an hour to play any thing. I just look

    We had to wear our blue clothes tonight with 14 buttons on them   sort of unhandy at times. ^{Ha Ha}

    I'd better stop writing. My time is up—

Good bye & my love
Homer

On the Home Front

"Tues, Feb 16, 43 Went up after Homer's letter he mailed in Helena Montana on Fri 12, 1943."

—Ruth's diary entry

While Homer adjusted to Navy life, Ruth adjusted to changes in her life, too. Ruth's job was in the upscale Kresge Dollar Store which sold fine women's clothing. The Kresge Company would be a good place to work.

As soon as Ruth acquired her job in Hannibal she found an apartment within walking distance of work. Frankly, she was a little scared at the prospect of being on her own and thirty miles from her family.

Downton Hannibal Kresge Dollar Store—third store from left

Ruth had grown up in a close-knit family. Four generations lived within three miles of each other. With Homer gone Ruth was lonely, but her family and friends made sure she wasn't alone.

Ruth's apartment house

Ruth's diary entries during the week after Homer left for boot camp record her day-to-day activities.

Ruth ready for work

Fri, Feb 12, 1943 Went to Briggs for supper last night. Laura Mae's birthday. Gave her lamps, made ice cream.

Feb 13 Went down home. Called long distance to Hannibal to tell them I would be there next Mon.

Feb 14 Cut out dress. Have an awful cold.

Feb 15 Mother made me a red dress

There was a lot to do if she was to be ready for work in one week. She didn't have clothes that were appropriate for her new job or money to buy any. Luckily, Ruth's mother and mother-in-law knew how to sew. With the help of Mother Yancey and Mom Norris, Ruth would start her new job looking like she just stepped out of a band box.

It took four days for Homer's first letter to get from Montana to Missouri. The day it arrived Ruth wrote a long entry in her diary.

Feb 16 Went up after Homer's letter he mailed in Helena Montana on Fri 12, 1943. Would get in Idaho that night. Called Ma Norris. Sent order to Sears for print dress. Made black dress.

Navy photo album

This was her last diary entry for several months. For years Ruth's diary had been a running narrative that chronicled her most personal life events. Seven days after Homer left she stopped writing in her diary. With Homer gone the activities of each day were just too painful to record. Ruth tucked her diary away in her cedar chest and started filling scrapbooks with cards, letters, newspaper clippings, and photographs.

Homer's letters tell his World War II experience, and Ruth's war time story is revealed in memories she saved in scrapbooks.

Smile, Boys, Smile

"Don't worry about me   I think I will take care of my self all right."
—Homer's letter 2/20/43

The Navy had its own way to do everything. The Navy way to get to the mess hall, the drill field or the lake was to march, and sing songs in cadence with their steps. Homer sent Ruth a copy of one of their marching songs with a note that said, "a song we have to sing each morning going to colors." [Colors was the morning raising of the flags.]

Once Homer learned to march, it was time to learn about K.P. [kitchen patrol].

```
Pack up your troubles in your old Seabag
     And smile, boys, smile—
While you've the lucifer to light your fag
     Smile, boys, that's the style—
What's the use of worrying, it never was
     Worth while, SO
Pack up your troubles in your old Seabag
     And smile, boys, smile.
```

18 Feb 43
Thursday 8 P.M.

My Dear Ruth,
   Sure was busy today   we got up at 4:15 A.M. washed, shaved, made up my bunk, check 55 bunk to see they were made up right   I do that every day before chow.
   Then we put on white clothes for the first time & marched ¼ mile to

chow. This K.P. lasts for a week   we served until the 7,000 men had eaten then washed the mess hall   We got back to the barracks at ten went back to the mess hall at 10:30   got back to the barracks at 2:15   go back to the mess hall at 3:30   that's the way things go in the Navy   no wonder I don't have time to fart.

For breakfast I served small boxes of Rice Krispeys and for dinner we had beef steak   the first good thing I've had sence I been here. Every company has a week of K.P I sort of like it.

I sure would like to get a letter from home sort of home sick but not bad   when I get some letters it will be a lot better   dont suppose I will get any mail for ten or twelve days   tomorrow will make me a week here. its lots of mountains here snow about 18 ins deep.

We rolled our clothes today   a little rope is tied around both ends. Our clothes are suppose to be rolled hard enough to knock a man out.

We get some more shots tomorrow

I love you
Homer

Saturday 20th 4:30 pm

Hello Ruthe,

I think I'll have time to write to my dear one. I had another typhoid fever shot, my arm is sore   Lots of the boys are having chills, I had chills last night. I went to bed feeling like an old wash woman, took two aspirin put two blankets over me and sweat all night, don't feel so good today.

In the drill hall there are 14 basketball courts, and a swimming pool that is 75 yds around. We went swiming yesterday you had to swim 75 yard to get out of swiming lessons. I was lucky enough to make it, only 26 out of 117 made the 75 yards. We have to be able to swim 75 yards to get out of boot camp.

After supper we washed our clothes   did we have a time   washed *in a bucket   hung the clothes with ropes to the wire line. We have to wash our clothes every other day, wish I had our washing machine here.*

The mail just came in but none for me   I would like to know what is going on back home. Tell everybody hello. Don't worry about me   I think I will take care of my self all right.

Good Bye and Lots of Love
Homer

P.S. I had to break my first five dollar bill today to buy books   one 69 cent, one 7 cent   I have to buy every thing it lookes like it to me   I thought every thing was furnished but====

Homer was shocked at the number of Navy recruits who could not swim. What he didn't know was that nearly thirty percent of enlistees could not swim![7]

When Homer left for boot camp he only had $10 in his money belt because frankly he thought Uncle Sam would foot the bill. He was wrong! During the first two weeks of boot camp he spent $3 on haircuts, supplies, books, and life insurance. The Navy was getting into Homer's money belt, and he didn't like that.

The only good part about boot camp was getting acquainted with the other recruits. Living with 116 men was a new experience, but for the most part they were a swell bunch. Homer had worried about how he would stack up to the other men. Many recruits were 18-19 years old and Homer was 22, so numerically they were about the same age—but he felt a lot older. He was married, and that made a difference. He had also worked with older men at the brick plant, and had been his own boss as a farmer, so he was accustomed to hard work. Once he started his boot training Homer was pleasantly surprised to discover that physically he was as fit as any of the men and stronger than most. After one week at boot camp Homer concluded that this Navy stuff was something he could do. In fact, he was already working on a plan to take care of Homer.

Service School

"I want to go to school if I can. . . . Roscoe wants to go to sea   but not me"
—Homer's letter 2/21/43

Ruth's mother always told her when she had to make an important decision she needed to put on her thinking cap. By week two Homer had his thinking cap on and was working on a plan so he could stay in the states as long as possible. Apprentice seamen got their orders when they graduated from boot camp. Either they went straight to sea duty or stayed in the states for additional training at service schools. The last thing Homer wanted was sea duty.

According to *The Bluejackets' Manual,* service schools trained radiomen, signalmen, quartermasters, cooks, hospital corp, gunners' mates, storekeepers, and electricians.[8]

Homer's goal was to get accepted into electrician's school; maybe those electrician classes he had taken back home would help him. It was not easy to qualify for school and Homer would have to give his best effort on all the physical and mental tests.

21 Feb 43
Sunday Morning

Dear Sweetheart
 I'm going to church at ten. I'm feeling fine today   the worst shots are over now.

Back from church now   had a good preacher   there was fifteen from this Co. of one hundred seventeen, we can go to ship service this afternoon think I'll get something good to eat.

It won't be long until we get to smoke, we can't smoke until eleven twenty on Sundays   can't smoke my troubles away very well

Our Co. commander Mr Wilson said we might get out of boot training in seven to ten weeks if we do good. If we go to sea we get nine to eleven days leave but if we go to school we may not get a leave until after we get through school, I want to go to school if I can. The fellow gives us a talk about going to school   he said electric was a very good course to take. I hope my grade is good enough to go, Roscoe wants to go to sea   but not me.

I wrote Mother & Dad this morning. It will soon be chow time   hope we have ice cream.

After chow now   we had a swell dinner T-bone steak, ice cream, mashed potatoes, gravy. Myself and Harold went through the line twice, got a double dinner.

Well its about time for me to go to ship service so I'll have to close

I love you
Homer

Ruth knew that the most important morale booster for a sailor was getting mail from home, so she began writing letters as soon as she had his address. And sure enough, on his tenth day in camp Homer was the first sailor from Missouri to get mail call.

Monday 22, after chow

Hello, Honey!

I was the happiest boy in the camp today at eleven when I got your letter   it was received with pleasure and I don't mean perhaps.

I read part of it before chow   couldn't hardly eat for thinking about it   ran back to the barracks and read the rest of it know one else around St Louis has got any mail yet, sure glad you mailed it air mail.

Say! Note this; we had a strength test this morning and I tied for first place in the whole Co. of one hundred and seventeen men with a total score of 352   the record is 444 with ~~some~~ a lot of practice I believe I can beat it.

Glad you got a job in the dollar store   I'll bet it will be a good place to work. Is the work anything like at Perry   I expect it is.

I have got to stop writing and study from seven to nine. We take our mential test tomorrow   it takes all day.

Love me Honey

Receiving Ruth's first letter was a turning point for Homer. Suddenly the man who hated to write letters took every opportunity to do so. Now they had a two-way conversation, albeit a slow conversation. It took four to eight days for a letter to get to him which meant waiting two or three weeks for a reply to any question they asked each other. However, a slow conversation was better than none. From that day forward when Homer wasn't studying for a test, he was anxiously waiting for mail call.

February 23
Tuesday night Six oclock

Hello Ruthie,

We took that mential test today   we didn't have time for me to finish, I got most of them. We won't get our scores for a week.

I'm on guard duty from 2-4 a.m. Tonight will make three nights that I have gotten up at one thirty & go back to bed at four thirty.

The boys have a guitar in here tonight and are having a good time. Mr Wilson our C.O.P. came in this afternoon   he said this place looked like a hog pen, it was so dirty, he was right too. We had to wash the floor with brushes about two inches wide and six inches long. About half of the boys won't do what they are told   it makes it bad on the rest of us. I guess they will learn I don't know when.

Mr Wilson is a good looking fellow and a nice man but he can get hard if necessary. Some of the boys have been talking after taps at nine. Mr Wilson said today if we didn't quiet down he would get us up at 3:30 AM and work us harder so we would sleep when we go to bed. It is just a few that think they are just — it on a stick.

We had our pictures taken today. Roscoe got a picture of his wife   I'll be glad when I get yours   I'm going to look at it half the time no fooling.

Lots of Love
Homer

The boot camp barracks put men from all over the country in very close quarters and unpredictable things happened with regularity. Most of the problems they caused were petty offenses. They got out of chow line, folded their blankets the wrong way, talked after taps, overslept, tied sea bags to the ceiling, and square danced in the barracks. When they got caught they had to wash windows, sweep and mop the floors, stand guard duty in the middle of the night, and do extra drills. As frustrating as it was to get extra duty because of a few fools, sometimes Homer enjoyed watching their antics. For the most part Homer was proud of the men in his company.

Friday 26th, six oclock

Dear Honey,

Tonight makes us two weeks here. We had our rifle shooting today. I got a score of 145 out of a possible 150. Probably too good for my own good.

We had another dam shot today its for yellow fever   My throat is sore as the devil   this afternoon I went over to the sick bay   they gave me two white pills for my cold and sprayed my throat & nose   I sent Roscoe to ships service to get me some aspirins but he brought me a candy bar instead he forgot what I asked him to get. I hope I feel better tomorrow.

We had to get another dam hair cut today . . . just something to get the fifteen cents for.

We go to see about school courses tomorrow and find out what grades we made. Think I will stop writing and go to bed. We are not suppose to go to bed before eight but I'm going at seven   the hell with them.

Your sweetheart
Homer

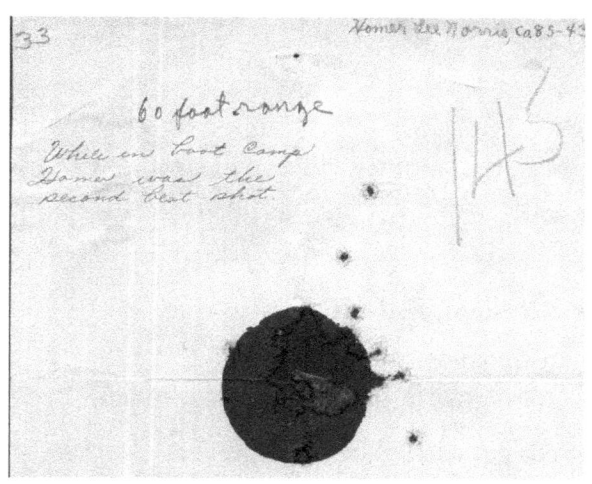

Homer's rifle target

Ruth proudly put his rifle target (complete with bullet holes) in her scrapbook with a note that said, "While in boot camp Homer was the second best shot."

The only obstacle that stood in the way of Homer getting into service school was his mental test. *The Bluejackets' Manual* said that a score of at least seventy on the General Classification written test was required for entry into service schools.

Sat 27, 1943
seven pm

Dear Ruth,

    Say I'm going to SCHOOL. Passed my examination   not so bad 73 G.C. test

    Some big shot said he would represent me for a school so that is something, and also said I would get a rating as soon as I get out of boot camp.

    I went to ship service tonight I had a ham sandwich and was it good. I bought candy bars (5) for 5 cents each   sold them today for 10 & 15 cents each.

    I have lots of money eight dollars $^{Ha\,Ha}$ I had to pay 75 cent for cutting my five pair of pants off and putting a stripe around the right arm of our shirts   that got my goat.

    A boy in here got an iron today   he sure is busy pressing pants & shirts havn't had mind pressed yet, costs 50 cents a suit don't think I will, not necessary here.

    I love you honey sure would like to get another letter. So far I have only got two cards and one letter. Write often honey.

                            Good Bye Honey and lot of Love,
                                    Your Dear Husband

Homer's score of seventy-three was only three points above the required seventy, but he didn't care. Maybe now at the end of his boot training he could stay in the states and go to service school. If he became a Navy Electrician's Mate it might keep him out of harm's way.

Making Money

"Every time I can make a little money on the side I do."

—Homer's letter 3/21/43

After two weeks of boot camp Homer was frustrated that money kept going out of his pocket, and none was coming in. He hadn't always been so concerned about money, but if he was going to start farming again he and Ruth had to save every penny. His goal was to find a way to make some spending money so he could send his entire military paycheck home.

He didn't go to Ship's Service with the intention of buying candy bars to resell, but when he made a profit—it gave him an idea. Apparently some of his fellow boots had money and were willing to pay someone else to do their work.

Then he started thinking about the huge quantity of laundry they had to wash, and the boy with the iron who made fifty cents for pressing one suit. From that day forward Seaman Norris would be on the lookout for ways to make a little money on the side, even if it meant doing extra work.

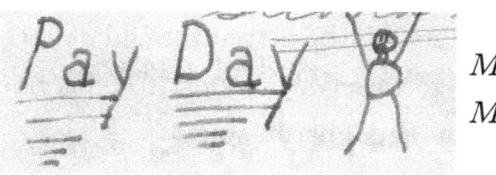 *Mon night*
March 1st

Hello Honey,

I got those pay day blues   got my first money today and can't spend it.
Ha Ha

We made our dependent allowances today   you won't get any for another month   you won't get a cent from my first months pay   they hold it back so we can go home. In case you didn't want me to come.^{Ha Ha} *I don't think about YOU   only 24 hours a day.*

I got your grand letter today   I'm sure glad to get your picture   the boys like to had a fit about you. Nothing like getting mail. The first name called was mine.

I took in a washing tonight for 50 cents   five garments   not bad money   I have a contract tomorrow night just like that, I'll do that every night if I get that money.

We washed 200 double windows   took all afternoon   I have got to go to ship service tonight to get me some toothpaste...wish you were going with me. . . .

I just got back from ship service   got 3 pgs. cigarettes sold one pack, got some tooth paste & hair oil.

I've got to sew some buttons on my "P" coat so I better close for now.

*Love,
your sailor husband
Homer*

Homer's "P" coat

The "P" coat Homer referred to was a heavy wool coat that had been the signature Navy overcoat for more than a hundred years.[9] The name comes from the pilot cloth that was used in the first coats.

It was dark navy blue in color with an oversized collar that could stand up and protect the sailor from winds. The coat had several corduroy-lined pockets to compensate for the pockets that were missing from sailor pants. Down the front of the double-breasted coat were ten large buttons with the USN anchor insignia.

Mail Call

"I sure like to get mail."

—Homer's letter 3/3/43

Mail was a sailor's lifeline home. Unfortunately, when the military needed to move troops or supplies, moving mail became low priority. Homer received his first letter from Ruth on his tenth day in camp, and then five days passed without any letters even though Ruth wrote every day. Homer's mother wrote every week and some of her letters had an extra page from his dad. Homer also got mail from his mother-in-law, his friends, and occasionally a card or short letter from a total stranger. Several of the women who worked with Ruth wrote to Homer because they knew how important it was to get mail.

It was customary to send "Good Luck" cards. One card in the scrapbook says, "Good Luck to You in the Service," and has a plastic horseshoe with a penny in the middle.

Each card and letter reminded Homer that he was in the thoughts and hearts of the folks back home.

The best mail call was receiving a soapbox package. Ruth used sturdy cardboard soap boxes to mail cakes, candy, toiletries, and Christmas presents. Sharing soap box food was a real treat for Homer and his buddies.

Wednesday March 3
eight oclock night

Hello, Honey

I sure like to get mail. I just received three letters   one from Mother & Dad Norris & one from Mother & Dad Yancey & one from you—that was the ONE. I hope you don't get as lonesome for me as I do you   this is the shirts.^{Ha Ha}

We drilled all morning with dummy rifles   learned to tie knots this afternoon   we had a hell of a supper tonight. it wasn't fit for a dog to eat. We have beans for breakfast twice a week and carrots in everything we eat. I wish the hell that they would have let me farm and eat a good cooks meal.

A boy just passed around a box of home made cookies and are they good! I did another boys wash this afternoon for 50 cents   makes me a dollar for two washes   not bad money if I only had more time   don't take about twenty minutes to wash.

Last night I did such a big wash it took me two hours   I wish I was washing your stockings and pants instid   maby I could get in your pants. (oh boy)

I got a letter from Mother & Dad today They think as much of you as they do of me. Know kidding why shouldn't they? Write often honey
Lot of Love & Kisses
Your Bee Honey

While Homer was at boot camp, his favorite time of day wasn't meal time, it wasn't free time, and it wasn't even taps. The most important moment of his day was hearing, "Mail call for Homer Norris."

Mar. 5
Friday 8 oclock

Hello Honey

Boy! Did I ever get mail tonight   three letters   one from you, two from Mother & Dad and $5   may come in handy. Glad you write every day even if it isn't but one page just anything to hear from you, I love you honey.

I've got your lovely picture out in front of me. I was sure home sick last week, I could have set down and boo hoo any time but didn't   but this week it hasn't been so bad   I'm getting mail now and that sure helps.

I'll answer your questions now   I think we can get $250 for our car we can stand fast for a while and then if you can't get that try to sell the car for $225.00

You can't come to see me now at all   they don't allow it here. You can come to see me when I go to school   I don't know where I will go.

Glad you asked the questions, anything you want to know just ask your old man   he can tell you. Ha Ha

I had two teeth filled   they weren't bad, they have the best equipment money will buy here. They do good work too.

So long til tomorrow night.

Good night Honey
Your Honey

Like Homer, Ruth's favorite part of any day was receiving a letter from her sailor-husband. Each night before she went to bed she wrote to Homer and then re-read letters from him. We are grateful that Ruth saved Homer's letters, and wish we had the ones she mailed to him. Sadly, her letters are lost. Lack of storage space and frequent changes in location prevented Homer from keeping them. In many of his letters Homer answers questions Ruth asked, and this gives a glimpse into what she was thinking. Some of Ruth's day-to-day activities are revealed through her scrapbooks and also from diary entries written by Homer's mother (Mom Norris).

First Liberty

"We get a 14 hour liberty next Tuesday   don't know where we can go but any thing would beat this place."

—Homer's letter 3/6/43

Between 1940 and 1944 the number of U.S. troops grew from fifty thousand to twelve million, and President Franklin D. Roosevelt encouraged private organizations to handle the on-leave recreation needs of the armed forces. In response to President Roosevelt's call, six civilian agencies including the Salvation Army, Young Men's Christian Association, Young Women's Christian Association, National Catholic Community Services, National Travelers Aid Association, and the National Jewish Welfare Board coordinated their war efforts and resources to form the USO (United Services Organization). At its high point in 1944 the USO had more than three thousand clubs which boosted morale by convincing the armed forces that the country was behind them.[10]

Small communities in northern Idaho (like the town of Coeur d'Alene twenty-six miles south of Farragut) opened USO centers to provide sailors from Farragut with a home away from home.

After a three week quarantine period, the Navy rewarded Homer's company with a pass to leave the base and go on a short liberty. Homer had heard good things about the USO in Coeur d'Alene and looked forward to going.

Monday night 8th
Seven o'clock

Dear Wifee

We got our idenification cards today   my picture is terrible (Wanted for Killing). We get a 14 hour liberty tomorrow   Got our tickets for our liberty cost 70¢ to Coeur d'Alene. We also got our finger prints put on our dog tags.

I'm going to be a good little boy on my liberty. The only thing I want to do is have my picture taken and see the city. We wear our Donald duck caps tomorrow. Won't get to write tomorrow we don't get back until about midnight. We got paid $10 today for our liberty   Have more money than I'll know what to do with (like hell).

I'm on guard duty tonight from eight to ten   I'm not a bad guard, but I can't do anything else. Well I have to go to guard muster, so will have to close.

Good bye honey
Your old Man
Homer

Bright and early Tuesday morning the men in Homer's company were dressed in required attire for apprentice seamen on liberty, including leggings (boots) and wearing "Donal Duck caps." At 10:15 A.M. they boarded the bus and headed to Coeur d'Alene.

The day after his liberty Homer had lots to tell Ruth.

March 10
Wednesday afternoon 2:30

Dear Honey

Yesterday was our liberty. We never left until 10:15 a.m. We got to Coeur d'Alene, Idaho 11:00   it's a town of about 10,000   they had a good U.S.O. center. Radios victrolas, ping pong tables, picture show about fish, deer & mt. goats sure was interesting. Had a big bowl of home made cookies   sure was good   every thing free.

We had an 85 cent T-bone steak for dinner   it was from a ten year old bull I think   couldn't chew it. I spent eight dollars   got my honey a pin $1.50, got pictures $2.90, a bag I had to have to put my small things in cost $1.65, dinner cost $1.00   We got back at 11:00 PM so didn't get much sleep last night. Some of the boys got drunk but not many   they were sober when they came back.

I didn't have a good time on our liberty at all   it made me home sick to see people that wasn't in uniforms. Roscoe and Harold felt the same way.

We are going to have to fall out right away so I had better close. I still have 15 bucks   some of the boys are broke so I did right well.

       Good bye honey I love you
        Mr Homer Norris

P.S. The salt peter sure works no kidding.^{Ha Ha}

A Lovely Sailor's Wife

Easter, 1943

Ruth really was a lovely sailor's wife, and lovely person. She took things to heart, and most of the things Ruth did came from her heart. She cared about other people and strived to be a good wife, daughter, daughter-in-law, granddaughter, and friend.

Ruth diligently tried to fulfill any request Homer made. His first request was for a picture he could show the boys to prove he was married. She immediately sent some of their wedding photos, and hoped these pictures would keep him happy until she could lose a little weight. A few weeks later new photos of a thinner Ruth were on the way to Idaho.

Ruth missed Homer "something fierce," and tried to stay busy hoping to make the time pass more quickly. Twelve days after Homer left, Ruth started her new job and took home $10.88 the first week.

While Homer was gone Ruth also did a little wheeling and dealing. The responsibility for selling their 1938 black Chevy sedan fell on Ruth's shoulders. Homer suggested she should try to get $250 or $225. He always said Ruth could sell ice cubes to Eskimos so he was not surprised when she sold the car for $250.

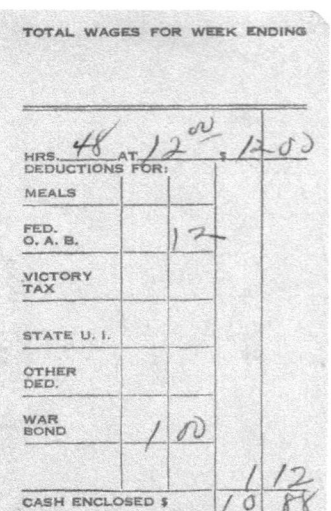

Without the car Ruth didn't have any transportation, so she hitchhiked the thirty miles from Hannibal to Perry on weekends to visit family. Sometimes she took the bus, but that cost money; hitching was free. Oddly enough, no one seemed worried about Ruth's safety since hitchhiking was a common means of transportation during the war. A lovely sailor's wife like Ruth surely wouldn't have long to wait for a ride.

Ruth and Homer knew that a long-distance relationship would be fraught with challenges, and went out of their way to show their love. While Homer was in boot camp Ruth made him a personalized ration book with coupons for kisses and hugs. She sent him a little black book that became Homer's address book, ledger, and calendar. She also mailed numerous soap boxes filled with cigarettes, gum, candy, and a jam cake—his favorite! Homer thanked Ruth for every thing she did, but he wanted to do more to show his appreciation. Finally he saved enough money to buy her a gift.

Thursday 11th,
Seven o'clock

My Darling Wife;

Sure got a grand letter from you honey   wish I could write like that. Honey don't think for a minute I don't miss my loving because I do but it doesn't do any good writing   it makes things worse for both of us.

You sure are a darling sailors wife surprising me like you did with that jam cake. It sure is good   gave some of it away but going to eat half of it myself.

I got this pillow slip over at ship service while on work detail over there, we mopped the floor and cleaned tables   we ate candy, drank coca's, had a malt and a sandwich so I didn't go to chow.

Roscoe & Harold are going to get something to eat but I'm not, I've got cake to eat and it's my favorite kind too.

I have this ration book you sent me out looking at it and your picture too   be glad when I get your other picture.

Its impossible to tell you in words how much I love you so I'm sending two stamps from the ration book   but they mean more than one kiss & hugs.

Well I'd better sign off

Love
Your old man

Homer wasn't very good at writing sentimental letters, but he knew that one thoughtful gift would make up for fifty letters. He was right.

Ruth was so excited about her gift that she even put the package envelope in the scrapbook. On it she wrote, "My blue satin pillow case Homer sent me from Farragut, Idaho." Every package and letter was a reminder of their unwavering love. If any two people could keep a long distance love strong—it was Ruth and Homer.

The Navy Way

"There are three ways to do anything   right way, wrong way, and the Navy way."
                                                              —Homer's letter 3/21/43

By the end of week four Homer had settled into Navy life. One night he had some extra time and in his letter to Ruth he actually drew pictures of the semaphore flag signaling system which allowed long distance communication between ships at sea.

Friday, March 12
Seven o'clock

Hello Honey,

   I got some good news today, we are going to get through with this training from one to three weeks early   they have never done that before and we would get a leave as soon as we get through with boot training.

   I'm going to show you the semi four we have to learn this is a rear view. use flags in your hands

A B C D E F G H I J K L
M N O P Q R S T U V W X Y Z

that is a picture of me doing it. Ha Ha   the other afternoon we went though that about 15 or 20 times straight sure got tired in my arms.

Well we didn't do a thing today we didn't do yesterday so this is my end of the letter.

Sunday March 14
six thirty

My Sweetie Pie

    I'm back now from K.P.   I have been eating enough for 3 men since we have be on K.P.   if I gain weight it won't be my fault.

    I have been getting your letters lately from one to two a day. I have had more fun about the card you sent kiss & hug special & the big feet & etc. *Ha Ha*

    I just took inventory   I have $14.78 I also have a dollar loaned out its good.

    Saturday night I went over to ship service expecting to come right back, got playing a game sort of like bowling but you use flat pieces of iron about 3 in. in diameter, you slide them down a board about 18 inches wide and twenty ft long, it was a lot of fun and didn't cost a thing, that's the first game I've played since I've been here and I didn't get back to the barracks until twenty till nine.

    I'm going to bed right away   its eight oclock now   have been eating, talking and a very little writing. Will close now. Yours truly, seaman Norris as I'm known these here days

Bye Honey
Homer the sailor man

Ruth kept track of the Idaho weather and lately it was cold, cold, cold with blowing snow. Since most of the sailors who trained at Farragut were sent to sea duty in the Pacific, Homer thought it would have made sense to train them in a warmer climate. Unfortunately, the Navy didn't think that way.

Tuesday Mar 16th
five oclock

Dear Ruthe Gooffee

Today we were busyer than a cat covering up s - - - on a concrete walk. We sure have to work but don't hurt me, almost killes some of the boys that never did any thing. We drilled outside all morning almost froze didn't have our coats on. Its about zero, the wind goes through me. Its been snowing like the devil since noon has snowed about five inches all togeather I expect. These mountains are sure pretty now after the snow.

Sorry I didn't write yesterday but I never had but one hour all day off, and made $2.75 that hour washing clothes. Last night I started washing clothes at 4:30 never got done until after 8:20. I sure was tired I have two washings tonight make a little more money don't have water in the wash house so have to carry it in buckets. Suppose to roll clothes tonight. Mother asked me if we ironed our clothes we don't just roll them.

I want to go to ship service tonight but don't know wheather I will or not a malt sure would go good now.

Today we had our pictures taken in a group. We can get one for 60 cents I'm going to get one.

I better go and clean up a little and get ready for chow.

Good bye sweetheart
I love you truly
Homer

Rush Like Hell Sailor Mail

COMPANY 85-43, REGIMENT 2, BATTALION 6

BOTTOM ROW (Left to Right)	SECOND ROW (Left to Right)	THIRD ROW (Left to Right)	FOURTH ROW (Left to Right)	
Corpus, R.	Phillips, R. B.	Howard, R. D.	Stausebach, N. E.	
Muir, H. J.	Jarosak, G.	Olynyk, J. E.	Helling, V. E.	
Schulte, J. J.	Anderson, R. G.	Pendzimas, F. G.	Shelton, N. J.	Renaud, N. L.
Beard, R. S.	Ables, O. L.	Brust, L. C.	Hammond, G. E.	Marsich, D.
Smith, R. W.	Walcott, W. T.	McManus, R. H.	Johnson, C. R. B.	Jensen, J. A.
Halls, D. E.	Schlens, E. E.	Reed, J. H.	Corless, F. G.	Maxwell, R. L.
Pewitt, L. M.	Brandis, F. M.	Letsch, K. B.	Norris, H. L.	Randono, E. C.
Wickland, W. W.	Baker, C. E.	Daws, C. R.	Albright, R. L.	Heise, H. J.
Wittman, N. W.	Jerin, E.	McDonough, R. E.	Walters, C. L.	Lang, P. T.
Powers, H.	Kaufmann, A. F.	Boos, H. B.	Davidson, J. H.	Nelson, L. O.
Daws, A. W. Jr.	Theiss, E. L.	Davis, R.	Theiss, E. F.	Crozier, J. W.
Wilson, J. R.	Sikorski, J.	Davis, A. W.	Green, R. A.	McPherson, A. R.
Schmidt, E. C.	*Rhoads, H.	Thorsen, G.	Hines, W. Jr.	Meese, D. L.
Sellman, W.	*Gibbs, R. C.	Roth, R. L.	Way, M. A.	Sullins, E. E.
Simokaitis, J. E.	Epperson, J. H.	Ray, A. F.	Edwards, R. R.	Davis, E. E.
Rockwood, R. H.	Kouba, C. A.	Kuehn, W. H.	Hollander, H. G.	Miller, E. B.
Sutherland, D. B.	Hurtado,	Upton, C. M.	Evans, B.	Mason, J. E.
Anderson, C. R.		Davis, L. S.	Beron, R. A.	Ronn, H. H.
Dishman,		Fischer, A. A.	Zachgo, V. A.	Rogne, R. O.
Patters		Lilienfeld, D. N.	Lawrence, D. M.	Scyphers, T. R.
Occhi		Lepiane, V. R.	Rodgers, E. M.	Johnson, K. L.
Eastl		Dyer, R. H.	Stevens, L.	Hurst, E.

FOURTH ROW (Left to Right)

Stausebach, N. E.
Helling, V. E.
Shelton, N. J.
Hammond, G. E.
Johnson, C. R. B.
Corless, F. G.
Norris, H. L.
Albright, R. L.
Walters, C. L.
Davidson, J. H.
Theiss, E. F.
Green, R. A.
Hines, W. Jr.
Way, M. A.
Edwards, R. R.
Hollander, H. G.
Evans, B.
Beron, R. A.
Zachgo, V. A.
Lawrence, D. M.
Rodgers, E. M.
Stevens, L.

After five weeks Homer summarized his opinion of boot camp in a letter to his long-time friends Lecil and Laura Mae Ulry.

Sunday March 21
Ten oclock

Dear Laura Mae & Lecil

This is a thing I've been wanting to do since I've been here but a person don't even have time to "wipe"   by the time I get those 13 buttons unfastened its time to fall out again. ^{Ha Ha} Well this isn't such a bad place just a step above hell. I lived though Navy shots, feeling good now. I sure have a swell wife   she has sent me two cakes and some candy   like a dam fool the first time I passed my cake out, didn't have but two or three pieces for myself.

I sure like to get mail even if I can't answer. It wouldn't surprise me if we don't get out of here in eight or nine weeks   since I have been here there has been about 14,000 men come here   that a lot of sailors in five weeks isn't it? Are running short of a place to put them.

I think we go to the lake tomorrow to learn how to row boats the Navy way. There are three ways to do anything   right way, wrong way, and the Navy way.

Just took a guard for 2 hour for 75 cents   Every time I can make a little money on the side I do. I made $2.75 one hour washing clothes one night but that will never happen again. I had $15 when I came back from liberty two weeks ago   now I have seventeen and I have been eating candy, cookies, bought a carten of cigarettes that was $1.30. Well had better close now

Good Bye and happy landings,
Homer

PS I'm almost nuts I think. ^{Ha Ha}

When the Navy told Homer's company they'd be finished with boot camp in eight weeks instead of twelve, he looked forward to skipping some of the boot camp experience. However, to his surprise instead of leaving out parts of the training, the Navy opted to cram it all in. Homer was even busier than normal.

Tuesday 23-March
Six oclock

Dearest Ruthie

Your old man is a little tired tonight   Had rifle drill this morning with a band, the rifles are dumbes 30-30ies   this afternoon we walked to the lake about three miles   rowed two hours and walked back   then we cleaned the barracks up   it is spotless. I want to practice on our rifle drill tonight.

Some of the boys won't get up at mornings   they have not been doing the jobs they were suppose to   so they took 12 of their names this morning and they have to stand guard duty from 12 to 4 AM   I expect they will get up now.

They are trying to have a square dance in here but they better not. Mr Wilson is coming over tonight and hell going to fly if they get caught.

I'm sure getting a lot of good out of the little memorandum & address book you sent me   it has a calendar in it, the only one I have excess to. Good night Honey

I love you truly
Your Darling Husband

PS Sure wish I could see you   its a lot I can't write in a letter.

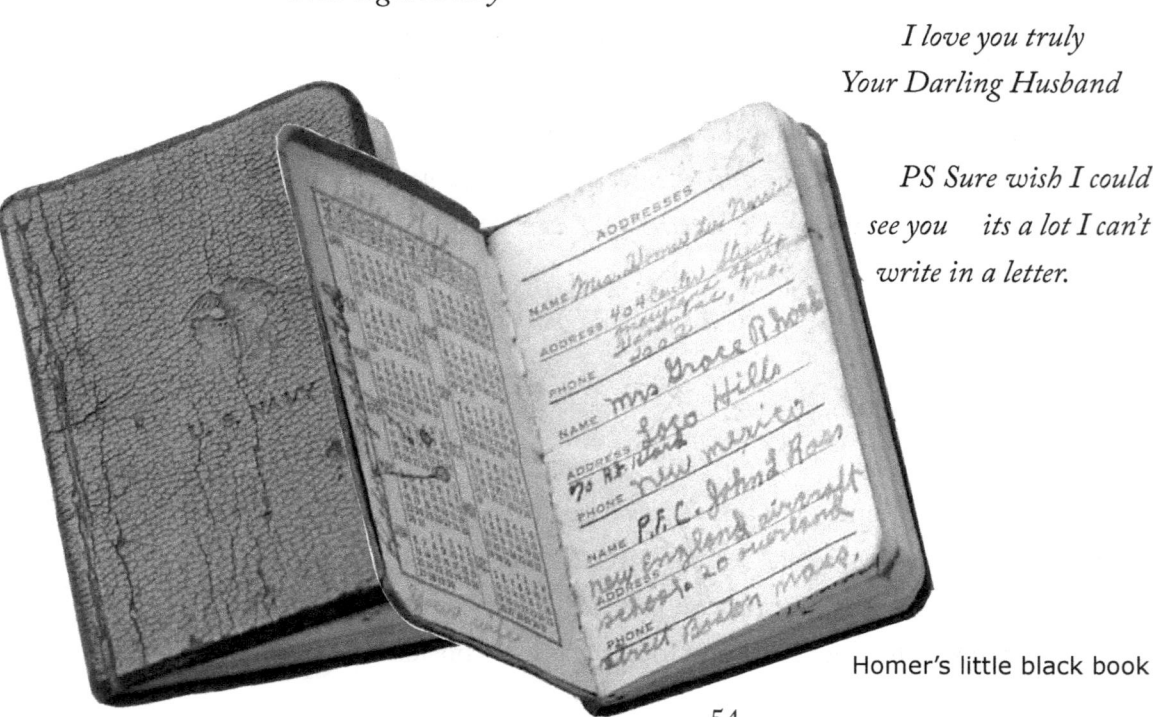

Homer's little black book

March 27
Saturday one twenty

My Ruth Marie

Honey last night I drove all over camp to deliver messages   some of the roads were almost impassable. This job is the first I have liked since I've been in the U.S. Navy

I was on guard this morning from eight to twelve noon. I just had a fried egg with fried ham sandwich   sure was good. Harold got some candy from home and I had to help him eat it. ^{Ha Ha} now eating an apple and cookies so I ought to write a good letter shouldn't I? I am on duty tonight from midnight to four in the morning so three hours sleep tonight—this is a lot of fun.^{Ha Ha}

Honey we are supposed to get out of here about the 9th of April! We got measured for our dress blues   that's the ones that have three stripes around the collar and a star in each corner. Well that almost made me lose my mind (with joy)   the sooner we got out of here the better it will suit me.

I sure feel good now. We had our final strength test   I never made but 379 points   I had boxed the night before and was so sore that I did well to get that.

I signed up for boxing so I may get my little "butt" knocked off "hope not." Sure wish we were going to Perry tonight   wouldn't that be swell. I guess I'll have to finish this tomorrow.

I love you my Dear,
Your old man Homer

Sunday Morning
Eight oclock

My Dear Ruthe

Here it is April 4 it won't be long until the 9th I still think we will graduate then. I'm sorry I couldn't write very much this week but we have been so busy. We have been going to shows on air planes, ships and a lot of other naval things and lectures my god I didn't know there was so many different things to know.

Well honey a lot happened last night from 4-8 while I was on messanger duty. Some of the boys tied others sea bags up to the celling and throwed eggs around the barrock and a duty officer caught them. This morning while I was on duty, I guess Mr. Wilson raised the devil and made the boys run about three miles without stopping and then made us drill. I don't know what else we are going to have to do for a few fools.

Last night at ten twenty we had a fire drill that was a lot of fun to get up and dress just to stand out side for ten minutes. I ran out this morning and went to early chow 6:30 then I came back shaved, washed my teeth rolled a suit of clothes, and now I'm writting. Have to write to Mother & Dad now.

Good Bye Honey
I love you My Dear,
Your old Man Homer

Ruth had worried about her "old man Homer" when he first got to boot camp. The shots made him sick, and then he caught a bad cold. As the weeks passed, she was relieved when he regained his strength.

She wasn't at all surprised when he started doing extra laundry and guard duty for hire. If anyone could figure out a way to make a little money on the side, it was Homer. Navy officers had also noticed Homer's work ethic and responsible attitude so he was getting some of the better work assignments—like messenger duty.

With graduation rapidly approaching, Homer was relieved to have the rigors of boot camp behind him. In his free time the farm boy from Missouri was getting to box, row, swim, and play basketball with boys from all over the country. He felt apprehensive about the future, but he was thankful that so far he had been able to adapt to doing things the Navy way.

Graduation

"Some of the boys are sure sick of getting sea duty . . . the longer I can stay from sea the better it will be."

—Homer's letter 4/7/43

The day before graduation a roster for Company 85 was posted indicating each sailor's next assignment. When he looked at the roster list Homer expected to see "service school" written beside his name. However, in the Navy you can't count on anything.

April 7
Ten thirty PM

Hello Darling

I should have a lot to write We are going to graduate tomorrow the 8th noon I think. We got our dress blue jumpers this after noon.

Some of the boys are sure sick of getting sea duty. There were 32 who get sea duty   Roscoe and Harold two of my best friends. I got B.G.   don't know what it is as yet but it last for 45 days then I suppose I'll go to school, the longer I can stay from sea the better it will be. Just two of us got B.G. out of this company of 116.

I'm going to send a telegram as soon as I find out what this B.G. is   you will probably get it before you get this letter.

I hope I can come home soon   it will cost around $47 a round trip. Maby if I can't come now I can after my 45 days before I go to school. I'm going to get a leave just as soon as I can. I sure would like to see my wife.

I hope I go to school close to home because I want you to come where I go   wont that be nice?

We made up one dollar collection each for our company commander. I'm not suppose to be up at this time of the night but I got off of guard duty at ten, now I'm in the officers room writing.

I got our group pictures today   will send tomorrow when I get some stamps. Will close now am getting sleepy.

Well good night honey
I love you
Homer

On April 8 Homer graduated, and was automatically promoted from Apprentice Seaman to Seaman 2/C [Second Class]. This promotion meant a $4 raise in pay to $54 a month.

After the graduation ceremonies Seaman 2/C Homer Norris was all dressed up in his new uniform with nowhere to go. Homer didn't get assigned to sea duty; consequently, when the other graduates left the base and headed home for a ten-day leave—Homer simply went back to the barracks. He was homesick as hell, missing his buddies, and desperate to see Ruth. However, he didn't have to ship out yet, so he still considered himself the luckiest sailor in Company 85.

Part 3: Ship's Company

Base Electrician

"Very few gets to stay here. I was sure lucky."

—Homer's letter 4/9/43

Instead of sea duty Homer's next assignment was B.G. He thought B.G. stood for Base Guard, but found out it meant Buildings and Grounds. Homer was one of only two men in his company assigned to the Farragut Ship's Company maintenance department—one of the best assignments you could get! During his boot experience Homer had apparently impressed someone with enough clout to get him an assignment better than he could have imagined.

The day after graduation Homer gathered his gear and moved to the Area J barracks reserved for the maintenance department.

He knew Ruth would be disappointed that he wasn't coming home on leave, and he hoped he could make her realize that in the long run this would work out for the best.

April 9
Friday 5:45 P.M.

My Darling
Well this is Homer, seaman second class writing in a new barracks new location.

We graduated four oclock yesterday there was 32 boys that went to sea. I'll get to stay here at least 90 days. Very few gets to stay here. I was sure lucky.

I'm an electrician here on base   my job is to rewind motors   I report at 8 A.M. tomorrow. As far as I know I'm the only person to get this job that isn't rated. This is sure a lot different than where I have been. We don't have to drill at all   go to bed any time we want   the lights go out at 10:oclock but we don't have to go to bed then if we don't want to. We have two mattrass (misspelle) to sleep on   the ships service is right across the street and the chow hall is too. We get a lot more to eat here, all you can eat. We can go to good movie shows any night we want.

I am going to find out what it cost for a train fare and if you can stay here so I can see you   some of the mens wifes are working here on the base and they get to see them ever night.

I inquired about the jobs here on base for women   they are civil service jobs pay $135 a month. Honey don't plan too big on that because the Navy life means "don't plan a thing" but it won't hurt to try because I sure would like to be with you.

I got paid $60 about a week ago, and I loaned Roscoe ten to get home he said he would give it to dad   I'm sure he will. I sure wish I could have come with him but not to go to sea. Thats one thing I'm going to stay out of as long as I can even if I don't get to come home. I think it will be better in the long run.

I had better go to bed because no one calls us at mornings   we get up at our own accord.

Well good night honey smack
Homer

My new address:
Homer Lee Norris S 2/C [Seaman 2nd Class]
14C3 Area J
USNTS Farragut Idaho

For the first time since joining the Navy, Homer realized that for some sailors life was pretty good. He might have been content except for one thing—he was in Idaho and Ruth was in Missouri. On his next liberty he planned to visit the nearest town and search for an apartment to rent.

Sunday Apr 11, noon

Hello, Honey

Here I am in Coeur d'Alene doing just as I please   I came in last night about 7 o'clock on my second liberty. I'm at the U.S.O. There are writting desks, easy chairs here cookies and coffee. They furnish the stationary and wraped my pictures for me   I don't think the U.S.O. can be beat. I stayed at a rooming house last night cost $1

I inquired about rooms for us   it would cost around two dollars a day beside board   a train fare cost about $100 a round trip   so I suppose we will have to forget about this thing of you coming out here

Its sure nice to get away from camp and sort of get my mind off of it. All I'm hoping is this war will be over soon

With all the love in the world,
your darling husband
Homer the sailor man

After failing in his first attempt to find a place for Ruth to stay, Homer vowed to try again the next Sunday. He had to get Ruth to Idaho even if the train fare was the equivalent of two months of his pay. Somehow he would find a way to earn extra money so he could be with his wonderful wife. In the meantime he would concentrate on his day-job as a base electrician.

Monday, Apr 12
Six thirty

Hello My Darling,

Well I lived through my first days work o.k. I wound one motor there are five fellows working there counting me. I don't know a sole where I am. They sure are nice they all try and help me with what I don't know and that's a lot. Its just what I had at that school I went to in Perry so it will come back. I go to work at eight oclock Then we get off at 4:20. I wish I had longer hours to work this way I have too much time to think about home.

I sent you a money order today forty dollars don't have but a five dollar bill now but that's enough this is no place to carry money that much anyway. If you need it it's yours. I'm also sending this two dollar bill home I got it about two weeks ago and didn't want to spend it, its so seldom I've ever seen a two dollar bill. Sunday I got the nicest little bible at the U.S.O. at Coeur d'Alene the new Testament

Honey I would like for you to send our iron These three men that do ironings have taken in 25 dollars the last two days that's better than eight dollars each not bad last night they worked until two thirty this morning so they earned it. They are going to be sent out some time soon so I just as well take up where they leave off. If I have good luck and can iron maybe I can save enough for you to come out or maybe I can get a leave, the lord only knows.

I bought a work jacket cost $1.10 they make a person buy almost everything. Six of us bought a glass coffee maker cost $1.66 each hot plate and all we can have good coffee now. We get the coffee, sugar & cream at the mess hall free that's about the only thing we do get free besides our eats know wonder the boys in the armed forces can't save money. I made a dollar tonight selling candy, cig. and ice cream but it isn't like it was in boot camp its too many others here doing the same thing. But when I get my iron look out then. ^{Ha Ha}

By the time I get out of this Navy I'll be a jack of all trades.
Good Bye Honey
You have all my love
your old Sailor Man

The iron he referred to was the electric iron Ruth's parents had given them as a wedding gift. Homer had never ironed before, but he was convinced that if these other men could learn to iron, so could he.

Homer knew it would take several weeks before he got the iron. In the mean time he was broke. He had sent $40 home and thought $5 would be enough to last until pay day. He was wrong. He didn't know he would have to buy a jacket and a coffee maker. He didn't plan on making several trips to Coeur d'Alene. He didn't know how hard it would be to earn a little "doe-ray-me." He was singing the "pay-day blues."

A Place for Ruth to Stay

"He [Roscoe] *said he would have you out here if you had to live in a tent, but I can't even find a tent.* ^{Ha Ha}*"*

—Homer's letter 4/20/43

Friday, Apr 16
Ten PM

Dearest Ruth,

I'm on a four hour telephone watch tonight   all I'm doing is watching the phone   haven't gotten a call. I'm taking a cold   my nose is running like a sugar tree in the spring of the year.

Oh yes I got your cake today   it is still fresh   sure is good   Honey you sure are a grand wife always sending me something to eat. I can't think of a better graduation present. When I get off watch I'm going back to the barracks and have cake.

I found out yesterday that I can't get a rating until I'm out of temporary ships company, that's what I'm in now   also I can't get a leave for 90 days   that's a hell of a long time if you ask your old Uncle Duddley.

We have a radio in the barracks now   I hear the war news ever night, its mostly good news but I don't see how this war is going to get over very soon but maybe the lord will help us end it soon, things have got to happen over the waters and on the water if it does, well so much for that. What I want is to come back home and live and raise a family.

    I suppose there isn't know need of telling how much I would like to see you   this is still a lot better than being out on the sea…the longer I can stay here the better. Its about bed time   I'll close now
    So long, never good bye

Homer

    P.S. Did you know, I love you? ^{Ha Ha}

And he sealed the envelope with a kiss.   S.W.A.K.

April 19, 43
Monday noon

My Darling Wife,

    Thought I had better write this noon because tonight I want to see if I can find my old buddies Roscoe & Harold   they should have come in this morning   back from their twelve day leave. They won't be here very long before they ship out.

    The men that are here working with me are mostly over 40 years old so I should be looked after.^{Ha Ha} Believe it or not the men don't tell jokes here   I don't know why   looks like some would doesn't it?

    This noon I went through the chow line twice making a pig out of myself.^{Ha Ha} Had custard pie, beef steak & gravy, mashed potatoes   right good dinner.

    Yesterday I went to Coeur d'Alene trying to find a place for an old woman to stay   but honey there isn't even one room   there are about 10 or 15 thousand here that wants the same thing   but I haven't given up yet   I'll try some place else the next time. I can't get a place any father away than Coeur d'Alene because it would be too far for me to come each night.

    I have to stop now and go to work.

So long honey I love you and always will
Homer

    P.S. Oh honey I got a Kodak "616" at the U.S.O. and had 5 pictures taken of myself. Will send soon as I get them.

Homer sounded pretty matter-of-fact when he told Ruth about the Kodak camera he purchased at the USO. We don't know how much he paid for the camera, but it would turn out to be the best purchase Homer made while he was in the Navy.

Tuesday 20th noon

Hello, Honey

I went over and hunted Roscoe up last night. I rode a bicycle (don't know how to spell)   it belongs to the electric department so I took it after working hours. I expect I rode four or five miles   thats my only exciser   I can't spell sh_ _ tonight.

Roscoe said that he stopped and saw Mother & Dad. He sure hated to come back   the train he got didn't have any beds   had to sleep sitting up, his clothes was just dirty as could be.

I told him that I had been looking for a place for you to stay. He said he would have you out here if you had to live in a tent, but I can't even find a tent. ^(Ha Ha)

Have you ever gotten any money from the Government? I'll get paid in two weeks I hope. I have a dollar and half to make out on, but I don't want you to send me any. When our iron comes, maybe I can make a little on the side then

Well I'm going to have to stop writing and go to work. I have 20 minutes to get there. Bye, Bye,

Your Old Man
Homer

When Homer asked if Ruth got any money from the government, he was referring to the 1942 Servicemen's Dependents Allowance Act which required married servicemen to contribute $22 from their monthly pay and the government added $28 dependents allowance to make a $50 monthly stipend for their wives. In March Ruth received her first check for $50 dependents allowance.

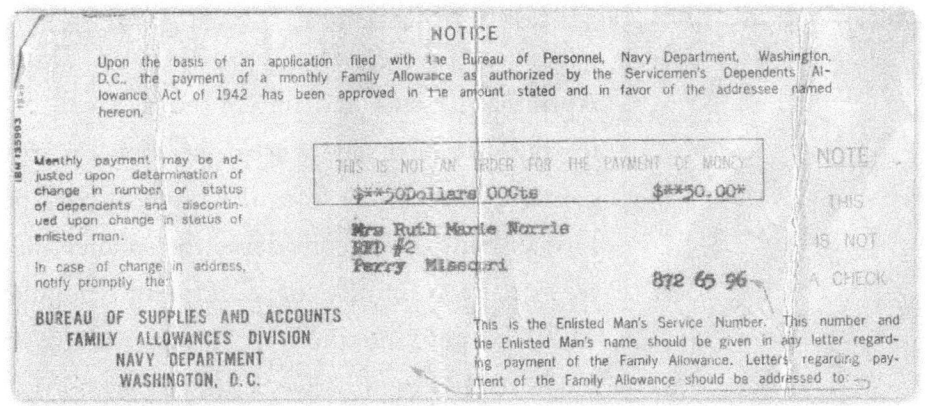

Thursday 22nd noon

My Darling Wife

I just received my pictures I took last Sunday   I think they are very good. I wanted to send you a gift for Easter, but haven't got enough "doe ray me" so the pictures will have to do.^{Ha Ha}

I got a letter from you today . . . and a box of candy from Mother & Dad   they sure are good. I'm eating candy and writting   don't be surprised if this had candy on it.

Say the first motor I rewound worked   aren't you supprised   I was and the second is going to work too.

I cleaned my locker, counted my letters   I have gotten 75 since I've been here. I think I'm going to have to destroy my letters   they are in the way. I still have the picture of you & me on our wedding day. I'm about to wear it out kissing it. That's all I have to kiss.   I l o v e you lots & lots.

Honey I'm trying my best to find a place for us to stay, I ask ever one I see if they know of any places   but no luck so far.

I don't expect I'll get to go to school now after this ship company. I believe I'm going to learn more here than I would have in school any way, maybe every thing will work out for the best.

Lot of Love & The Very best of Wishes,
Homer

P.S. . . . I love you

This would be his last letter for four months!

Homer on steps of USO

When Homer wrote to Ruth on Thursday, April 22, he still had not found a place for her to stay. The next day at work he met a man who commuted each day from the town of Sandpoint. Homer hadn't even considered the smaller and less crowded community of Sandpoint (population 4400) because he thought it was too far away. However, it was only two miles farther north than Coeur d'Alene was south.

Early Sunday morning Homer took a bus to Sandpoint. His first stop was the USO where he met several very helpful people. Before noon he was walking through a quiet residential area with nice homes that had been converted into apartment houses to accommodate the population explosion caused by Sandpoint's close proximity to the Naval Base.

In front of a two-story white house a sign said, "Rooms for Rent." The landlady Mrs. Prater showed him a two-room apartment, and agreed to rent the apartment to him without a deposit!

Monday at noon he sent a telegram to Ruth:

Sandpoint, Idaho April 25, 1943

FOUND APARTMENT=
WIRE $20 FOR RENT=
COME TO IDAHO.=
LOVE:=
HOMER

Wanted!!!!! A Wife AT Once.

"Ruth started to Idaho 7:20 P.M."
—Entry from Mom Norris's diary 4/28/43

Monday night Ruth got home from work and found a "missed telegram" notice hanging on the front door knob. The Western Union office was closed for the night so she had to wait until morning to get the telegram.

Tuesday morning Ruth arrived at work triumphantly waving Homer's telegram and hoping that her boss would not be mad at her for leaving. Two months earlier Ruth accepted the job with the understanding that if Homer got stationed in a place where wives could join their husbands she wanted to go be with him. Everyone at the store read the telegram and her boss, Mr. Smith agreed that Ruth should go to Idaho as soon as possible. Ruth gave all her co-workers warm hugs, grabbed a few of her personal items, and was on her way.

First, she hurried to Western Union and wired $20 rent money to Homer.

Then she phoned Homer's parents to tell them the news, called the train station to purchase a one-way ticket to Idaho, and then packed every suitcase she owned. When Homer's parents came to pick her up that afternoon she was sitting on a suitcase in front of her apartment house waiting for them. She spent the night at the Norris farm.

Wednesday morning Ruth was the first customer when the Perry State Bank opened. She withdrew the $250 from selling their car and left the bank with many best wishes for a safe trip to Idaho.

At noon she bid farewell to her parents and grandparents. It was difficult for them to think about her traveling so far by herself, but they knew there was no stopping her. Everyone knew Ruth would walk to Idaho if it meant she could be with Homer.

Wednesday afternoon Homer's parents drove Ruth to the train station. That night Mom Norris's diary reads, "Ruth started to Idaho 7:20 P.M."

Thursday Ruth rode the train—all day and all night. She couldn't afford a sleeper berth and sat up the whole trip. She was too wound up to sleep anyway, and passed the time visiting with the other passengers.

Friday was a very long day. It was Ruth's second full day on the train and she was anxious to be in Idaho. Homer had requested an "exchange of duty" for Friday so he didn't have to work, and spent the day with butterflies in his stomach. He must have looked at his watch a thousand times. He was excited, and for good reason—that night he had a date!

He packed some clothes and a few toiletries in his duffle bag, and put on his best dress blues. Then he walked to the Naval station front gate, and caught the Inter-Lake bus to Sandpoint.

F.N.T.S. bus (Homer in middle)

Getting off the bus, Homer went to the Sandpoint Drug Store & Soda Fountain and spent the last of his money on a box of chocolates for Ruth. Then he walked four blocks to the train station. Finding a bench on the station platform he sat down, pulled a pencil from his pocket, and wrote a short message on the bottom of the candy box. For the next several hours he sat, stood, paced, got a drink of water, went to the bathroom, paced, stood and sat some more.

At 7:43 P.M. the whistle of a not-too-distant train brought Seaman Norris to his feet. He smoothed his clothes, straightened his sailor's hat and tried to act calm even though his heart felt like it might explode.

At exactly 7:45 a train pulled into the Sandpoint station. Homer scanned the train windows until he caught sight of a very familiar face that beamed back at him. Minutes later a porter emerged, and offered his hand to a beautiful black-haired girl from Missouri.

She stepped off the train and reached up to adjust her hat. Her brown eyes sparkled as she hurried toward her handsome sailor husband. As they got closer she wondered why he had a mischievous look on his face. Beneath his chin he was holding something with both hands. Was it a box? A sign? Seconds later she burst into laughter when she read the note he had written on the bottom of a box of chocolates.

Glued to a page in Ruth's scrapbook is a symbol of one of Homer and Ruth's happiest memories—the cardboard bottom from a box of chocolates.

In the back of her diary is a calendar page with a circle around the date of Friday, April 30, 1943. In tiny letters Ruth wrote, "arrived in Sandpoint 7:45."

Summer in Sandpoint

"My first bike ride. Do my legs ache Uh huh."
—Ruth's note on back of photograph

Homer and Ruth picked up Ruth's bulging suitcases and left the train station heading toward their apartment house. As they walked past the business district, Ruth was amazed at the number of servicemen in the downtown area. The crowds thinned out once they reached the middle class family neighborhoods. Springtime leaf buds were just beginning to open on tall trees that lined both sides of the paved streets, but Homer and Ruth didn't even notice the trees or the heavy suitcases as they talked nonstop about everything and nothing. The sun faded behind distant mountains and street lights glowed to welcome them.

Six blocks from the train station they stopped at 413 Lake Street in front of their two-story apartment house. It was a well-kept modest home, painted white with lots of windows to allow in the fresh Idaho air. Like many of her neighbors, Nettie Prater

413 Lake Street Sandpoint, Idaho

converted every available space into apartments and became a wartime landlady.

Mrs. Prater liked Homer from their first meeting. And months later she wrote a warm letter of encouragement to Ruth saying how much she enjoyed having them there. Mrs. Prater's letter is in Ruth's scrapbook.

During the summer of '43 Homer and Ruth were far from home, broke, and fearing their wartime future. However, after spending ten weeks apart, they were ecstatically happy to be together. Their summer activities can be traced through Ruth's scrapbook filled with photographs, newspaper clippings, church bulletins, and receipts. For a few weeks they could assume a more normal lifestyle as they shared picnic lunches by the lake and skipped stones across the water.

They even went to the movies! Homer hadn't cared much about going

Lake Pend O'Reille beach

to movies while he was at Farragut, but going with Ruth was a lot more fun. According to the *Sandpoint Shopping Bulletin*[11] the summer movies included "Wake Island" with McDonald Carey and Robert Preston; and "Sunset Serenade" with Roy Rogers, Gabby Hayes and Lynn Merrick.

Homer's first responsibility was his Navy electrician's job on base. Monday through Friday he commuted by bus from Sandpoint to the Farragut Naval Training Station.

While he was at work Ruth took care of their apartment, ran errands and participated in local USO activities. The Sandpoint USO located in a big log cabin in the middle of town, was obviously the center of social activity. Women in the community donated sandwiches, cookies and coffee to keep the kitchen well stocked. The USO never charged servicemen or their wives for any food or supplies. A game room had tables set up for cards, checkers and dominoes, plus a few easy chairs and small desks where sailors could relax or write a letter.

Ruth made friends with other Navy wives and joined their bridge and pinochle club. In the scrapbook is a newspaper clipping from the Sandpoint Society Page.[12]

THURSDAY, JULY 29, 1943

SOCIETY

Navy Wives Meet

The Navy Wives met Monday afternoon at the USO with Mrs. Blanche Mock and Mrs. Rose Northrup as hostesses.

After a business meeting bridge and pinochle were played. Mrs. Violet Grisvold won the bridge prize and Mrs. Ruth Norris the pinochle prize.

❖ ❖

Dr. and Mrs. McKinnon Entertain

A delightful time was enjoyed by a group of children at a picnic supper

Beneath the article is a pinochle scorecard with Ruth's hand-written note, "My score at Pinnochle when I won the baking dish at USO Club in Idaho."

While Ruth was in Idaho she rode a bicycle for the first time. A photograph shows Homer and Ruth standing beside two bicycles in the back yard of their apartment house. On the back of the photograph Ruth wrote, "My first bike ride. Do my legs ache Uh huh."

To see you serve this Grand Old Flag
 Is most inspiring, Son —
Your Victory is sure, because
 THESE COLORS NEVER RUN!
But, on your Birthday, every thought
 Becomes a wish for You —
A loving wish for happiness
And luck to see you through!
Mother and Dad.

Homer and Ruth were away from home on their birthdays, but family and friends didn't forget about them. In May Homer received several birthday cards, including a special one from his parents in honor of his twenty-third birthday.

June 23 was Ruth's birthday and Homer's mother mailed a birthday cake to her. The cake arrived in perfect condition with twenty-one candles on top!

The Fourth of July had always been their favorite summer holiday because back home the Fourth of July meant picnics, music, dancing, and lots of fun. This year thinking about July made Homer and Ruth homesick. To their surprise, the Sandpoint celebration put the Perry picnic to shame. For weeks the festivities were the talk of the town, and the July 1 newspaper headline read:

Expect Farragut to Really Come to Town Sunday[13]

July 4 has been set as the day for introducing recruits of the naval training station to Sandpoint. We will have four or five hundred ship's servicemen plus a possible five hundred recruits in town Sunday. It is important that these men be properly fed. Because of the current food shortage, the U.S.O. requests as many donations of sandwiches, cakes and cookies as possible.

Dancing was a big part of the USO activities. The main room had a juke box that encouraged continuous dancing. According to the local newspaper, one Saturday night the USO dance floor saw fifty couples dancing while the Navy orchestra from the Farragut Ship's Company played.[14]

It's a good thing that many activities were free of charge, because Homer and Ruth didn't have much money. Their monthly income (including his Navy pay and her dependents allowance) was only $82.

The *Sandpoint Shopping Bulletin* made weekly references to food prices and ration coupons. Bread sold for 9¢ a loaf, radishes were 4¢ a bunch, Idaho potatoes were 100 lbs for $2.69, and bacon was 37¢/lb.[15] Meat was such a valuable commodity that while Homer and Ruth were in Idaho, his parents even sent them a home-cured ham.

In addition to food, rationing encompassed automobiles, gasoline, tires, and fuel oil. Before Homer went to the Navy he was affected by gasoline rationing and conserved as much as he could so he would have enough gas for his tractor. Ration books brought the war into the daily lives of the American people. Everyone shared the burden of war—whether they wanted to or not. Ruth's scrapbook includes several partially used ration books and a page with mills and ration coins that she collected.

While Homer and Ruth were in Idaho, Homer's mother kept them updated on the tittle-tattle back home. Mom Norris's diary mentions many cards, letters, and packages between Missouri and Idaho.

Ration stamps from Ruth's scrapbook

Homer's mother often sent *The Perry Enterprise* newspaper. The July 1 issue had an article about him in the section titled, "Our Men in the Service." A note in Ruth's handwriting says, "My Darlings' picture was in the paper!"

SEAMAN HOMER L. NORRIS

Homer Lee Norris, seaman second class in the U. S. Navy, son of Mr. and Mrs. Harry Norris, south of town, is stationed at Farragut, Idaho. Homer was inducted into service at Jefferson Barracks February 3, 1943 and enlisted in the Navy. He left Jefferson Barracks February 10th for Farragut, Idaho where he has taken his boot training. He is now in a ship company, maintenance department, at Farragut. His wife, the former Miss Ruth Yancey, is with Homer at his station.

"Our Men in the Service"
July 1, 1943

Homer and Ruth were together in Idaho for 101 glorious summer days. During that time war raged in the air, on land, and at sea as the U.S. Navy escalated its efforts to counteract the aggression of Japan. Names of faraway islands like Solomons, Aleutians, Gilberts, and Guadalcanal became common place. The outlook for the future was ominous. But at 413 Lake Street Homer and Ruth could shut out the rest of the world and enjoy the simple pleasures of everyday living. They went on bike rides, drank chocolate shakes at the soda fountain, held hands on long walks and shared romantic summer nights in their apartment where they pretended the world was at peace.

On Monday, August 9, the Sandpoint summer of '43 ended abruptly. Homer was working at his base job when he unexpectedly got new orders for a twelve-day furlough.

After his furlough he was to return to Farragut on August 24 to await orders—probably for sea duty.

Furlough

"Homer cried after he got on the train."

—Entry from Ruth's Diary 8/21/43

With furlough orders in hand, Homer quickly sent a telegram to his parents and grabbed the next bus to Sandpoint. Then he hurried to their apartment to tell Ruth the news. That afternoon they repacked all of Ruth's suitcases, cleaned the apartment, and made one last visit to the USO. After his furlough Homer would return to Farragut, but Ruth would have to stay home. Ruth hated leaving the friends she had met at the USO. She told them all "farewell" instead of "good-bye" even though she knew it was unlikely they would ever meet again.

The next morning (Tuesday, August 10) Ruth and Homer gave their landlady the keys to their apartment, and left Idaho aboard a train to Missouri. That same day Homer's parents received a telegram confirming that Homer and Ruth were coming home.

After six months in Idaho Homer was excited about going home. Unfortunately, the twelve-day furlough came without any vouchers for travel expenses or food. If a serviceman wanted to go home he did so at his own expense. Homer and Ruth spent $90.12 (more than a month's pay) on train tickets to Missouri.

Sometimes servicemen and their spouses were treated like second-class citizens when they rode on trains. Homer and Ruth rode in the oldest cars on the train and slept sitting up. They couldn't afford expensive dining car food, and ate sandwiches they brought with them. After traveling for two days they arrived in Mexico, Missouri Thursday evening. Stepping off the train they were greeted by Homer's parents, Ruth's mother, and their friends Lecil and Laura Mae Ulry. They shoved Ruth's suitcases into the trunk and drove the three miles to the Norris farm for a late supper of ham sandwiches and chocolate pie.

For the next eight days Homer and Ruth were treated like celebrities. On Sunday Mom Norris wrote in her diary, "Picnic in Perry Park for Homer and Ruth." Everyone knew that when Homer got back to Farragut his next orders would probably be for sea duty. If Homer was headed overseas, he would leave with their best wishes for a safe return. Homer received dozens of hugs and handshakes. However underlying their encouragement was the unspoken fear that they might never see him again.

The August 19, 1943 edition of *The Perry Enterprise* had an article about Homer under the section "With Our Armed Forces." It read, "A picnic dinner was enjoyed at the Perry Park Sunday, August 15th honoring Seaman Homer Lee Norris who with Mrs. Norris was here on leave." The article listed names of over forty picnic attendees and went on to say, "Homer has completed his boot training and his course in electricity and is now ready for active service with our armed forces."

Two days after the picnic Ruth and Homer drove to Hannibal to the Kresge Store. While Ruth met with her boss Mr. Smith, the Kresge girls chatted with Homer. It was the first time Homer had met any of her co-workers, but Ruth had written about them so much he felt like he already knew them. Ruth got her old job back and even managed to get another (even larger) room at the Maryland Apartments. She was glad for Homer to see where she would be spending her time while he was gone.

Ruth and Homer during Furlough

Homer with niece and neighbor boy

It was great to be home and away from the war, but all too soon his furlough was over. Friday evening friends and parents congregated at the Norris farm for Homer's farewell dinner.

Saturday, August 21, 1943 was the day they had all dreaded. Mom Norris wrote in her diary, "took Homer to Mexico to train 12:30 noon."

Six months ago when Homer left for boot camp, Ruth's feelings of sadness were awful, but what she felt now was a million times worse. Back in February Homer was just leaving for a few weeks of training. Now he was going to war.

When passengers began boarding the train, Ruth's heart raced but the scene on the station platform seemed to unfold in slow motion. She tried to savor every word Homer said, every time their eyes met, every touch of his hand against hers. For just a moment time stood still . . . then the train conductor hollered, "All aboard" and panic gripped Ruth. The moment she had dreaded was here.

Homer gently touched his cheek to hers, and his voice cracked a little when he whispered, "I love you always." Unable to speak, she threw her arms around his neck and her kiss said all the words she was feeling. Then he turned, stepped onto the train, and disappeared from sight. Her eyes scanned the train windows until she caught a glimpse of him taking his seat.

Looking out the train window, he searched the platform for Ruth. Their eyes met for one last time. Then his eyes filled with tears and he looked away. It broke Ruth's heart to see Homer cry. Overcome by the emotions she had choked down for so long, she stepped behind one of the platform posts so he wouldn't see her cry. Suddenly the train jerked, wheels squealed as they rolled forward, and he was gone.

Ruth hadn't written in her diary for months, but on August 21 she wrote,

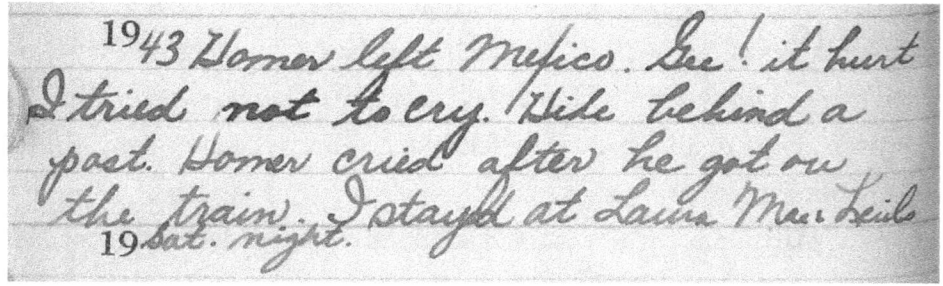

Part 4:
Preparing for Sea Duty

Ridin' the Rails

". . . the [train] conductor came along and told me I would have to move . . . so I did   madder than an old setten hen."

—Homer's letter 8/23/43

When the United States entered World War II, the American railroads were not prepared to handle the tremendous number of servicemen and women who had to be moved from one region to another. The Navy policy of training recruits far from home contributed to the crushing volume of train traffic and created a financial hardship on sailors who paid their own travel expenses to go home on leave. By the fall of 1943 trains ran almost everywhere! The Association of American Railroads boasted that the "230,000 miles of rails made the railroad the World's Busiest Highway."[16]

Trains advertised delicious dining car meals served on white table cloths. In reality few servicemen could afford to purchase any food on the train. On Homer's trip from Missouri back to Idaho his only food was a sack lunch given to him by the Red Cross at a trackside canteen in Sheridan, Wyoming.

The kindness shown to Homer by the Red Cross is indicative of the grateful mind-set of most Americans during the war. In dozens of towns across the country canteen volunteers set up refreshment stands on station platforms. They met troop trains—day and night and offered free food to millions of soldiers. Homer never forgot the kindness of the canteen volunteers.

We like to think that military men and women were treated well on trains. Unfortunately, when Homer was on his way back to Idaho he felt disrespected. It made him angry.

Aug 23
Monday Night
8 thirty

Dearest Ruthe

Here I am at the USO at Sandpoint   I got in at seven thirty   came up here and cleaned up some and had two sandwiches and some cookies   it sure was dirty on the train   I had an air conditioned car to Kansas City and from there on to Billings the Navy boys had to ride in old cars like the one we rode in from St Paul to K.C.   at Kansas City they told me to get on the old car and I did but walked on down to a good car   the conductor came along and told me I would have to move   so I got up and went to the other end of the same car, there an M.P. came and asked if I was supposed to be in that car and I said yes   then he went and asked the conductor and then came back and told me to move so I did   madder than an old setten hen well I suppose I was lucky not to get kicked off. Ha Ha

At (Sherdian)spell Wyo. the red cross gave us cigarettes (20) and sack lunches to take with us, an orange, milk, candy bar and magazine. The first night I never went to sleep until day light and last night I never got very much sleep. I guess I'll go out on the ten thirty buss tonight. Well I had better sign off for now.

Love,
Homer

When Homer's bus got back to Farragut, he slept in the Ship's Company barracks. The next day he moved to Barracks 11 reserved for out-going units.

Homer's letters reveal a negative attitude that was uncharacteristic for him. The Homer who had been so responsible and hard working during boot camp had been replaced by a sailor who broke rules, pushed limits, and didn't seem to care anymore.

Wednesday 25th
7:30 Night

Dearest Ruth;

I guess I'll be leaving in 2 days   I'm going to Port Hueneme near Sa Monical California   its about 45 miles west of Los Angeles right on the coast. I don't know what it is or how long I'll stay.

I'm suppose to work but they can't find me and they arn't as long as I'm here, I go visiting just before they line up to go work.

Well honey I'm going to make this letter short & I don't know about the sweet part. ^{Ha Ha}

Good Bye Honey

Homer

On August 27 Homer left the Farragut Naval Training Station for the last time, and boarded a southbound train to California.

By the time Homer got to California, he had spent five out of the last nine days on trains and traveled over 2800 miles!

Sun Shiny California

"It looks like I'm going to sea   don't know just when but I'm afared its coming   I may be put in the C.B. landing force...."

—Homer's letter 8/30/43

After a couple of train rides that were dirty, sleepless, and frustrating Homer was pleasantly surprised when his trip from Idaho to California offered comfortable accommodations, fascinating scenery, and lots of good eats.

Salem, Oregon
Saturday 28th

My Darling Wife,

Honey I give anything if you could be with me on this trip, now get your map out and I'll tell you where we've been   we started out yesterday (Friday 2 PM) from Farragut and went through Spokane to Seattle Washington   south to Tacoma down to Portland Ore.   now past Salem the capital of Oregon.

We're riding in a Pullman, I'm in a car with private rooms   the only one in the train of 12 cars   it's the same one the officers are in   its three beds in this room and three riding in it. The other two boys in this room are asleep. We have a private toilet wash basin.

In Washington they have a lot of wheat   I saw hundreds of thousands of bushels run out on the ground   no cover over it   so it must not rain very often there. Also lots of lumber mills, in every river they have big logs in them floating down.

Here in Oregon they have lots of timber, some corn   We just pasted a big pole bean field ten acres I expect   it looked like 12 or 15 people picking. Not many mountains. we went though an eight mile tunnel last night while asleep   an electric engine pulls the train through.

There are 165 men on this draft   its suppose to take three days to get to Calif. I'm not going to stay there very long because our orders said to further transfer so its probably sea duty. We're stopping at a little town so maby I can mail this letter.

I love you honey
Homer

The Navy didn't send Homer to California to enjoy the ocean view, but the boy from Missouri could not contain his excitement upon experiencing the ocean for the first time.

All construction battalions [C.B.'s] were sent to Port Hueneme [y-NEE-may] for final training and outfitting before they were shipped overseas. C.B.'s better known as "Seabees" did not go through boot camp. Instead they were recruited directly from the civilian construction trades. Homer hadn't been trained in construction but his electrician's training made him a good fit with the C.B.'s.

30-Aug-43
Monday Night seven thirty

My Darling

Honey here I am in sun shiny Calif, it sure is nice here   the Pacific so close here I can see it plain any time. We had a swell trip all the way. I saw the golden gate bridge. It looks like I'm going to sea   don't know just when but I'm afared its coming   I may be put in the C.B. landing force, that is about all there is here.

The weather is wonderful here. I went swimming yesterday in the Pacific ocean and don't think for a minute that it isn't salty and cold   I like to froze but it was a lot of fun   those waves are high as ten feet I expect   if you don't go over them they sure take you for a roll and I sure got rolled   got salt water in my eyes nose, mouth, but it was worth it.

I've got to wash clothes tomorrow. I took a bath this morning the first and only one since I left Farragut. I've got to write my folks tonight so good night honey and lots of love,

Homer

Homer soon discovered that there were many differences between the Naval bases in Idaho and California. In Idaho there were thirty thousand sailors on the base, but the surrounding communities still felt like small towns. In California when he left the base he was in the midst of huge crowds of people everywhere. One city blended into the next. Sandpoint's USO felt like a home away from home, but there was nothing homey about the Hollywood Canteen and Palladium Theater.

In Idaho the USO dance floor was crowded with one hundred people who danced to music from the juke box and ate free food. In California the Palladium dance floor held four thousand with music provided by the likes of Tommy Dorsey and Frank Sinatra. One dinner at the Palladium cost $3 plus the $1 cover charge just to get in the door!

Homer didn't know how long he would be in California, so while he was there he decided to enjoy the ocean and see all the sights. His letter home dated September 6 was written on stationery from the Hollywood Guild & Canteen.

Sept 6

My Darling

I have know reason not to have a good letter this time because I got a special liberty (48 hours) and a friend of mine Fred Smith a young chap 19 years old, blue eyes curley hair 6 ft 2 in so we were about the same size. ^{Ha Ha} [Homer was 5ft 8in tall.]

We started out Saturday hitchhiking and we went around & around until two o'clock   last night we went to Hollywood, Los Angeles, Santa

Monica, Long Beach and within fifty miles of San Diego. We weren't suppose to go but fifty miles away from the base and before we stopped we were close to 200 miles.

With four different rides we ended up at down town Hollywood   we went to the U.S.O. but didn't get to go to the Hollywood canteen   the line was a block long. At eight thirty (Sat night) we went to the Platium the bigest dancing place in Hollywood   Honey you can't realize how nice it was   after we got inside the rugs were about two in thick and the floor was as big as the patch south of my folks house. The music was furnished by Tommy Dorsey och. and it was real too. It lasted until one oclock. After that we went down to the Hollywood guild   its sort of like a U.S.O. only it has cots to sleep on   so thats where we stayed until ten oclock Sunday morning   got up and they gave us our breakfast corn flakes, milk, hot cakes.

Then we began hitch back to Ventura   then got a bus back to the base about two A.M. So that ends my trip. Sure wish you could have been along.

Its almost time for the lights to go out so had better hurry.

Good Night Darling
Homer

After spending the weekend in Hollywood, returning to base Monday morning meant an abrupt return to reality. Weekend liberties were fun and games, but during the week Homer trained for the game of war. In Farragut he had practiced with dummy rifles, now the guns were real. During his second week in California the training intensified. Homer realized that what he was learning now might be very important later when his unit had to unload their own gear while landing on beaches under enemy fire.

ACORN 16

"Our acorn got commissioned this morning... and I've found out what the duties are of the acorns."

—Homer's letter 9/9/43

ACORN was the Navy's code word for the organization of personnel and equipment necessary to rapidly build, operate, and maintain an advanced air base. Each ACORN unit had a construction battalion attached to it to build the airfield and base facilities.[17]

The mission of Homer's ACORN 16 unit involved going ashore on the heels of the Marine assault troops. His unit would work with the construction battalions to clear the aftermath of battle and build airstrips and base facilities. After the bases were operational the construction battalions would move on to other islands. ACORN units stayed to operate and maintain the control tower, field lighting, communication system, transportation, medical, and messing facilities. An unofficial acronym for ACORN was: Airfield Construction Operation Repair Navy.

Sept. 9,
Thursday 9:45PM

Dearest Wife;
We moved this morning, about a mile to the martime building   it's a big building (brick) where most of the officers work   it has 8 dormitories where the waves all stay but they have been moved, to where? I don't know. We eat here in the same building as we sleep   matter of fact we don't have to go out side for any thing [Ha Ha] *I got up at 5:30 AM   I have*

been out on the beach almost all day awaiting to get out gear   put away that's the Navy way, make us wait all day for what should have taken an hour at the most.

Our acorn got commissioned this morning now we are getting organized this afternoon   we drilled all afternoon and I've found out what the duties are of the acorns.

The marines take the island the C.B's build and we build on it and the acorns stay and maintain and protect them. So watch for the time after I get shipped I'll tell you that way where I am.

I just stopped and pressed two suits for a dollar   not as much as I got at Farragut but it helps, thats the first I've pressed since I've been here.

I expect it will be almost a month until I leave but honey there isn't a place around here for you to stay   ever house, store, and old shack has people in them working in war plants.

Italy blowed up this morning   sure was glad to hear it and Germany going to do the same thing with in the next three or four month is my guess. I'll sure be glad when we turn loose everything we've got on Germany   I want this damn thing to get over so I can come home to honey and raise us a family   thats something to wish for isn't it?

Its blackout here   you see all the cars driving with parking lights only. They are turning lights out so good night darling

I love you,

Homer

Now that Homer knew he was headed to an island in the Pacific he wanted to remind Ruth about their secret code system—the **Norris Code**. While they were in Idaho they heard stories about the military censorship policy which did not allow sailors to reveal their location once they left the states. So Homer and Ruth devised a code system to circumvent the Navy censors. They assigned a number to each letter of the alphabet. For example, #1 = "A," #26 = "Z." Homer told Ruth to "watch for the <u>time</u> after I get shipped I'll tell you that way where

I am." His plan was to write the time of day on his letters and when she transcribed his numbers into letters she would know his location. So far the Norris Code was yet to be tested.

Sunday morn
Ten oclock
Sept 12

Dear Ruth;

I'm in Ventura (misspelled) at the U.S.O. am going to church at eleven   its only two blocks from here so I'll have time to write my honey a letter.

I went to a dance here at the U.S.O. last night   it was over at eleven then I went down to a hotel and slept in the lobby on a davenett. I will go back to the base this afternoon.

I had bacon & eggs for breakfast and coffee 65¢ sandwiches are 40¢, T-Bone steaks $1.75. Idaho is cheaper than Calif.

Well honey I'm going to sign off now and go to church.

Bye, Bye, Darling.

P.S. I've received two letter from you

16 Sept 43
Thursday night six thirty

Dearest Ruthe;

I hit the jack pot and got six letters today. Four from my love, two from Mother & Dad

So my wife is working again   I know you were happy that you could get your old job back

Boy am I tired   they sure are putting us over the road now. This morning we mustered at eight oclock then two buses took a lot of us out to the rifle range about 10 miles from here   we got rifles and then drilled all morning then the buses came after us for dinner and took us back after dinner   we practiced shooting 30-30's and taking them down and *putting them back togeather again. Are my dogs tired?* ^{Ha Ha}

Some one stole two of my hats night before last   now I don't have but two. I wanted to go up to see my commanding officer today about my rating but I didn't get time. I'm going up and raise plenty of hell if I don't get it. They say where there is a will there's a way so I have plenty of will in looking out for Homer.

Im going to Hollywood this week end. It will probaly be my last time. Will close for now, so long Darling.

Your old Man

Homer

Lots & lots of my best love

Being stationed at Port Hueneme was a lot different than Farragut. The morale was low, tensions were high, theft was rampant and he frequently overheard men plotting to go A.W.O.L. When they got orders to ship out, some men chose to run the other way. Homer didn't have any intentions of deserting; in fact, he was relieved to be in the ACORNs. He still didn't want to go overseas, but at least he knew his work would be relatively safe. He was grateful for that.

He would be even more grateful if his promotion came through. The Navy had said he could get a higher rating (and pay raise) once he was out of temporary Ship's Company at Farragut. However, he was moving around so much now that it was difficult for the Navy's paper trail to catch up with him.

Riding the Emotional Roller Coaster

"The morale is very, very low among the boys   I think half of them don't think they will come back but not me."

—Homer's letter 9/24/43

When Homer got a Liberty pass on Saturday (9/18) he and a friend decided to forget about war for awhile and hitchhike their way around town.

September 20
Monday Seven oclock

My Darling Wife;

Honey I've got a lot to tell you about my week end. Saturday at 12 oclock Fred and I started from here. He's the nice boy I told you about   we got in to hollywood at 1:30 which was very good time for hitch hiking better than 60 miles. It sure was hot.

We went to a show then to the U.S.O. Then we went to the Platum neather of us wanted to dance so we started to hitch hike to the Grill   the place we stayed the other night.

We walked I expect a mile and a man in a big Buick stopped and asked us if we wanted a ride so we got in with him, he asked us where we were going   I told him that we were hunting for a place to stay all night. He then asked us to come up and stay all night with him so we did.

He was a man fifty years half gray weigh about 180   he had a modern home nine rooms. He wasn't married I don't think because it looked like there hadn't been a woman in the house for some time.

He fixed beds for us and we didn't get up until noon yesterday   he had rolled oats and toast and coffee and then we left

We are the luckiest two boys getting rides that ever was. Cars would pass other boys up then stop for us   just plain luck.

Honey I think I've told you about my trip as well as I can and that's all I have to write about. Will close for now.

Lots of Love & Kisses
Your Old man

Communicating long distance was tricky because written words could get misinterpreted and lead to a long, painful ordeal. For months Homer and Ruth had experienced very few misunderstandings, and they knew better than to fight through the mail. But in the fall of 1943 it happened!

In August when Homer's furlough ended Ruth resigned herself to the fact that it would be months, or even years before they were together again. Then Homer wrote about the sunny California weather and beautiful ocean, and it frustrated her that he was still in the states and she wasn't with him. The more she stewed about it, the madder she got. Against her better judgment she wrote to Homer and accused him of not wanting to be with her. She also complained that he didn't seem to be writing every day. The minute she mailed the letter, she regretted her actions, but it was too late.

It took five days for Ruth's letter to get to Homer. In the meantime she received several letters that had been backlogged. In these letters he had explained why she wouldn't be able to be with him in California. So when Homer innocently opened Ruth's angry letter her blistering words took him completely by surprise.

Tuesday night 21st
Six thirty

Dearest Ruth,

Boy did my ears burn when I got that letter you wrote last Monday night   you must surely been tired and in a bad mood. I think I have written to you ever other day since I've been here, except the week end I went to Hollywood.

Yes honey I've been getting your mail, got 4 one day from you. I'm most sure I metioned them too.

Darling there's a war going on, and I'm not running it eather, you seem to think I don't want you out here, but please don't be that way   being married two years to me you should know better than that. In case you don't know it I'm going to sea in about two weeks, to some island in the Pacific. I just wanted to let you know that letters like this isn't very well enjoyed. Honey this paper is to good to write like this on   I should have written on toilet paper. ^{Ha Ha}

I got a shot yesterday a booster for tetnus. my arm is sore today. we have inspection tomorrow in dress blues

Darling I just can't think of anything else to write now so I'll close with

All my love & kisses
Homer

When Homer mailed the letter, as far as he was concerned they'd both had their say and he wasn't going to waste any more time fighting. It took a couple of weeks, but by the end of September Homer and Ruth's first and last long-distance argument was history.

Ever since Homer arrived in Port Hueneme it seemed like his training was conducted with a sense of urgency, but without any particular time table or organization. Homer and thousands just like him were being kept busy until some unknown moment when they would get orders to ship out. It might be tomorrow, in three weeks, in the middle of the night, or right now. When Homer got up each morning he had no idea what he would do that day or where he'd sleep that night. The unpredictability added a tremendous emotional strain. Every man felt it, and for some it was just too much pressure.

Fri 24th 7:30 P.M.

Dearest Ruth

I got two letters from you today darling, sure was glad to get them. I got paid today $50 intend to send part of it home before I leave. I'm sorry I wrote a letter to you like I did on Tuesday but I was in one of my bad moods like I have ever so often.

Just got done doing a washing for a boy that went on liberty gave me $1.25 to do a suit of dungaress, suit of under ware and two hats.

We had two lectures on guns (rifles) that lasted all day. I got a package from Mother & Dad today some cake sure is good. I also got the Perry Enterprise but havn't looked at it as yet.

I got me a pair of Bausch & Lomb antiglare glasses yesterday they sure are good on my eyes the sun is so bright here that it hurts your eyes. Smith & I were looking at them in Hollywood they were $6 to $10 and I got these for $3 here at the Ship's store.

I haven't had any luck with my rating yet doesn't any one know any thing about it the officer I want to see was in a car wreck over the week end and hasn't gotten back as yet.

We got orders that we would leave around the first of Oct. We have a pep talk about ever other day half of the boys are A.W.O.L. The morale is very, very low among the boys I think half of them don't think they will come back but not me. I'm thinking of my honey and our to be family.

I love you very much darling

Homer

Realizing that he had zero control over his current state of affairs, Homer tried to cope by being flexible. On Sunday September 26 he woke up in Port Hueneme and went to sleep that night in a barracks near San Diego. Three days later he was in Tijuana, Mexico.

> Sept 30 Thursday
> Seven oclock

My Darling Wife;

Honey I'll start out from the beginning, we left Port Hueneme Sunday at 9 A.M. in two trucks twenty of us. we ate dinner at Long Beach and got down here at the navy training center about 5:30 PM just in time for chow

We have to go about twenty miles to where we are getting our schooling   we have been shooting 20 m.m. machine guns which will shoot 60 shots in 7½ seconds. The shells are almost 1 inch in diameter. My shooting was fair   my test score was 3.5 which was probably too good for my own good   half of the boys shooting was considered poor   we shot at a sleeve pulled by an airplane which was about ten ft long and two feet in diameter. Which was pretty small up there in the air. We done our shooting on the beach at a gunner school.

We went to town (San Diego) two nights in the truck. Here at Diego you can go for miles & miles and all you can see is service men. A lot of French & British sailors are here going to school.

Last night we went to Tjuana Mexico about twenty five miles south of Diego. We couldn't take the truck over the line so parked it on this side and walked across   didn't but five of us go   the rest was too young   had to be twenty one years old before you can get a pass to go over. The two officers that are with us went too.

I hope you like what I got you. It's something to let you know that I think your the most wonderful wife in the world.

We are going back in the morning after chow to Port Hueneme. Honey I can't think of anything else now but will probably be telling you for a week what I've done   so good night darling.

Lots of Love & Kisses
Homer

Homer thought the nights in San Diego and Tijuana were probably the last time away from training before they shipped out. So he was surprised to get a special weekend liberty when they got back to Port Hueneme.

October 2
Saturday 11 AM

My Darling Wife;

I'm sort of going around and around   yesterday morning we left San Diego at eight o'clock and got in the base at two and found out that we had a special liberty that started at eight A.M. and we got paid a special pay   I got $10. so at six oclock I left the base again and came down here to San Barbara just to get away from the base.

I didn't want to go on liberty because we had just gotten back off a sort of a vacation but it may be my last liberty before going out

I think I'll spend most of this day writing letters   I get so disgusted at times I could almost go over the hill but that would never do.

I'm going to see about my rating again Monday   the officer I wanted to see is back now. I will close now and write to your folks.

I love you,
Homer

Monday he went to see about his rating and they said they'd check on the paper work. Somehow Homer knew he'd ship out before it came through. Then he'd have to start all over again with new officers at his next location. Oh, the joy of military red tape!

Orders to Ship Out

"This was sure a surprise to me."

—Homer's letter 10/5/43

Oct 5
Tuesday 8 PM

My Darling Wife
 At two oclock this afternoon we (about 100 men) got word to get our things packed and be able to leave by 4
 Now it's eight oclock and they can't find transportation for us   so don't know what time tonight we will leave   we are going to San Frisco for about four or five days and get shipped out from there.
 This was sure a surprise to me. I've got my envelope addressed so if they come after me I can mail it. I haven't shaved yet today should do it now but I wanted to let my loved one know what's taking place. I'll write as soon as we get there so good night honey.
 I'll love you forever darling,
 Homer

For several days Homer played the "hurry-up-and-wait-game." Each day he got dressed at 5:30 in the morning, marched to the harbor, waited all day for a ship that didn't come in, then marched back to his barracks for another sleepless night—only to begin the whole scenario again the next day, and the next. By week's end he was sick of waiting. To use Homer's own words, he was "madder than an old setten' hen." Then he got a very special mail call that changed his whole attitude.

8-Oct-43
Fri Night Six thirty

My Dear Wife,

Honey I sure am a proud boy I received one of the prettiest rings today it sure is a honey. If you were here I might even give you more than a kiss for it. ^{Ha Ha} Darling I love you.

I hope you are as pleased with your neckless as I was with the ring. I think that was the prettest neckless I ever saw its solid gold so it won't rub off. ^{Ha Ha}

Well it looks like I'll never get out of here we are still standing by. Yesterday two hundred new boys came here from other stations to be in Acorn 16 and they have our beds. Every one that is supposed to go to Frisco are sleeping on cots no mattress.

I didn't think I would be here this long but it looks like we won't leave until tomorrow now, unless they get us up tonight. Honey this is a hell of a life and I don't mean _____. One thing about it I don't have to go anywhere only just wait.

Station XYZ signing off with love to a wonderful wife.

Homer

Ruth had coincidentally mailed Homer's ring to him the same weekend he was in Tijuana buying a necklace for her. Ruth thought her necklace was the prettiest she had ever seen. It was a beautiful heart-shaped gold locket, engraved with the initial "R" bordered by delicate scrollwork. Homer's ring was gold banded, black onyx, with the letter "N" on it.

Homer's ring   Ruth's locket

If his ship had come into the harbor even one day sooner, he would have left before his ring arrived. As it worked out he received it and was able to write and thank Ruth before he shipped out. In his last stateside letter "Station XYZ" signed off by sending all his love to a wonderful wife.

The day after Homer received his ring he got up at 5:30 in the morning, dressed, packed and marched to the harbor— just like he had done on the four previous days. Finally, on October 9, Homer's ACORN unit shipped out.

Part 5: Anchors Aweigh

Remember Pearl Harbor

"It seams the men are taking a greater interest and work harder   they are beginning to realize what its all about."

—Homer's letter 10/27/43

It was customary for the Navy not to tell sailors their destination until the ship was at sea. Ruth was left wondering about the fate of her sailor husband. One week passed then two, then three; still no word from Homer.

Now that Homer was "overseas" his mail was slower because his letters had to go through scrutiny by the dreaded censors. He had heard stories of people back home who received letters that had sections marked through or cut out. The Navy didn't want sailors to say anything that would be of value to the enemy, such as their location or the number of troops in an area.

In the Northern Pacific passenger train schedule Homer and Ruth had seen an advertisement that advocated censorship. It had a picture of a sailor's hat floating on water and the sailor's hand disappearing to infer that the sailor drowned because the enemy got information from someone. The ad said, "Somebody Blabbed-Button Your Lip!" [June 20, 1943]

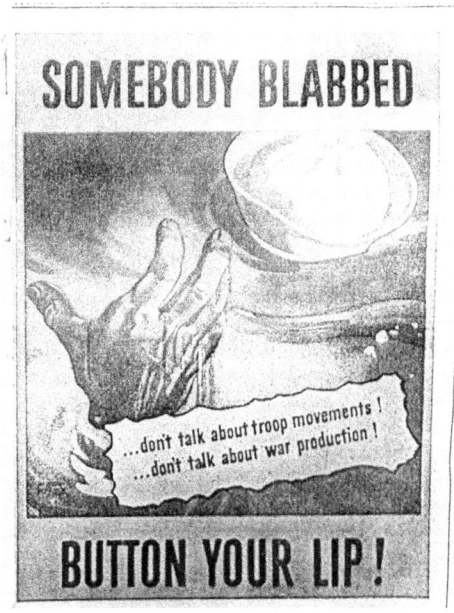

From now on each time Homer wrote a letter he would put it in an unsealed envelope for a censor to read. It was intimidating to think of his letters being read by a stranger.

Three weeks after Homer shipped out Ruth finally received a letter. Imagine her surprise when she saw that a censor wrote "Ha Ha You said it!" on Homer's letter! It gave her the creeps to think of a censor reading Homer's mail. She wondered how many others would have censorship notes or cut-outs.

Ruth forwarded Homer's letter to his parents so they could see that he was all right. At the top of the page she wrote, "I got this letter just last Wednesday. It surely was the first letter he wrote after he got overseas."

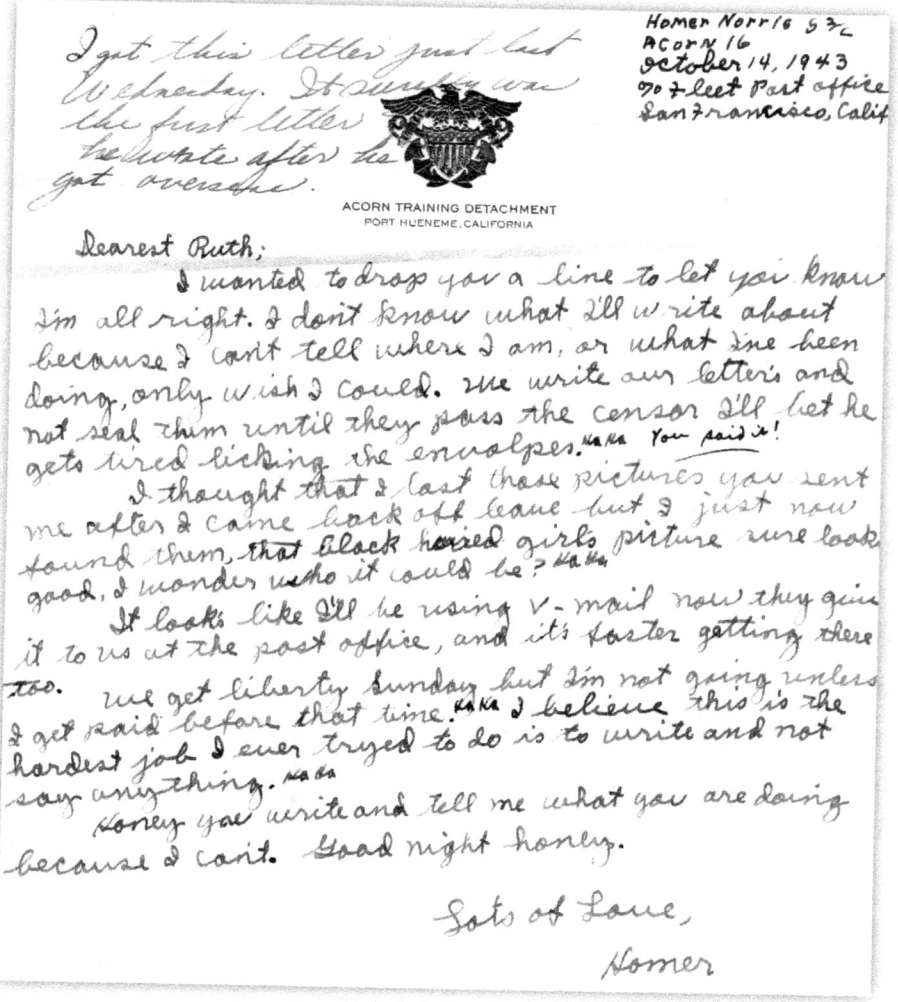

Ruth's letters weren't censored, and Homer encouraged her to write about anything and everything. Ruth wrote every day, however, when Homer's ACORN unit shipped out, the mail didn't and he went into a mail call drought.

The Navy knew it was important for the morale of sailors to get mail from home. So they developed V-Mail, an elaborate way of transmitting mail photographically. Servicemen and women stationed overseas could write letters on a special V-Mail form provided free of charge. V-Mail letters were photo copied onto microfilm, and placed on reels which contained up to 18,000 letters each.[18] The film was developed and letters were printed on photo paper and mailed to the addressee. The military launched a huge publicity campaign to persuade everyone that using V-Mail was the patriotic thing to do.

Unfortunately, there were problems with V-Mail. When the letter was photo copied onto a 4x5 inch page, the handwriting got reduced by about 30% and became too small to read. The purpose of V-Mail was to speed up the mail— but it failed miserably. Ruth wrote her first overseas letters using V-Mail, but it was eighteen days before Homer received a single letter. Air Mail letters arrived in only six days. So they decided that it was worth a few pennies to send by Air-Mail and get letters days or even weeks faster.

Homer was so intimidated by the censors that he forgot to use their secret code to tell Ruth his location. In his next few letters he started dropping hints to let her know where he was.

16 October 1943

Dearest Ruth;

Think maby I'll have a little more to write today. Yesterday eight of us tryied out for truck driving and I was the only one that pass but still didn't drive very much   expect I will before long. Last night I saw a good show. Think I'll go again tonight. It's a good way to pass the time away. This morning I washed clothes   most all my things were dirty. I never knew I was so dirty when you were doing my washing, I wonder why.[Ha Ha]

Honey you should be here   pineapple sure is cheap and plenty of it. I sure don't look like I did when I was at Farragut   I have a good sun tan now. Tomorrow is payday and they have me marked no money   suppose I'll have to draw a special pay   but don't send me any because I'll get paid before it could get here.

How do you like this V-mail   hope you can read it all right because I know you want to hear from me often   I also hope I don't write anything this censor disapproves of   write and tell me if they do cut any thing out.

I sure like this place   always told you where I'd go. ^{Ha Ha} But its not like I thought. We had a good swim in the pacific this after noon   got both eyes & mouth full of salt water like I always do   but I still wont never turn down a chance of going. Well honey ever one has gone to chow around here but me   expect I had better go before its to late. I want to write Mother & Dad tonight too, have got to get writting   I expect to get mail tomorrow   some of the boys got mail today from Hueneme so I should tomorrow. Good Bye Honey

I love you
Homer

When Homer's ACORN left California he had no idea that three days and 2387 miles later his transport ship would dock in the world's most famous Naval port—Pearl Harbor, Hawaii. Homer had told Ruth he hoped that someday he'd get to see Pearl Harbor, so when he wrote "always told you where I'd go" she knew exactly where he was.

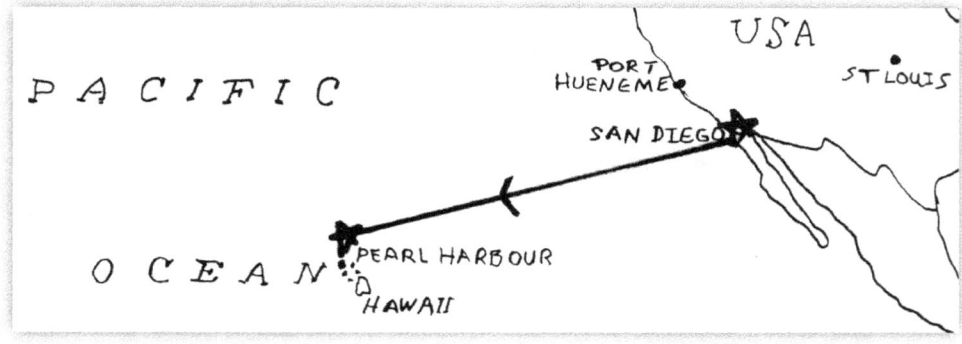

The whole world had seen newspaper pictures of the horrific destruction from the Japanese attack on Pearl Harbor, and Homer expected to see a harbor in shambles. Instead he observed a bee hive of activity. During the past twenty-two months the military had been very secretive about the extensive repairs that were intended to get the U.S. war-time ready.

Every man trained in construction had been sent to Hawaii. In 1943 the construction battalion at Pearl Harbor contained as many as 20,000 men.[19]

The scope and urgency of rebuilding was unprecedented. Seabees worked at a frantic pace to rebuild and expand the base facilities. At the Naval Industrial Yard other skilled crews worked under camouflage covers to salvage and refurbish the Pacific Fleet. Homer was witnessing one of the greatest salvage feats in all history, and he couldn't even tell Ruth about it. So he continued to write about his daily activities which he considered much less exciting.

18 October 1943
Monday night

Dearest Love;

I was sure I'd get some mail today but didn't   may get some tomorrow   sure hope so. I went to the show this after noon   helps pass the time away   not doing anything else except cleaning the barracks once a day   just takes about an hour.

As soon as I go to town I'll send a card of the island so you can see where I am. We can't write and tell but can send cards home telling where we are if we don't put our return address on them or our rate   isn't that foolish.

I went swimming this morning and I never had as much fun a swimming in my life I don't believe. A boy loaned me five dollars last night so I'm all fixed now. I went over to ship's service and got me a can of sardines   they were sure good for a change.

I've been reading some V-mail and the writing is so small that I expect mine is almost unreadable. Tell me if it is and I won't write V-mail any more I'll write air-mail. Honey you should see what some of these boys

write home it keeps the censors pulling their hair what has it. ^{Ha Ha}
I believe this is all I can think to write so I will sign off for today.

I love you Honey,
Homer

Homer worked in the mail room and saw that V-Mail was slower, so he wrote his next letter on regular paper and sent it the old-fashioned way.

Sun Oct 24

My Darling Wife;

I've been helping sort mail for the last two days and I can't even find one for myself, so I must be a poor mail man. ^{Ha Ha} *This kind of mail, not male.*

I don't mind my work in the mail room. I go to work at eight oclock in the morning and get off about five at night   an hour off for dinner so its almost like your work only its seven days a week. I'm enjoying my work more than I did at Farragut but not my nights.

I see in the papers that the blackout has been discontinued in the coastal states   I'll bet the people are sure glad.

How is ever body around home? How many new babies has there been the last month? Darling write and tell me everything even if it doesn't seem very important because its news and there isn't very much of that around here   the day I read the wars over   that will be what I call good news. Well I guess this is about all I've got to write.

Lots of love,
Homer

Wednesday 27th
4 PM

Dearest Ruth,

Well it's the same old thing mail and more mail but none for Homer. I know it isn't your fault   the mail is being held up some place.

I'm in charge of all the mail now but have to have a rated man go along to get the mail because a non-rated man cant get it. I can't see why in the hell I can't get my rate if I must say such a thing. If I hadn't studied so hard when you were with me I wouldn't care. But the way it is I deserve it and know it. Tomorrow Im going to see about it again.

One thing about this place we have good eats   and our mattresses are about five inches thick   I believe I could sleep 23 hours a day and eat the other hour. ^{Ha}

I ran across Fred Smith, the boy I ran around with at Port Hueneme. He has gone tattoo crazy   he now has both arms covered and a big one on his chest   the last one he got on his chest cost $16.50 and took two hour and ten minutes to put it on. I wouldn't even get a fly speck tatooed on me.

Today I got two pairs of shoes (heavy) two pairs of pants and two jackets, a big hat and a pair of leather gloves   so we must be going to do some work. ^{Ha Ha}

It seams the men are taking a greater interest and work harder   they are beginning to realize what its all about.

Well I have got to quit writing now, I'm transportation driver this afternoon, so long honey.

I love you ever,
Homer

While they were in Sandpoint Homer passed the examinations to get a promotion, but left Farragut before it came through. Then he shipped out from Port Hueneme before the paper work was done. Now he feared that if he left Hawaii before his promotion was finalized, he might never get it. Once again Homer went to see about his rating, and this time he raised a little hell.

My Darling,   *Mon Nov 1*

I got the most welcomed letter yesterday I ever got in my life   it was written the 25th and I got it 31st. I have already read it three times and I'm not kidding. Honey keep sending your mail air-mail, it comes so much faster   I'm not sending any more V-mail.

Honey I don't know if you know it or not but your mail isn't censored so write just anything you like. I saw a dirty joke I would like to send you but the censor's might like it to well and keep it.^{Ha Ha}

This letter was the first one I had gotten since you had got your locket   I though you would be pleased with it, the way it looks now it may be your Christmas present if I don't get payed pretty soon

There is a boy sitting besides me thats from St. Louis   boy did we ever have a time talking over old Missouri.

Well honey I'll sign off with all my love and that's a lot.

Homer

The next week a transport ship from California arrived with hundreds of mail bags filled with letters and paychecks! The mail room was swamped.

Sat night 6th

My Dear Wife;

Our acorn got five bags of back mail from Port Hueneme today. Boy did I ever hit the jack pocket   I got eight letters   sure made me feel good. I wish I could answer all the questions you asked but its not a lot we can say

I got payed so I'm going on liberty Monday and will send you some cards that might be of interest to you   but your sure a good guesser

I was in the brig today for half an hour   always wanted to see what it was like but didn't think I'd get in it. ^{Ha} *I took a release over for a boy in our acorn that had been A.W.O.L. in Hueneme.*

I just met a boy from Centralia Missouri. He knows a lot of kids from Perry that played basketball with you and I'm going to ask him if he knew you.

Honey I'm sorry I'm not going to be able to send many Christmas presents home but I'll sure try and let you know that I'm thinking of you all the time. I think I'll go to bed.

Good night Darling.

Lots of love from your husband,

Homer

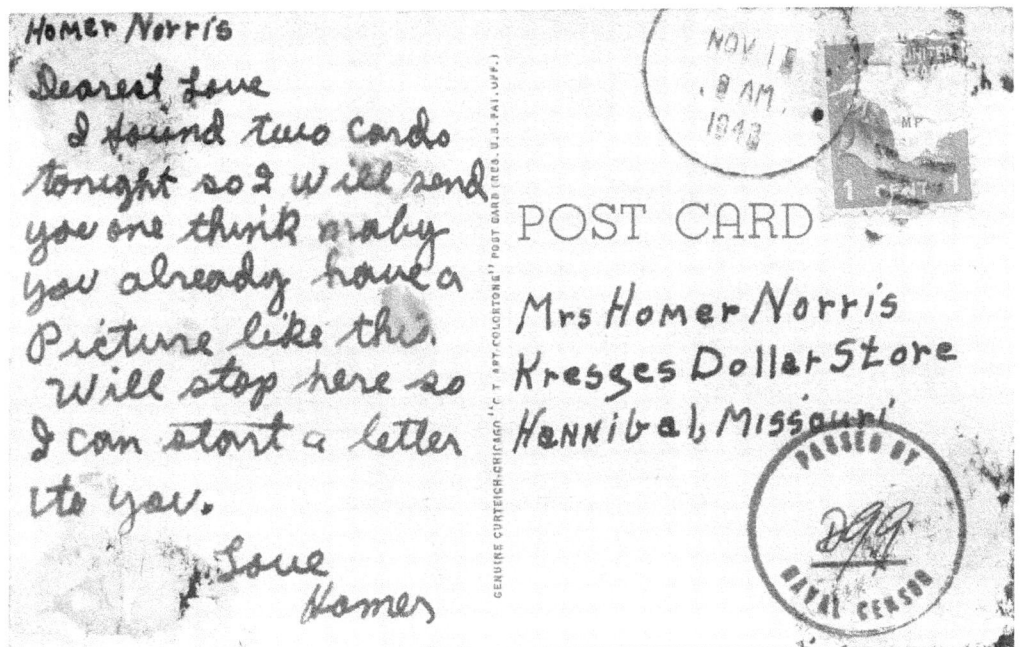

Postcard Homer sent from Pearl Harbor, Hawaii

Pineapple Field near Honolulu, T. H.

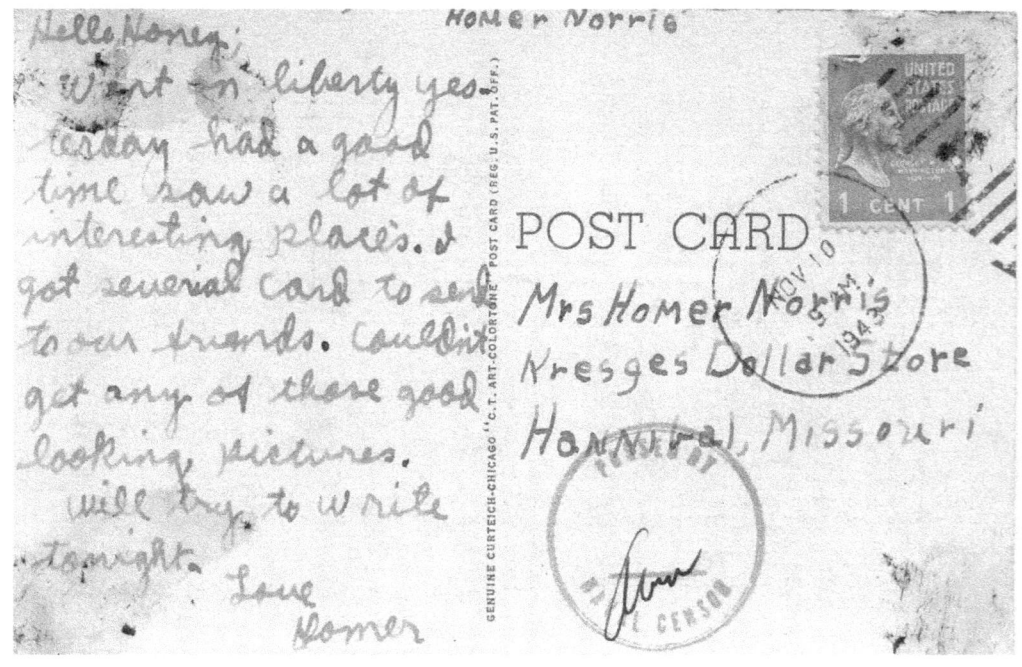

Hello Honey;
Went on liberty yesterday had a good time saw a lot of interesting places. I got several card to send to our friends. Couldn't get any of those good looking pictures.
Will try to write tonight.
Love Homer

Homer Norris

Mrs Homer Norris
Kresges Dollar Store
Hannibal, Missouri

Ruth had already guessed that Homer was in Hawaii, but it was confirmed when she received the postcards.

In the months ahead Ruth knew there would be many days of waiting for a letter from her husband. For now she was content knowing that Homer was swimming in the ocean, having good eats, sleeping on a comfortable bed, and thinking about home instead of war.

Nov 12 '43
Friday night

My Darling Wife;

Honey this letter isn't going to be all B.S. because I can say one thing I've been wanting to say for a long time   I findlly got my rating   I guess that little hell I raised done a little good   your old man is now a petty officer, electriction mate third class. Same as a sergant in the army and also an addition in pay of twenty-four dollars a month which will help. With my twenty per cent over sea duty we are drawing $121.60 a month now which isn't so bad for war duty.

Honey I'm getting your mail regular now   get one from you ever day   its sure is something to look forward to is a letter from your wife

All I have been seeing is mail, mail & more mail. I sent some cards today   I'm writing on my knee so it may be hard for those poor censor's to read.

I'm getting the last of my gear this afternoon, a complete field pack, will tell you what the pack consists of as soon as I know for sure myself.

I got myself six cartons of cigarettes, six bars of soap and a carton of gum.

It's almost time for the lights to go out so I had better sign off.

From the one that loves you most,
Homer

Now that Homer was stationed overseas, he got paid twenty percent more. Following is a summary of their monthly income:

Homer's Monthly pay after boot camp	$54
New rating	+24
20% for overseas duty	+16
Ruth's Dependent's Allowance	+28
Ruth's take-home pay from the store	~58
Total Monthly Income	$180

Due to limited funds Homer only went on one liberty while he was in Pearl Harbor, but he made it count. He shopped a little with Christmas in mind and even put on his biggest smile as he posed for a couple of pictures. They wouldn't be his last photos surrounded by palm trees, but they'd be the only ones with him dressed in his sailor whites.

Homer in Pearl Harbor, Hawaii November 9, 1943

When Homer arrived in Pearl Harbor he joined thousands of Marine, Army, and Navy troops training for a top-secret mission. Homer still didn't want to go to sea duty, but seeing Pearl Harbor was the equivalent of hearing the world's best motivational speech. He knew that going to war was one way to honor the memory of those who paid the ultimate price on 7 December 1941.

As Homer prepared to ship out the lyrics from the 1942 song, *"Remember Pearl Harbor"* kept playing in his mind.

Remember Pearl Harbor on a beautiful morn,
Remember Pearl Harbor and what came with the dawn.
A foe lighted on us with bombs bursting in air,
But they couldn't beat us, for our flag still waves there.
Our Army and Navy just fought with all their might,
And our planes from the air shot the foe right out of sight.
Remember Pearl Harbor, remember-
And the boys who died for liberty.

("Remember Pearl Harbor," 1942, Lyrics & Music by Johnny Noble)

Operation Galvanic

"... there's a big job to be done before I can come home to my darling wife."

—Homer's letter 11/17/43

Note: Unless otherwise cited, material in this chapter is based on "Operation Galvanic: The Battle for Tarawa November 1943."[20]

The attack on Pearl Harbor crippled the U.S. Naval Fleet and gave Japan free hand to occupy first one island, then another and build a Japanese empire in the Pacific. By the fall of 1943 the U.S. Pacific Fleet was once again a formidable force; the stage was set for the Allies to fight back.

In September, while Homer trained in California, a conference was held in Hawaii and Navy Admiral Chester Nimitz proposed an island-hopping campaign—code name Operation Galvanic.

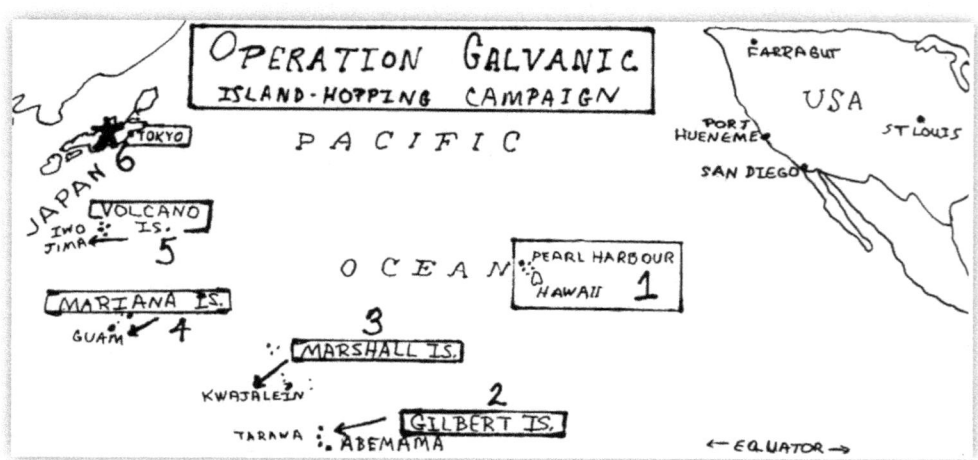

In Operation Galvanic targeted islands would be attacked from the air, sea, and land in a carefully orchestrated plan. The Gilbert Islands became the opening move of this major offensive which was to continue across the Pacific Ocean during the year that lay ahead.

To re-conquer the Central Pacific Islands Admiral Nimitz had 13 battleships, 19 escort carriers, 35 destroyers, 15 cruisers, and 35,000 Allied troops.[21] The surprise attack on the Gilbert Islands would bring the battleship big guns into play for the first time in the Pacific Theater.

Admiral Nimitz and his top advisors formulated the following plan to reclaim the Japanese-occupied Gilbert Islands of Tarawa, Makin and Apamama.

Phase 1: Allied fighter planes and battleships simultaneously bombard Japanese strongholds to weaken enemy defenses. Marines come ashore to take the islands by force and remove all enemy.

Phase 2: Attack forces move onto the next targeted islands, and Marine occupational units arrive to scout the best location for building a military base.

Phase 3: Construction battalions and ACORN units come ashore with heavy equipment to construct air strips and facilities to support future operations against Japanese bases in the Marshall Islands.

The 95th Construction Battalion and Homer's ACORN 16 were part of Phase 3 of the mission. D-Day for Operation Galvanic was 18 November 1943.

During the second week of November, troops began to ship out from Pearl Harbor on huge transports and battleships. Fearing that he could leave at any time, Homer wrote his last letters from Hawaii with a sense of urgency. Writing wasn't easy because Pearl Harbor was still under blackout.

Wed night Nov 17

My Darling Wife;
I have got to write tonight if I have to write by a flash light, have been so busy the last two day I hardly knew which end was up. I have so much gear I don't know just how I'm going to carry it all, mosquito netting, 30-06 rifles, rain coats, steel helmets, knives, mess kits, tents (pup)   we got our gas

mask this after nooon. I'll be damn if I don't beleave I'm in the army. ^{Ha Ha}

Mother ask me if I'm in the C.B.'s I'm not but just as well be. I sent more clothes home today because I'll never ware them until I get back to the states and that's not going to be very soon because we're going the wrong way.

Honey this will probably be the last letter you'll get from me for a long time so don't worry if you don't because there's a big job to be done before I can come home to my darling wife   and I'm sure coming too   just as soon as this things over.

My darling sure is writing a lot but honey I really enjoy them   so keep the good work up and I'll write as often as I can. I'm not keeping your letters now   I've got so much to carry now I don't know what to do with it all.

Honey I can't think of any other things to tell or had better say that I can tell you only that I love you very very much and always will.

oodles and oodles of love and kisses
your old man
Homer

Operation Galvanic commenced on the morning of 18 November 1943, when Allied fighter planes and battleships initiated a relentless attack on the Japanese-controlled islands of Tarawa and Makin. Back in Hawaii, Homer got orders to ship out.

On 19 November, while the Pacific fleet continued to bombard the Gilbert Islands, Homer's ACORN prepared to leave.

The morning of 20 November, U.S. Marines invaded the Gilbert Islands, and Homer's ACORN 16 and the 95th Construction Battalion shipped out from Pearl Harbor. The third phase of Operation Galvanic was on its way across the ocean.

Part 6: Journey Into War

The SS *Robin Wentley*

"The Gilbert Islands are small dots in the midst of a vast sea, 2,400 miles southwest of Hawaii, 3,000 miles southeast of Tokyo. Toward them . . . moved the mightiest naval force ever assembled in the Pacific."[22]

—*Pictorial History of the Second World War*

In his pocket Homer carried a half-page of stationery. There were stains on the thin paper and deep creases from being refolded many times. Dotted lines divided the paper in half down the center. On the right side he wrote names and addresses of family and friends. On the left side he listed his service identification number, rankings he held while in the service, and important dates.

After being in Hawaii for five weeks, Homer added the following important date to his page of notes, "Left Pearl Nov 20."

Homer didn't know his specific destination, but for a man whose greatest wish was to go home to Missouri, he could tell he was going the wrong way.

On this trip across the Pacific Homer was on board the SS *Robin Wentley*, a heavy cruiser that was transporting 1500 men from the 95th Construction Battalion and Homer's ACORN 16, plus enough heavy equipment to build a military base and airstrip.

The SS *Robin Wentley*

The experienced Merchant Marine crew took care of everything, so there wasn't much for the troops to do on the ship. Homer's personal recollection of his crossing revealed the following information:

> "I remember going up on the huge deck of the ship. A lot of fellas were up there because they were sea sick, but I went up on deck to smoke and spit over the side. It sounds kind of silly now, but spitting over the rail helped pass the time while we were at sea.
>
> We'd heard lots of stories about the initiation pranks they played on new sailors and we were real worried. But the Captain took care of that all right.
>
> The first day we were at sea, the Captain called everyone on deck and said, 'These men are going to war and it's our job to get them there. You will treat every man on this ship with the respect due a war hero, because that's what they are.'
>
> That stopped any pranks. I never heard one more word about anybody being a first timer."

The mood on board the ship was somber—and for good reason. They were just days away from the Gilbert Islands and war. Had they known what was taking place in the Gilberts they would have been even more worried. Allied troops landing on the Islands of Tarawa and Makin were encountering unexpected obstacles.

Back in September Admiral Nimitz and his advisors had tried to consider all the variables when planning Operation Galvanic. Unfortunately they grossly underestimated the force of Mother Nature.

The attacks on the Gilbert Islands were to be the first American assaults on fortified atolls. An atoll is a ring-shaped coral reef and series of small islets with a seawater lagoon or pond in the center. Surrounding the atoll are razor sharp coral reefs that can make the island impassable to landing craft. Troops going ashore had to traverse the treacherous reefs in open rubber landing craft then wade in waist-deep water for several hundred yards while under enemy fire.[24]

On paper the plan looked good. In reality the invasions of the Tarawa and Makin atolls were fraught with problems. The Marines who landed found that the naval bombardment had failed to inflict much damage on the Japanese entrenchments. Only the sheer will and determination of the Marine beach busters allowed them to overcome the well-entrenched Japanese.

The invasions of Tarawa and Makin were examples of the perfect plan gone wrong. In the taking of Tarawa and Makin 4877 Marines were killed or wounded.[25] Too many Americans paid the ultimate price. However, there wasn't time to learn from the mistakes because while Tarawa and Makin were under attack, sixty-five miles to the southeast, the beaches of the Apamama atoll were under surveillance by periscopes from the huge American submarine USS *Nautilus*.

On a map of the Pacific Ocean the Gilbert Islands appear as small dots, and Homer's troopship was headed toward the smallest dot of them all—Apamama (also spelled Abemama). Located just north of the equator, the Atoll of Apamama consisted of a tiny group of islets, and was only fifteen miles long, six miles wide.

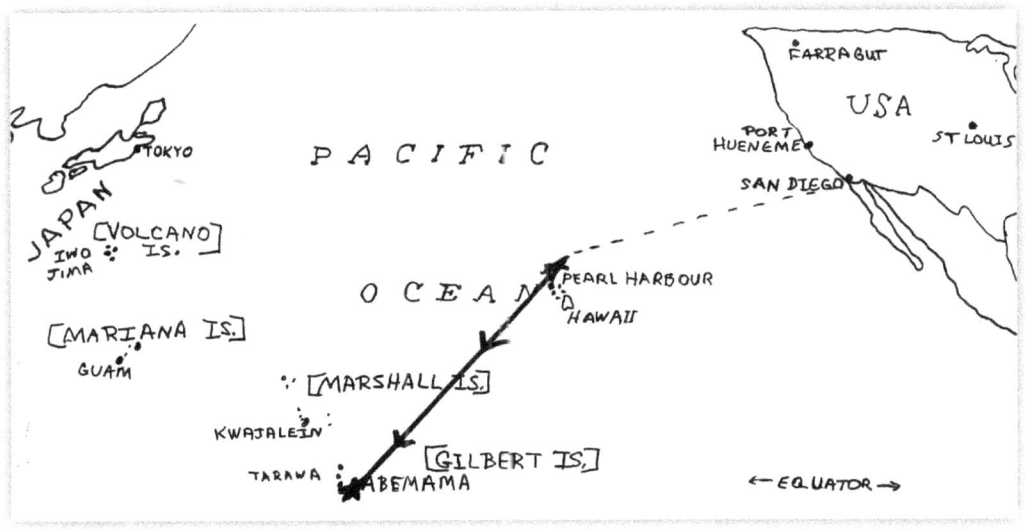

Operation Boxcloth

"Life was simple and peaceful on the beautiful atoll of Apamama. The sun rose like a red globe in the East and set with a green flash in the West."

—Tolbert, Sgt. Frank X. [1945] "APAMAMA, A model operation in miniature"[26]

Note: Unless otherwise cited, material in this chapter is based on the Tolbert article found in Ruth's scrapbook. The newspaper was distributed to troops in the Pacific Campaign.

Apamama in the Gilbert Islands

Before Pearl Harbor, Apamama was a tiny island in the vast Pacific and inhabited by one-thousand religious, handsome, warm-hearted and intelligent natives who called it home. Also, there were eight white persons, including two Australian nuns and four French Catholic priests. The only structures on the islets were a Catholic mission built by the British and the native Kabangake village comprised of thatch-roofed huts. The native language was Gilbertese, but the nuns taught English to the native children.

Soon after Pearl Harbor, two companies of Japanese Imperial Marines occupied the island without opposition. In the fall of 1943 the Apamamese were into their second year of slavery when a decision was made that would change their lives forever. Over 2400 miles away at a conference in Hawaii Navy Admiral Chester Nimitz looked at a map of the Pacific Ocean and pointed to the Gilbert Islands as the starting point for Operation Galvanic. He included the island of Apamama because it contained a large, well-protected lagoon with an extensive anchorage area which could provide good support as an air base for future island-hopping maneuvers to reclaim the Central Pacific Islands.

Code name for the invasion of Apamama was Operation Boxcloth.[27] By the evening of 20 November, Allied forces were within spitting distance of the atoll of Apamama. The Apamamese people were about to be liberated.

Shortly after midnight on 21 November, the American submarine USS *Nautilus* heaved out of the sea. On board were seventy-eight Marines who had come to scout out the island and determine the strength of the hostile forces prior to the invasion by American troops five days later.

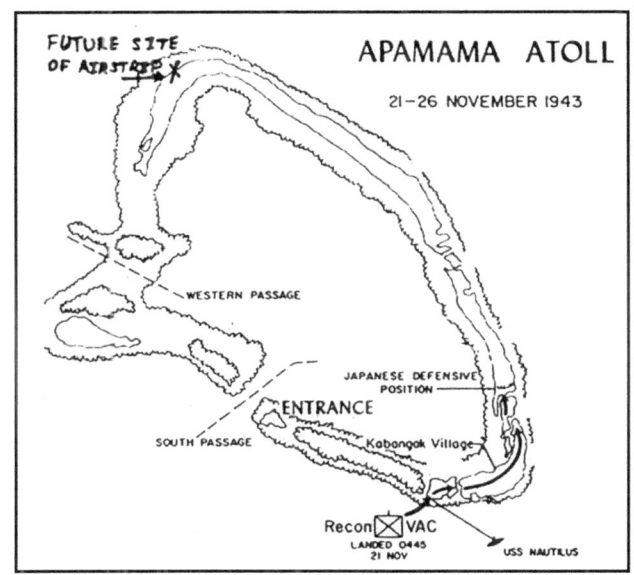

Heavy rain squalls drowned out the outboard motors of their landing craft. All hands paddled against the current that pulled them toward the treacherous reef. At 4:15 in the morning they reached shore but the men were in pretty bad physical condition after their nightmarish ordeal in the rubber boats.

At the first light of day they went out in scouting parties. Accompanying the Marines was Lt. George Hard, a small, baldish Australian who had lived in the Gilberts for many years before the war and knew the people of Apamama.

Minutes after the patrol set out, Lieutenant Hard recognized two Apamamese wading across the reef and called to them in Gilbertese. The natives informed the lieutenant that there were only twenty-five Japanese on the island, but they were well entrenched with machine guns, mortars, rifles and grenades. Word of the Marine landing spread quickly throughout the island and the Japanese ran to their fortifications while the natives nonchalantly headed for the brush.

On Day 2 the Marines patrolled the island and made plans for an attack the next day. On the morning of Day 3 the units moved into position about 150 yards from the Japanese, set up machine guns and started shooting. The Japanese gunners returned fire from their entrenchments. One Marine was killed and three others injured while trying to get him to safety.

Late in the day several American ships appeared on the horizon. The Captain of the destroyer agreed to shell the Japanese positions on the following day. Early on the morning of Day 4 the Marines began to get some strange reports from the natives. The story was that the Japanese commanding officer had made a long speech to his men waving a pistol which fired accidentally. He received a fatal wound in the belly. After witnessing this shocking scene, all of the remaining Japanese dug their own graves, lay down in them, and shot themselves with their own pistols in a mass suicide, also known as hari-kari.

The Marines started to bury their enemies when out of the coconut groves the native people reappeared from their hiding places to help on the burial detail. The Apamamese had been liberated.

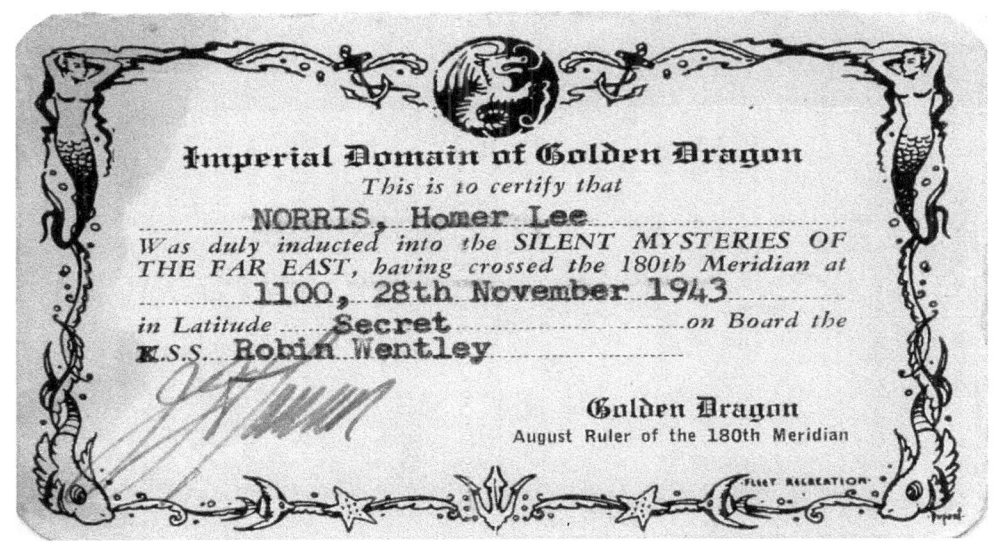

Homer received card for crossing the 180th Meridian

Four days later at 1100 hours on the morning of November 28 the SS *Robin Wentley* crossed the International Date Line, also known as the 180th Meridian. In recognition of the crossing a ceremony was held on deck and all men crossing for the first time were duly inducted into the **silent mysteries of the far east**.

Crossing the 180th Meridian earned the troopship another Battle Star for sailing into a war zone and also brought them within spitting distance of the Gilbert Islands. After cruising southwest for eight days the SS *Robin Wentley* dropped anchor. Homer was 6157 miles from home. On his little page of notes he wrote, "*arr. Abemama Nov 28.*"

Part 7: Apamama

DECEMBER
Norris Code

"My Darling Wife . . . I landed safe some where in the south pacific   had a nice trip   sure been busy since we landed . . ."

—Homer's first letter from Apamama 12/2/43

The SS *Robin Wentley* was too large to drop anchor near the beaches of Apamama. Landing craft navigated through strong currents to get the incoming troops as close as the treacherous coral reefs would allow. Loaded down with heavy equipment packs, Homer's ACORN 16 and the 95th Construction Battalion waded waist deep through warm aqua blue ocean waters. The island was supposed to be clear of enemy forces, but Homer and the other men felt better once they reached the sand beaches.

Apamama Beach

Fifteen hundred men came ashore and immediately went to work. Bulldozers, trucks, jeeps and other heavy equipment quickly surfaced from the bowels of the ship. Some men set up a temporary camp, others scouted the island for building locations. The scene was organized chaos.

The first three days melted into one endless day as troops worked round the clock in shifts. When Homer wasn't working he ate field rations, slept in a pup tent and bathed in the ocean. On day four Homer finally got his sea bags from the ship and wrote his first letter from Apamama.

#1 Dec 2 Time 1016

My Darling Wife

Its been a long time since I've had a chance to write you a letter so I'll see if I can't write you a short one any way to let you know I landed safe some where in the south pacific had a nice trip sure been busy since we landed. I got off work at 1131 yesterday and will go to work tomorrow at the same time.

We have been washing in the ocean but today I got my sea bags with a bucket in them so I took a bath in the bucket.

Its sort of like being on a fishing trip but no fish. I washed all my dirty clothes this morning   we have mess halls now   is a lot better than field rations.

We are doing a lot of hard work but ever one is in there doing their best so it don't take very long to do a big job. There isn't much I can say because all our work is suppose to be secret and I hope it is. Will close for now will write as often as I have time.

Lot of love & Kisses

Homer

Homer knew Ruth wouldn't be satisfied with knowing he was "some where in the south pacific," so he tried using their secret coding system to tell her his exact location. According to the Norris Code when Homer wrote the time of day in his letters she was to assign a letter to the numbers to spell out his location, for example, #1 = "A," #26 = "Z." He hoped from these numbers she would spell A-P-A-M-A-A-M-A.

Unfortunately, there was a problem with the coding system. The numbers Homer listed were 1-0-1-6-1-1-3-1-1-1-3-1, but Ruth couldn't tell where to separate the numbers. For example 1-0-1-6 could be 1-16 (A-P) or 10-16 (J-P), or 10-1-6 (J-A-F). The more numbers there were, the more confusing it became.

Ruth tried several different combinations as evidenced by all the names of islands she wrote on the back of Homer's letter. First she tried to spell from his code, and then she listed names of islands that she had read about in the newspapers. It was like searching for a needle in a haystack. For now she would have to be satisfied with knowing that he "landed safe."

Ruth's attempt to decipher the Norris Code

O'Hare Field airstrip on Apamama

The secret work Homer referred to was the building of a 4000 x 150 foot airstrip. Starting with nothing but jungle and coral, the construction battalion was to build an airstrip as fast as possible so planes could use Apamama as a base for attacking the Marshall Islands. Bull-dozers pushed the tropical jungles back and removed top soil along the runway area to reach the hard coral.[28]

The task at hand was Herculaneum in scope. There was so much to do that every able-bodied man worked—including the native men. Out of 1000 natives living on the island 426 native men were employed to handle cargo and place coconut logs for pier construction.[29]

The first plane landed on O'Hare Field December 12. The airstrip was formally named O'Hare Field in honor of Edward "Butch" O'Hare, a pilot who was killed in the invasion of the Gilbert Islands.[30]

Homer didn't mind the hard work, but jumping into foxholes during air raids disrupted many a night's sleep. Nightly blackouts made it almost impossible to write letters.

#2 Tues night, Dec 7

My Darling Wife

If they don't find me I'll write my honey a letter   about the only time I have to write is after dark and a person can't see with out a light. You should see my little cellar   some other boys dug it for me while I was working yesterday   its about four ft by nine   room enough for four men maby five.

You should see how the native women dress   I think I'll dress you that way when I get back and not let you go out of the house. ^{Ha Ha} *Only I'll through the grass skirt away.*

I'm numbering all my letters so you'll know if your getting all the mail or not. I hope you can read this letter   it's hard to write on your knee. I'll close for now   I love you darling always.

Lots of love & kisses
Your old Man Homer

Josefo

During the construction of O'Hare Field Homer befriended one of the native men named Josefo Tmereta. Once the airfield was finished his friend went back to the Kabangak native village fifteen miles south of the airfield, but their friendship continued.

Kabangak Native Village

Homer thought the Apamamese people were exactly like he would have expected island natives to be. They were athletic-looking, brown-skinned people. Young barefooted boys could skinny up a tree in nothing flat to knock coconuts from the tip top. Girls wore flowers in their straight, waist-length hair.

Both men and women wore grass skirts—only. That was the first thing Homer noticed about the natives—they were topless! That's why Homer wanted to dress Ruth like the native women.

Native boys climbing tree

Homer knew some of his letters would get lost, so he started numbering each letter; however he only made it to number three and lost count.

In his third letter home once again he attempted to use the Norris code to tell Ruth he was in the G-I-L-B-E-R-T-I-S.

With the airstrip complete some of the CB's worked to extend the runway, others erected a mess hall, hospital, officers' quarters and tent barracks. Homer's ACORN began building a communication system to make the air base operational.

#3 Friday Dec 17
8:30 P.M.

My Darling Wife;

Honey I hit the jack pot today   got three letters from Mother & Dad, and nine from my darling and was I tickled. Dad wrote a page congratulating me on my rating. Be sure to tell Mother that in coming mail is not censored. She said in one letter that she was afaired the Japs would get something from her that would help them. I'm the one that's got to be careful what I say. Honey this is the third letter that I have written since leaving Hawaii. You should see me   I haven't worn a shirt since I've been here. Almost as brown as the natives.

I've had my dirty clothes soaking for two days and haven't had time to wash them. I have 11 pairs of dirty socks. The only time I get a chance to wash clothes is after dark and that doesn't work very well.

This is the first time I've had to write for some time I'm working from day light to dark on telephone lines one day we will lay them, the next day go along hunting for trouble. I'm in charge of three or four men. I've been climbing trees with climbers. Like my work all right   have a swell officer to work for.

My yesterday schedule   I went to work at 7:09 got in at 12:25 and last night I got back at 18:20 and went to bed at 9:19, so you have my days time right to the minute.

Honey I have to go to bed now   its nine thirty   Good night my darling I think of you often, I love you ever.

Your darling old man
Homer

Homer climbed trees with an apparatus strapped to his ankle and shin. He used his legs to jab the spikes of the climbing apparatus into the trees. Once he reached the top, a safety cable added protection while he worked on lines. Since the trees were over twenty feet tall, the climb up and back down was extremely dangerous.

While Homer strung telephone lines near the air strip, five miles away work continued on a new camp site. With such a huge labor force, construction happened very fast, however communication between Missouri and Apamama was very slow. Letters took weeks, packages took months. Homer was on the island nineteen days before his first mail call. Once the mail started to arrive, he was pleasantly surprised to discover ever so many letters and Christmas presents!

Homer climbing with tree spikes

Nobody loved Christmas more than Ruth Marie, but this year she dreaded the holidays. How was she going to make this Christmas special for Homer? Back in October Homer was still in California when Ruth received his overseas mailing address. She and Mom Norris began planning presents for their favorite sailor.

On Thanksgiving Day Homer was aboard the SS *Robin Wentley*, but packages were already on their way from Missouri. Homer received his first Christmas present on December 18, and they just kept coming. Two days later Homer had his mouth full of home-made candy while he wrote Ruth's letter.

Mon December 20
nine o'clock P.M.

My Darling Sweetheart

Nine oclock is as early as I can ever get started writing. We have a new camp site now but I haven't moved yet   expect to in a few days. We have a screened chow hall down there   its about four or five miles from where I am now so it takes a long time to go back and forth.

Honey I've gotten some Christmas presents and ever thing was so nice   sure never expected to get so much. I've gotten seven packages and seventeen letters since I've been on this rock. I've been eating a lot of candy   I don't know how I'm ever going to get time to write and thank ever one because I can't even get time to write my darling as often as I should.

Honey to my greatest surprise today I walked up to some marines and started talking and there was a boy I used to work with at Farber, Elmer Hull, Tom Hulls son. Elmer has been in the Southwest Pacific for 17 months.

It was sort of funny today I got a letter from you wishing me a happy Thanksgiving and its only five days until Christmas but it can't be helped   I like to get the letters even if they are a month behind. I love you so much darling I realy can't tell you how much. I must retire honey   will close for now with all my love.

Lots of love & kisses
Homer

Back in Missouri it was Christmas season at the Kresge Dollar Store and Ruth was hard at work during the busiest time of the year. Her time card shows that she worked forty-eight hours each week and her take-home pay was $14.46. On December 24 she also received a $5 Christmas Remembrance and was strongly encouraged to buy war bonds and stamps with her bonus.

> In sincere appreciation of your loyalty and service during the year just ending, may we extend our thanks. We wish you a
>
> **Merry Christmas and a Happy New Year**
>
> S. S. Kresge Company
>
> BUY WAR BONDS AND STAMPS WITH YOUR CHRISTMAS REMEMBRANCE

Christmas at the equator didn't feel like Christmas at all. The calendar said December, but the heat and humidity felt more like August. While Homer wrote letters holding a towel to keep the sweat from dripping onto the paper, his dad pulled out his wool long johns. Missouri was having a nasty winter. It was so cold at the Norris farm that they cut pond ice twice a day so the livestock could get water.

A week before Christmas Homer's parents had just come in from cutting ice when Ruth called from Hannibal to say she was sick. Mom Norris went to Hannibal to take care of Ruth and the next week Mom and Dad Norris both came down with influenza. They were so sick that the doctor had to help with the farm chores.

By December 24, Ruth was over the flu and took the 7 o'clock bus to Perry to spend Christmas Eve with Homer's family. While she struggled to sleep, Homer struggled to stay awake to write a couple of letters.

Christmas Eve
Eleven oclock PM

My Darling Wife

I'm going to have to get busy if I get this written Christmas eve   I just got done writing Mother & Dad a letter   the first I've written since leaving Hawai   I never got in tonight until ten. This sure will be a Christmas I'll never forget   we had a good dinner turkey, mash potatoes, gravy, corn, peaches, apples, cake, ice cream, coffee, and candy. It was far the best meal I've ever gotten off the navy.

I'm sure getting sleepy but I'm going to get my darling a letter wrote tonight. We got a big kick out of those jokes you sent   it's four of us boys living togeather so we have a big time. I got 11 letters yesterday, the third I had gotten. Today was the first Christmas I ever went swimming. I've got our pictures sitting out on the table in front of me   I can look and look at them and never get tired. I sure missed my darling today worse than ever   sure hope I'm home next Christmas

Good night to the most wonderful wife in the world.

Lots of Love Homer

While Homer was in Hawaii he mailed a beautiful Christmas card to Ruth. He didn't know where he might be, but he wanted to make sure Ruth knew he was thinking of her at Christmas.

Card Homer sent from Hawaii

One week later the month of December finally ended, and the Norris family was relieved to have the holidays behind them. They hoped Homer would be home for next Christmas. In the meantime they were braced for a very long 1944.

Calendar from Ruth's scrapbook

JANUARY
Un-Happy New Year

"We should all be praying for the boys in the Marshalls   for God's sake they need it."

—Homer's letter 1/30/44

Ruth celebrated the New Year by getting all dressed up in her best suit, hat, and high heels—with a fox fur wrapped around her shoulders. She wasn't going out on-the-town; she was going to have her picture taken to send to her honey.

Photographs show Ruth on a sunny winter's day with the Lick Creek Bridge in the background. When Homer saw the pictures he knew exactly where they were taken.

Sun. Night
Jan 2, 10 oclock

My Darling Wife
I've sure been getting a lot of mail from a swell lady in Hannibal   It was hotter today than it has ever been I believe   we had a nice shower last night. We have to go about four miles to get my breakfast so I have to get up to

early to suit me very well. Its two of us and we stay in bed just as long as we possibly can to make it   one morning we never woke up and we missed chow.

We had ice cold lemonade for dinner   about the third time we had anything cold except beer & coco cola I don't like beer and two bottles of coco isn't very much for a week.

Honey I just found out that we can get films developed here on the island so if you can find any 6-20 films I request you send them, all you can find, beg, borrow or steal. We have a Kodak and I want to get some pictures of these natives and their huts, they are very interesting.

Darling I wish I could write in so many words how much I love you but its impossible. Well honey, I'd better sign off for now its getting pretty late

I love you lots & lots.
As ever, your old man
Homer

When Homer said that they could get films developed, he was referring to a make-shift darkroom some fellas had set up to develop black and white film. Homer was glad he had packed his Kodak camera in his sea bags. Now all he needed was film, lots of film.

The first week of January Homer was so busy that he started his letter three times.

Jan 3
Jan 4, eight oclock
Jan 5th Wed night
Eight oclock

My Dearest Ruth,

It sure looks like I never get to write to the one I love most   we are having a black out ever night   Last night I wanted to write but had to move my gear about four miles and the truck ran out of gas. I'm getting with the rest of the acorn now   have been away from them so I could shoot trouble on the telephone lines at nights.

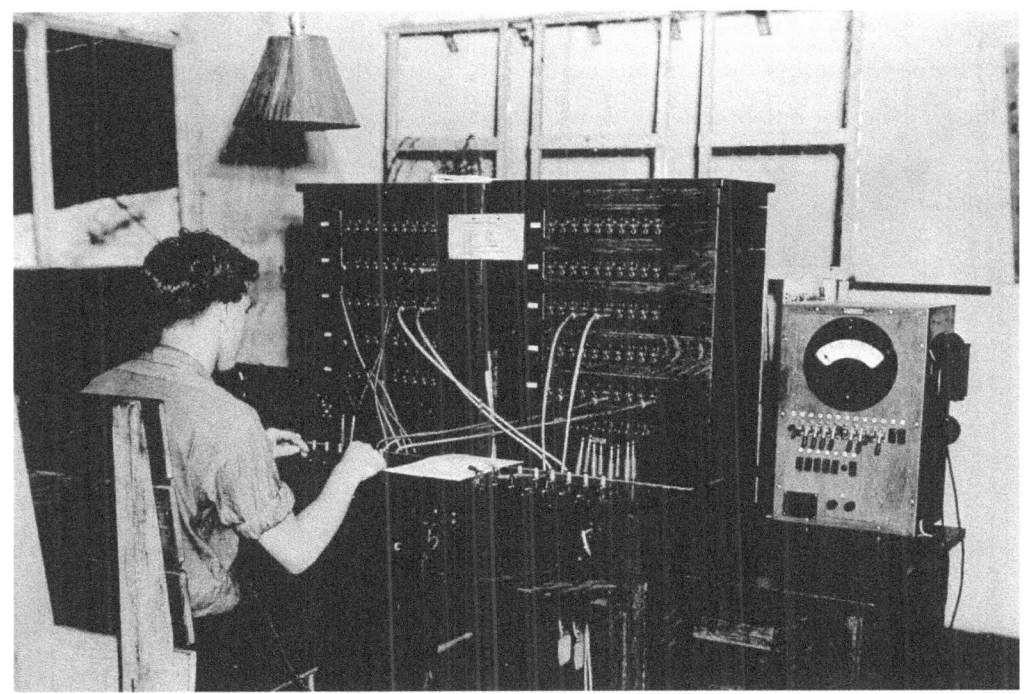
Telephone switchboard built by Homer's ACORN 16

We are putting in a 100 drop telephone switch board and we have been so dam busy that I almost don't have time to unbutton my pants   if it wasn't for a lot of brush I'd never make it. ^{Ha Ha}

I saw one of my marine buddies Elmer Hull and got three light bulbs so I can have a good place to write and he got me a tray to eat out of   I've been eating out of mess kits   they are to small and ever thing is mixed up when you do get it. We're getting a lot more to eat now and better food. Elmer gave me a can of peanuts   they sure were good.

Honey I think you are a poor guesser on part of your guessing. I looked in my book for the name of that part to the stove that's broke. It's either 1-2-5-13-1-13-1 or 1-16-1-13-1-13-1 They should know at the store any way.

Good night my darling   I hope to write sooner the next time.
Love & Kisses Homer

On Homer's third attempt at using the Norris Code he separated the numbers so there would be no confusion. Ruth already knew he was in the Gilbert Islands, but didn't know which island. When Ruth got this letter her "hen-scratching" notes on the envelope attest to her determination to decipher the code, and her ultimate success.

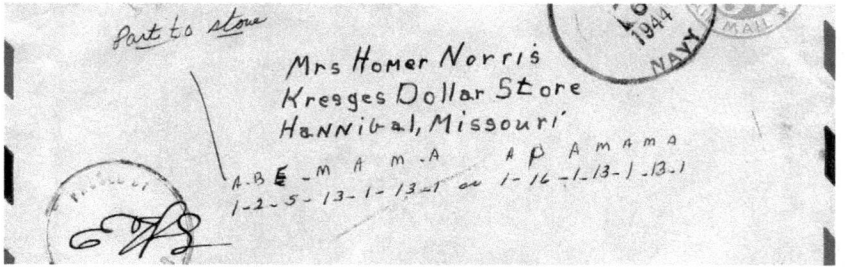

Notice Ruth's attempt to decipher the code

Mon Jan 10
8 o'clock

My Darling Ruth;

    Its sure not much I can write about only that I feel fine   I suppose thats the most important thing.

    I got a card saying that I was getting the readers digest for a year from Russell & Jane for a Christmas present   that was sure nice of them wasn't it?

    They have canteen now where we can buy candy, nuts, tobacco, soap and such like. We got paid twenty dollars day before yesterday   I didn't draw any   think I'll live on loans for a while. I loaned money out about two months ago and this is about the first chance they have had to pay it back.

    You have the wrong idea of our life   it isn't what you think it is at all. You said something about if I ever went to town, this island hasn't got but one building on it with a tin roof and made out of sawed wood and it's a church the British built. This island is owned or use to be owned by the British and their flag is still flying in the native village   there was one white man and three women here when we got here that were Catholic's.

British priest and nuns

Exterior and interior of British-built church

No town or anything of that sort   no roads I'd better say no nothing. Only coconut trees and a few natives. Know buildings except natives huts.

The only thing I can see that they had to eat was coconuts and a few different wild things that grow here   I'm pretty tired tonight   I haven't had but ½ day off since I've hit this rock and that was Christmas day and I had to wash then.

The way I feel I'd better turn in and hope I'll see you in my dreams, if dreams would only come true   I dream half of the time about you now   honey your a swell wife, I love you.

Good Bye Darling Wife
Your old man

By week eight life on the rock improved a little. Living at the main camp was better, but still very primitive with only a hole in the ground for a bathroom.

Homer was learning to appreciate simple things like light bulbs, a tray to eat on, and a canvas roof over his head. Thank goodness for Marine buddies who had access to all the good stuff that Homer's ACORN unit didn't have.

Telephone and Telegraph Hut

Homer liked his tent mates and his work. The men in his communications unit were so proud of their new switchboard they even hung a sign over the Quonset hut door that read "Apamama Tel and Tel."

Snow removal in Missouri

Wed. Jan. 19
Seven oclock

My Dearest Wife;
I received the snow pictures today   I showed them to ever one
It doesn't seam possible that it could be that cold any where.
Our eats consist of beans beans & more beans. If we don't blow the Japs away it won't be the navy's fault. We have spam and corn beef   thats about all the meat we have   if you can call it meat   I'd give anything to have a slice of bread with good old cow butter on it   we have some sort of lard on our bread. Ever thing else is from the states and it can't be very fresh.
I got two letters today one from you and the one from Mother   oh yes I got a box of candy from mother today   it sure was good.

nine o'clock
I just got back from the hospital to see my friend   Time for lights out
Good night my darling
Homer

After a busy Christmas season at the store, Ruth took a week of vacation to visit family and friends. She sewed a new dress with her mother's help, embroidered pillowcases, went to movies with friends, played lots of cards, and relaxed a little.

The following Monday Ruth went back to work and her boss Mr. Smith announced her promotion to Manager of the Ladies' Lingerie Department. Ruth was thrilled about the increase in salary. It would take several weeks for her good news to travel to the Pacific Islands.

Sunday Jan 23
eight o'clock

My Darling Wife;

Tonight has got to be my writing night   I got four letters today. Two from my darling one from your folks & one from my folks. I'm going to write your folks just as soon as I get done with this one, your mother was apologizing for not writing and I haven't even writting to them since I've left Hawaii.

The boys have been making so much noise here at the switch board where I'm writing   We have a black out ever night so we can't have lights on in our tents. We haven't had an air raid for several days.

We lived in pup tents awhile   now we have big tents   there are five in our tent, have a lot more room.

My buddy and I have it fixed up pretty good   we have a chest each made out of ply wood   I haven't gotten mine done yet but I'm putting a shelf in the top to put my small articles in.

I'm in charge of four men putting up telephone lines and never a one of them ever climbed a tree before yesterday   they sure had a time. Never any one fell. We are running cables now for our telephone lines   its sure a lot better than just plain wires.

Homer's five-man tent

Honey I was sure glad to get your pictures I've got them on the table in front of me I never miss looking at them each day. I better close now and get some shut eye.

> *Good night my darling*
> *Your old Man*
> *Homer*

The only problem with the bigger tent was that it leaked whenever it rained—and it rained all the time. The communications gang didn't know how to prevent the roof from leaking, but the Apamamese natives had a solution. One day while Homer and his buddy Jack were out checking lines, they took a little detour to the native village at the other end of the island. Two hours later they returned to camp with a thatch roof draped across their jeep. Homer and his tent mates placed the thatch roof over their tent—leaky roof problem solved.

Thurs Jan 27
3 P.M.

My Darling

This is the first time I've started to write my honey in the day time since before I left the states   I got the day off today another boy and myself cleaned up the tent   took us all morning   I was going to wash my clothes this afternoon but some natives came along and I got them to do it   I was thinking of taking a nap but it's to hot   only would be a sweat bath

I'm writing on a table we built   it has two big wire spools and a piece of ply wood for top   sure is a good table to write on. The only time I can write on this table is in the day time because we have black out ever night   have lights in the tent and can't use them. We sleep on canvas cots with mosquito nets over us. The Navy is giving some things away now   two cartons of cigarettes, one tooth brush, listerine tooth paste, a colgate shave stick and a bar of swan soap.

Natives washing clothes

We had apple pie last night   it sure tasted good. I'd give five dollars for all the eggs fried sunny side up I could eat. Haven't had any eggs or milk except powdered since Pearl Harbor. So I'm getting pretty dam hungry for something good to eat. Just think of my good cook wasting her time at a dollar store when she could be cooking for her old man. Darling I love you lots & lots.

I have a lot of news but can't write very much...can't explain but if they read the papers closely you can probably find out why.

Better sign off now.   I love you always my dear.

Your old man
Homer

The news Homer couldn't write about was the planned invasion of the Marshall Islands (D-Day 1 February 1944).[31] The Gilbert Islands of Apamama, Tarawa, and Makin had been occupied to provide base support to conquer the Marshalls. By mid January O'Hare Field was fully operational, telephone lines were laid and the switchboard was good to go. The atoll of Apamama was about to become a key player in the invasion of the Marshall Islands.

Japan had held the Marshall Islands for twenty-five years so they were well prepared to withstand enemy attack. In anticipation of an Allied strike, the Japanese had increased their forces in the Marshalls to over 8000 men and 110 aircraft with strongest fortifications along the outer ring of islands.[32] Instead of attacking the outer ring, Navy Admiral Chester Nimitz ordered an invasion of the main Japanese naval base on the Atoll of Kwajalein (kwäjə-lən) in the very heart of the Marshalls.[33]

Allied warships and planes subjected enemy installations on Kwajalein to a three-day bombardment unparalleled in history.[34]

Homer knew pilots who took off from O'Hare; some did not return. Others came back with bullet holes in the planes. Homer's letters reveal his mixed emotions.

O'Hare Field control tower and planes

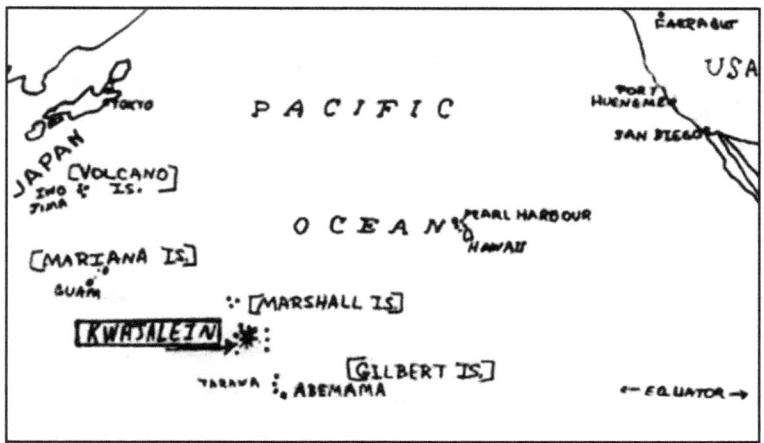

Pacific Islands including Apamama and Kwajalein

Sunday Jan 30
eight o'clock

My Lovely Wife;

I went to church tonight and it sure done me a lot of good. By what I can hear its sure tough going in the Marshalls now. We should all be praying for the boys in the Marshalls   for God's sake they need it.

We will take the islands but I wonder what the cost will be. I got my first letter today for about a week. Our mail isn't coming very good just now but it will get here better in a few weeks when things get settled down in the Marshalls.

I've been working on a new switch board   I sure like that kind of work. This afternoon a tree was chopped and fell across our lines and broke 14 pairs and we had to stop and go fix them   and we still had trouble on one line tonight   so after chow we went out to fine the break in the line and after an hour of checking found out that a peace of paper had been put between the bells to keep it from ringing. Oh! What a life. ^{Ha Ha} Maw said there would be days like this. ^{Ha Ha}

My light just went out its nine oclock so I just lite up a candle and go on as if nothing happened. You asked me about buying a bond I wouldn't advise anyone to do that   I wish we didn't have any bonds after seeing what I have and the way the money is wasted that has bought

Homer repairing telephone lines

157

bonds   its unexplainable. If the people in the states only knew, they wouldn't be complaining about gas rationing or anything else   they would be dam tickled to walk where they do have to go.

I'm going to sign off now darling only wish I could be there to kiss you good night.

Here is a kiss from
Homer

For the next six days wounded men were flown into O'Hare Field and taken to the base hospital. Homer and his unit maintained the telephone lines and switchboard to allow communication between the air strip and base hospital.

The bases on Apamama, Makin, and Tarawa provided crucial support for the invasion of the Marshall Islands, and significantly reduced the number of casualties. The final count showed 372 Allies killed and 1592 wounded compared to 7870 Japanese. Not one Allied ship was sunk in the invasion of Kwajalein.[35]

FEBRUARY
Rear Base

"…going to stay here for six more months as far as we know   in a way we are lucky."

—Homer's letter 2/18/44)

On 4 February Old Glory waved over Kwajalein and every man on Apamama heaved a sigh of relief.

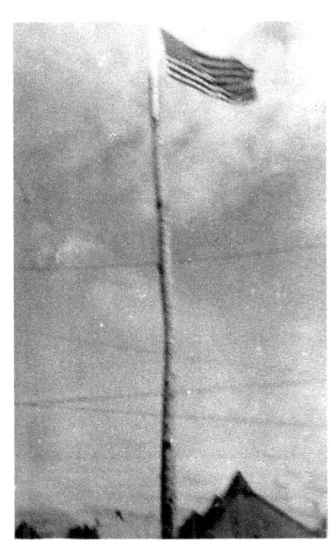

The original mission of Apamama was to give base support during the invasion of the Marshalls. With that mission complete Apamama began conversion to a rear base. Over night the work of ACORN 16 changed from construction to maintenance and the 95th Construction Battalion prepared to transfer to the Marshalls to work their magic there.

Sat Feb 5
eight oclock

My Dearest Ruth
I got your Valentine   it sure had a swell verse on it   I read it two or three times. I'm drinking a coco-cola now I've got to tell you about our food. Almost all our food had been dehydrated except what canned food we had. We were so sick of powedered eggs we couldn't hardly eat them.

At noon we had green beans, soup beans, warm ice tea and bread & butter. Tonight just soup beans bread butter & tomato juice. I've got a big washing to do tomorrow. I want to write about a dozen letters tomorrow   expect I'll get one or two written. ^{Ha Ha} I got six letters today and four day before today   that was yesterday. ^{Ha Ha}

I believe we won't have to use our fox holes any more   sure hope not anyway.

Natives dancing

I was playing horse shoe last night and pitched one and hit a boy in the head   he sure had a hard head   didn't even knock him down. He said he saw stars and I'll bet he did to.

I went to a show in our camp and the natives put on a dance. The funniest dancing I ever saw. The girls danced sort of like they do in Hawaii but its almost impossible to explane how they dance so I'll just drop it.

This being Saturday night sure wish I was with you (as if I don't all the time) having a swell time.

Good night my darling I love you very, very much

Homer

By mid February ships and planes arrived with mail and other supplies that had been held up due to the war effort. One day Homer was dealing with life and death situations, and the next day he was playing horse shoes and scouring the beaches to pick up sea shells and hand grenades!

Sunday Feb 13
noon

My Darling Wife

My day off and I'm due to write my honey a letter. I just got done knocking down some hand grenades I found yesterday   want to bring one back for a souvenior   I got two letters from my honey today.

We're trying to keep our tent clean and sort of live for a change. I guess we are going to start getting ever Sunday off   ever other Sunday I will be subject to call in case of trouble which won't be bad at all. I went to a good show last night   I really enjoyed it, don't expect you would   it was all about boxing Jim Corbett and John. L. Sullivan.

Boy oh Boy we had baked chicken for dinner, chicken gravy, mash potatoes, and ice cream. I think our chow is going to get better as time goes on, they are going to get big refrigerators and be able to have fresh food most of the time.

I just got back from one of the best shows I ever saw in my life can you imagine me going to a show on a desert island like this but we sure enjoyed it. "Your always in my heart." it sort of made me home sick but expect to get that way every so often   sometimes worse than others. But the name of the show is just like me   darling your always in my heart and always will be   I love you so much.

Nine oclock now, what a day. I'm afraid the lights will go out before I can get it finished so had better hurry. Tapps...

They have turned the light out and I'm writting by a candle. A boy gave me some Vatalis and I sure smell good now.

I want to let you in on a secret (I love you)   don't tell anyone. ^{*Ha Ha*} *I enjoy the jokes you have been sending me.*

Good night my Darling
Homer

Ruth and Homer both appreciated a good joke—especially a good dirty joke! Ruth sent jokes that she heard or cut out of newspapers and magazines. Copies of some of them are in her scrapbook.

If the censors had read incoming mail, many of the jokes Ruth sent would never have made their way to Homer.

"That's fine — but can you cook?"

Friday Feb 18
seven thirty

My Darling Wife

Boy do I feel good   just came back from the show Fibber McGee & Molly Charley McCarthy & Edgar Bergen. Laughed so much I'm almost sick.

I got four letters today one from your folks, one from Mother and two from the most wonderful woman in the world. Darling I miss you more each day.

My poor wife is back to work now I believe   you must have enjoyed your vacation at least I hope you did. It seems like I've been here for a year but havn't been here three months   going to stay here for six more months as far as we know   in a way we are lucky

We had beef stake yesterday noon and pancakes for breakfast   I went around the serving line twice each time. Today is pay day but I'm not drawing anything. Fifty dollars is as much as you can draw. Honey, you asked me if I need money, if you only knew, I can't write so you can understand what conditions we are living under I've spent about one dollar the last three months I expect. A person has got to save money out here if they want to or not.

I had to get up at eleven oclock last night and go out on the line we had four lines broken didn't get back until four. I never worked very hard today The boys are coming back from getting payed and there is a lot of noise Will sign off for tonight.

I love you lots & lots,
Your old man

The last thing Homer wanted to do was stay there for another six months. But he knew there were a lot worse places he could be stationed. Apamama was boring—but at least it was safe. In the luck of the draw, Apamama really was a lucky draw.

MARCH
Pecking Order

"Its not what a man knows in this navy its who he knows, and thats no kidding."

—Homer's letter 9/24/44

The military adheres to a clearly defined hierarchy, or "pecking order." There is a **formal** pecking order based on rank. There is also an **informal** pecking order. The men at the top of the informal pecking order are the ones who have learned to circumvent military regulations and get what they want—by hook or crook.

Wed Mar 1
eleven thirty

My Darling Wife

I just got two letters from you. One was post marked Oct 9   it was the one thanking me for your neckless and picture   it was sent to Port Hueneme and I'm just getting it.

We got two more cartons of cigarettes given to us yesterday   makes me 134 packs of cigarettes now   don't think I'll ever run out. We are getting caught up on our work now. There's still plenty to do but know hurry   we can take our time with it.

You was saying that you were going to a lot of shows   me, too   we have shows ever night and I don't even fall asleep. ^{Ha Ha} *It looks like rain   don't expect the boys will see all the show. I hope it does shower tonight   it cools off so we can really sleep then.*

I was up to see Elmer Hull tonight before dark. He thinks he's leaving soon   don't know where. I sure hope he gets to come home soon.

Tonight was coca-cola night but its hot and there's nothing much worse than hot coca so I'm saving mine until I can steal some ice.

We have a girls picture in our tent with pretty legs like your's   it makes me home sick ever time I look at her and thats most all the time. ^{Ha Ha}

Good night my darling, I love you very very much

Homer

Homer's ACORN unit was stationed on Apamama with about three thousand Marines. At first he didn't know any of them, but the Marines had all of the supplies. So Homer started getting acquainted. By March he had worked his way into the good-old-boy network, and hooked (or crooked) enough building materials for a new house.

House built by Homer and buddies. Notice dog on front step.

Friday March 3
eleven oclock p.m.

Dearest Ruth

We have moved, just a little ways   we (the five of us) built a new house. Board floor 16'x16' plywood side two feet high, screen wire four foot high, tent roof. And a two hundred watt light bulb in the middle. I can write any time at night. We have been working until midnight almost ever night for several nights.

Notice Homer's ring and casual shoes

We're sure proud of our new home   can walk around in our sock feet now and not get them dirty. Ever one has gone to bed now and I'm getting mighty sleepy.

Tomorrow is clean up day   we have inspection every week now started last week. Another boy and myself put out two of the biggest washings this morning   we used a washing machine and took three hours   we washed four blankets. We have a well dug right close to our tent now and good wash water and so handy.

We had a little card game last night some boys came over had a right good time. The boys have their sail boat finished and are sailing today   they joined the navy and have to make their own boat to be able to get in the sea, thats a laugh isn't it?

You asked about my ring   I still have it and you needn't worry about me losing it, it fits perfect. I sure love you a lot and wish so much for us to be togeather again.

It won't be long until farming time will it   sure wish I was back a turning over old mother earth again.

Well honey I'm going to turn the light out and go to bed now so good night my darling,

I love you a lot
Homer

Homer had the soul of a farmer. Even on the equator, his internal radar knew that back home the seasons were changing, and he started thinking of spring planting. He longed for the farm he would have someday—after the war. Inside Homer's head was his **imaginary** farm of the future, and he had plenty of imaginary money to buy land, tractors, and livestock. To make his farm a reality, he would need **real** money. While stationed in the states, Homer washed clothes, took extra guard duty, and ironed to earn extra money. Now that he was stationed on a primitive island, he feared it might be impossible to make a little money on the side.

Back in January word got around that Homer had a camera; he was immediately welcomed into the photography gang. He soon discovered that printing photos was a very lucrative business. Everyone stationed on the island wanted pictures of the island, especially the topless native women.

Page from Ruth's scrapbook

The Apamama base actually had an elaborate darkroom where military photographers developed film and printed surveillance photographs. But the military wasn't going to let a bunch of guys use the official darkroom to print pictures of half naked natives. However, a few industrious men set up a photo lab in their tent.

During the month of March the Marines shipped out, and Homer and his buddies inherited the darkroom. At first they didn't know how to develop film or print pictures, but if they could make a little "doe-ray-me" that way—they were willing to learn.

Mon March 13
nine oclock P.M.

My Darling Wife

I got three letters from the most wonderful wife a man could have. All the boys are gone   they are trying to develop some films tonight   I will send some pictures if I get hold of any.

Congratulations on your promotion. You should be able to support me now, so when I come home I won't have to go to work.^{Ha Ha} *I'll think I'll get a money order and send some money home some time soon. Honey don't do without anything you want to save money.*

I went to small stores today and got some hair oil   bet it makes my pillow slip dirty dont you ^{Ha Ha} *also got stationery, gum, peanuts, mattress cover, pillow slip, two combs   thats about all. I sprayed our tent and the bugs are getting in my hair now. Bet they stick to my hair oil.* ^{Ha Ha}

The army has come to release the marines. Our family is going to increase we're going to get six dogs   one old dog and five pups, the marines are leaving and turning the dog family over to us.

We had steak for dinner   its the first food we have had for a week that was fit to eat. Honey it doesn't seem like I can think of anything to write, will have to quite. I love you honey.

Your old (gray haired) man
Homer

Fri March 24
Ten Thirty PM

Dearest Ruth

The first thing I want to tell you is that I still love you even if I haven't written to you for severial days.

We got some bunks from the marines today   they have rubber springs, will be a lot better than cots   those cots get pretty hard. A boy just turned our mosquito bomb on and the bugs are falling so I just put my hat on to keep them out of my hair.

Honey, looks like I'll be here a year, sure would like to come home but have little hope for a long time.

We have a radio speaker here in our tent so we have news, music, and stories really enjoy them. We are fixing up a shower   have already had our well dug but know water in our barrel yet Ever one else on the island has had shower's but the acorn for its always a month behind anyway.

This letter to be continued tomorrow.

Water Tower

Sat March 25
ten P.M.

Dearest Ruthie

Just took a shower in our new shower sure was fine to take a bath in fresh water it was the best shower I had since I left Pearl. Today the army opened a new ship store   they have almost anything a person would want   we got cookies, grape juice, candy bars, gum, hair oil, stationery, cigars, planter peanuts (in cans). Thats what we made our supper of tonight.

Homer's "Johnnie"

I got my first Readers Digest yesterday   they sure are interesting   I think we are going to take some pictures tomorrow of our house, dogs, ourselves and other things around here.

Everone wants to send me something   I realy dont need anything but I'm going to request a picture album   small one about 5"x8" or 6"x10" something like that. I'm going to get some pictures and I cant send them all home, so I'll just bring them.[Ha Ha]

It's past ten oclock now   past my bedtime. It looks like I've written all I know for now. I love you sweetheart and miss you more each day, no fooling. Good night my one and only

Love & Kisses
Homer

It was hard for Homer to say good-bye to his Marine buddies. Most of them were headed to the Marshall Islands to build airstrips. He hoped Elmer Hull would get to go home. Homer was happy about inheriting the rubber bunks, but it reminded him that his ACORN had been at the bottom of the pecking order. Things were getting ready to change.

Soon after the Marines left, the Army maintenance battalion landed and Homer had one of those ah-ha moments. The arrival of new troops meant a whole new pecking order, and ACORN 16 wasn't at the bottom for a change. Homer and his buddies were now the island old-timers who knew how to work the system. While laying telephone lines for the Army, doing a favor here and there got them access to lots of supplies the Army brought to the island. Homer always said that in the military it's not **what** you know but **who** you know that counts.

APRIL
At Ease

"We should have a lot of fun some day looking at these pictures."

—Homer's letter 4/9/44

By April Apamama was no longer on high alert. For Homer this was too much "at ease" so he spent his free time trying to make a little money on the side.

Sat April 1
noon

My Darling

Time sure flyies by   today is April and hotter than he_ _ have been laying wire under ground and its a lot of work that's the reason we notice the heat so much.

We had a rat killing last night at three oclock a boy woke up and found a rat in bed with him so we all got up and killed Mr Rat after a half hour fight.

We took pictures this morning of all the boys that worked around here they were taken with a big camera. I don't know if I told you or not I'm growing a mustache   I almost shaved it off tonight.

Darling your sure a swell wife   you write to me almost ever day and some times its a week between my letters   should have my little butt kicked. I got my Easter card   sure was nice.

I'm going to bed early tonight   pretty tired   been climbing trees all day putting up telephone lines. Here's a salute to the one I love,

Homer

Homer's ACORN 16 Unit

All thirty-four men had on their sailor hats and work shirts which came off as soon as the picture was taken. Now Ruth could see faces of the men Homer mentioned in his letters.

Homer and his buddies had honed their darkroom skills by printing from the negatives they already had; then it was time to take some new photos. On Easter Sunday Homer unpacked his camera and realized he had a big problem.

> *Easter Sunday April 9*
> *nine thirty p.m.*
>
> *My Beloved Wife,*
>
> *Honey what do you think about sending your camera out here to me or would you reather buy a new one. The one we had is know good now   it got salt water in it and rusted it so bad that it will never work again   sure hated to lose the one we had. We should have a lot of fun some day looking at these pictures.*
>
> *I ran around all this morning   and after noon chow I did a hell of a washing by hand*
>
> *We have sold two of our pups for ten dollars each and have two more to sell. Honey the boys have all come in now & ever one is talking to me. Think I'll close for now. Good night my darling wife.   I love you*
>
> > *Your old man*
> > *Homer*

Sat April 15
noon

Hello My Dear;

Another month half gone and I'm still sweating the time along. It rained all last night and the sun came out bright this morning and it's been so hot we can't hardly get our breath.

We cleaned up around our yard this morning   hauled a truck load of ashes and wire out. Are going to set up a sixteen by fifty foot tent to put our supplies in   its going to be close to our tent so we can watch it.

We have been printing pictures   expect I have almost fifty if not more.

Our food for the past two weeks has been very good. We have roast beef and pork almost ever day for dinner   and have been having hot cakes for morning chow. Ice cold lemonade for noon, and hot coffee for breakfast.

If you notice our address has been changed. The acorn-16 is now ships company of a naval air base. We still do the same things we have been doing. We have been laying telephone lines for the army the last two days.

We only have one pup now   think we will keep this one he has fleas now have been spraying him and every thing else trying to get rid of them. Things like that happens in the best of familys I suppose.^{Ha Ha} Our mother dog "Pattsy" is a chicken dog   she very seldom catches one but is always after them. She always rides on the truck or jeep ever time we go out.

I love you so much   I haven't been feeling very perky today think I'll go to bed early tonight for a change.

Good night my darling sleep tight.

Your love,
Homer

Homer with dog and chicken

When Homer's ACORN became part of Ship's Company they moved considerably higher in the island pecking order. Since they maintained base communications and electricity, no group had more clout or access to supplies than the Ship's Company.

Thurs April 20
nine thirty night

Dearest Ruthie

Jack, Josefo, Homer

Another boy and myself just went up to see a boy in the hospital.

Honey I have a grass skirt for you   A little native boy ten years old brought me a grass skirt today

A native friend of ours came sixteen miles day before yesterday just to see us. Was the first time in four months he had been on this island   there had been a lot of changes made. They don't like our food very well   eat coconuts mostly some dried fish they catch   dry them in the sun. Don't worry about me getting moved   think maby I'll be here for a year   that's a hell of a long time isn't it. But you'd better not start hunting for another man, you might do worse, if possible. ^{Ha Ha}   *I love you very, very much my dear*

Homer

Homer's native friend (Josefo) came to the north part of the island to deliver souvenirs he had crafted and to invite Homer to Sunday dinner. Because of censorship Homer couldn't tell Ruth about how he and Josefo were selling souvenirs to make a little money on the side. Homer's goal was to make some money to send to Ruth for Mother's Day.

Thurs April 27
eight oclock

My Darling Ruthie

I just picked out some pictures to send to you Darling I was sure glad to get your pictures   am about to wear them out looking at them.

Honey can't you get in a mail bag and come to see me, you know make yourself little like a mouse.^{Ha Ha}

I'm going to send this money order so don't forget Mother's day. For yourself as well as the others. Only wish you were a mother. I love you so much darling

We have a lot of packages at the post office   I'm hoping to get some films in the mail tomorrow   if so I'll take some pictures Sunday. Will close for now.

Lots of love, loads of hugs & kisses

Your old man

P.S. I know something I could put in good use   you might send me, "don't faint" its a Webster Dictionary. Thanks.

Homer and Ruth wanted to have children in the worst way. In fact, Ruth wanted to get pregnant before he went overseas; Homer disagreed. So they decided to wait until he came home to start their family. Telling Ruth to get herself something for Mother's Day was his way to let her know he hadn't forgotten how much they both wanted to have children. Having Homer say, "I only wish you were a mother" was in itself a very special Mother's Day present for Ruth.

MAY
Native Friends

"I had a wonderful time Sunday   went to see a native friend we know."

—Homer's letter 5/3/44

In Homer's little black book he wrote the names and addresses of only twelve very special people—including the names of a native friend and his wife: "Native Friend: Josefo Tmereta and wife T Lana Susuga on Kabangak Abemama Gilbert Island." Homer met Josefo while they were building the airstrip and they forged a lasting friendship. Several of the photographs Homer sent home are labeled, "my native friend."

The last Sunday in April Homer and his buddy Jack went visiting at the south end of Apamama in the Kabangak Village.

Josefo's family

Wed May 3
eight oclock

Hello My Darling;
I had a wonderful time Sunday   went to see a native friend we know, and had fried chicken and sunny side eggs   it sure was a treat. We got several souvenirs and I have my box packed ready for censorship. I'm sending two of my blankets and my watch and a lot of other little things I've picked up here and there.

Honey the natives don't wear shoes   they go bare footed all their lifes. They don't wear many clothes because they dont have any.

We took a lot of pictures Sunday   hope you enjoy them, the picture of me, I think is pretty good. I took severial of the boy with me and he also took severial of me.

We can buy Ritz crackers at the Army PX and we have bought two cases of six boxes each. We had cold Pepsi Cola tonight I sure enjoyed it.

I never write a letter that I don't look at the pictures you sent me. Well honey I guess I'll close for now   wish I was going to bed with you instead of by myself.

Bye, Bye

Love, Homer

Sitting on native boat

Homer and Jack came back to camp with lots of souvenirs—some to sell, some to send home. Homer sent home extra souvenirs for Ruth to give to all the people who wrote letters and sent Christmas gifts to him.

Monday May 8

seven oclock

Hello Sweet Stuff;

Our native friends family has increased   now they have a baby girl   he sent a man about fifteen miles to tell us about it. It happened three days after the picture was taken. Honey I have been invited out for ice cream   boy oh boy sure bet it will be good   special made. It will be at eight oclock, can hardly wait. Wish you were here to go with me.

At last I have a package on its way   got it censored today. This package has a purse for Mother and you can do what you want with the rest.

I'm getting a better boat made for us so you can give the boat away   and you can give some of those neckless away I'm getting some more of those too.

There's something this native wants and that is dye. If you can get severial boxes of that all colors he said that he would make us some big mats.

Native women with mats

My Darling I think its about time for ice cream   I dont want to be late. Oh yes   I got eight letters yesterday five from you   honey your so nice to me   I love you lots and lots and always will.

Your old Man
Homer Lee

A U.S. Customs packing slip from the Naval Air Base is in Ruth's scrapbook. In brief it lists the package contents with one small omission.

Homer forgot to mention that he had also included two **hand grenades**. It was risky to send hand grenades through the mail, and he hid them among the souvenirs.

On May 14 Homer turned twenty-four years old. The only good thing about being thousands of miles from home in a war zone on his birthday was that the erratic mail delivery spaced out the arrival of cards and presents over several weeks. This allowed Homer to be continually reminded that lots of people back home were thinking about him.

Ruth wanted to send him something really special so she scheduled an appointment for a professional portrait session in Hannibal. The portraits arrived four days before Homer's birthday.

Thursday May 11
ten oclock

My Darling,

Honey I received your pictures. They sure are swell. I've looked at them all day.

I sure thank you a lot, I love you so much. I also got the package with two rolls of films a box of candy which was in very good shape, a wash cloth and towel, shaving cream, razor blades. Also got the box with a 6-20 Kodak so dont worry about us not getting the films taken. Also got a package of stationery from Mother.

I just came back from the show In Old Oklahoma, it sure makes a person wish for his loved one. Honey God only knows how much I love you and dream of you day and night.

We have to drill two days a week   a half hour a day   and Monday & Tuesday are our days   maby they don't think that we get enough exercise which is a laugh.^{Ha Ha} *Don't think anything about this B.S. I'm spreading on this page.*

Good night my dear, I love you lots & lots

Your one and only
Old Man

Ruth Marie, age 21

Homer's family remembered his birthday, but when the actual day arrived **he** forgot.

My Birthday

My Darling;

When I started this letter and looked at the date   May 14th   its seven oclock and now was the first time I'd thought about it. I'm 24 today! I sure hope I don't have another birthday in the service. Don't we all?

I've had a very enjoyable day. Houck and I went down to our native friend's   saw their week old baby girl   I almost stoled her but don't think I'd make a very good mother. I'm sending you a picture of the baby and wife of this native friend of ours   the baby was five days old when this picture was taken.

We had fried chicken, eggs, potatoes, peanut butter, some kind of fruit, bananas and coffee. What a dinner. Tonight we are going to have ice cream getting state side.^{Ha Ha}

I got another native boat today and some shells.

I got a beautiful birthday card from what I think is the most wonderful young woman in the world. Honey I'd better sign off and go help freeze ice-cream.

Lots of Love and Loads of kisses,
your old man,
Homer

Souvenir 12" replica of native boat

When Ruth saw the baby's picture she wrote "Little Love" on the photograph and put the picture in the scrapbook next to a picture of a native boat. Then she went shopping for a little dress to send to the islands.

Ruth enjoyed seeing the native group picture from Homer's birthday celebration, but she was surprised to see that many natives were wearing clothes. When the troops arrived on Apamama, the men sent letters requesting towels, shirts, dresses, cloth, and thread. Wearing clothing showed the effects of the military's influence on the native people.

Monday May 22
six oclock p.m.

My Darling Wife,

If my mail gets much quicker getting here it will be like state side   today I got a letter that was mailed only seven days ago   that pony express Missouri has must be pretty good.

I have my birthday card at the head of my bed   I liked it very much. I sure miss my brown eyed, black haired wife   its a shame we have to be so far apart.

Honey I've got some pictures on the road now   I had close to one hundred and twenty five pictures censored today. It may be a month before you get them. I have a few that didn't pass censor so I'll bring them home.

I just sprayed the tent for bugs and its so strong this bug that is writing is about to get down. Three native boys here now and they are making so much noise I may be writing almost anything. I was showing some native boys your picture a while ago and they said very nice   so well I think that too. The native boys like Pepsi-cola but don't like beer   they say to much beer make head go around & around.

I want to write Mother and Dad a line to let them know I'm still kicking around as perky as ever.

Well good night my love I'll be thinking of you in my dreams.

Lots of love and load of Kisses,

Homer

Native friends

Homer Norris E.M.2/C
Saturday May 27
Six oclock

My Darling Wife

Honey, believe it or not I'm second class. It was posted yesterday   that was the first time I knew about it. I thought I would make it by my birthday but had given up. I wanted to surprise you. I hope I did. It means eighteen dollars a month more. That's what I'm interested in most. Besides getting home thats the most I could ask for.

Honey, how much money do we have in the bank? I asked you a long time ago but you must not have gotten that letter.

Tomorrow we will be here six months so tonight we're having a party of some sort   are having some beer, sandwiches and a native show.

Oh yes honey be sure and write about the hand grenades I sent home   I sure hope they came through all right   they are all safe having had the powder and caps taken out. The yellow one is an American and the black one a Jap.

I made a picture holder twenty four inches long and twelve inches wide and I put 21 pictures that you have sent me and I have them hanging over my bed so I can see them all the time   not meaning I stay in bed all the time.[Ha Ha] *I had to laugh when you said you had sent a surprise in a package and hoping they didn't get damaged. Then you said, "You know how I hate to have my picture taken." Its just like you. I know how hard you would try to keep a secret then give it away.*

Lots of love & box car loads of Kisses
Homer Lee

P.S. On May 16 I got your cable gram wishing me happy birthday! Honey I love you a terrible lot.

All things considered Homer had a very nice birthday month. Ruth sent oil portraits, their Kodak camera, a soap box care package, a cable gram, and a special birthday card. Mom Norris mailed home-made candy and a box of writing stationery (hint-hint). Homer spent his actual birthday at the native village eating a delicious fried chicken dinner with friends and had home-made ice cream that night. His new rating on May 26 was the perfect way to end the month.

JUNE
Island Adventures

"... after dinner we went sailing in the boat we built and never got back until after mid night last night ... wet as a drowned rat."

—Homer's letter 6/17/44

Sometimes the activities of a normal day on Apamama turned into a full-blown island adventure. Thursday, June 1 was one of those days.

Friday June 2
Nine oclock

My Best Half
Is it ever nice now   has been raining almost all afternoon and now it's just good and comfortable.

Homer and Jack

Yesterday three of us went to check a telephone line that was out on another island   we went across to the other island when the tide was out and while we were across the tide came in and we had to wait until ten oclock at night until low tide then the jeep wouldn't start. We called in and two boys came after us in another jeep and we got in it and it wouldn't start   so there five of us were   the tide was coming in again, so we stayed all night and another truck had to come after us and pull both jeeps in.

We sure enjoyed ourselves even if we did have to sleep on concrete with the mosquitos.

Tomorrow is another inspection day, we'll have to get up early in the morning and clean things up a bit.

Well honey, I've about ran out of anything to write about so will close for now.

I love you more each day honey,
Your old man Homer

When the communications crew had a little free time they didn't know what to do with themselves. In order to stay busy Homer and his tent mate Jack Houck built a sailboat. Homer had zero sailing experience and quickly found that there was a lot to learn about sailing and even more to learn about unpredictable island storms.

Homer on the boat he built

Saturday June 17th
seven oclock

Hello my Dear,

I had intensions of writing yesterday but after dinner we went sailing in the boat we built and never got back until after mid night last night. we sure had a ride   about seven oclock we had a rain and hard wind, then about ten oclock a storm came up and we were about two miles out   almost turned over but we findly made it o.k. but wet as a drowned rat.

I bought some blue pants and shirt and I have a blow torch now heating water and boiling the starch out of them   I hope they don't burn. Be right back   I've got to take my shirt out and boil my pants a while.

The other day one of the boys in the tent got one of the pictures he sent

185

home to his girl friend back saying she didn't care for that type of picture. Then we all begain wondering about the ones we sent home. We have seen so much of the way the native women dress that we don't think any thing about it any more   a few ware under shirts that boys have gave them. But after that happened we got thinking I'll bet it is sort of a shock to the people back home. These natives are a lot more modest than Americans are. It's just because they havn't got the clothing is why they don't ware them.

I want to write to Mother & Dad tonight. It has just started to rain, will be able to sleep good tonight. I love you sooooooomuch

Bye Bye My Love, Homer

Homer wanted to do something special for Ruth's 22nd birthday, but he was pretty sure she wouldn't appreciate getting sardines or men's hair oil from the Army store on Apamama. So he asked his mother to pick out something special. The week before Ruth's birthday Mom Norris sewed a silk dress. According to Mom's diary, she finished the sleeves on June 8.

Ruth's birthday was on a Friday, and she worked all day. Saturday morning Ma and Pa Norris drove to Hannibal and brought Ruth to Perry for the weekend. On Sunday the whole family gathered at Ruth's parents' house for a surprise birthday party. Monday morning Ruth was back at work wearing a beautiful blue silk dress.

Friday June 23
nine oclock p.m.

My Darling Wife;

It happens to be the twenty-third of June today. Happy Birthday Honey. Darling I hope you like the birth day present. Mother said it was a pretty one. I got a letter from them today Mother said they had been working pretty hard putting up hay.

It has been raining for the past two days   I don't know if the battles up north are causing it or not but I can't keep from believing it does.

Its been some time since you have received a letter from me, but I've been pretty busy working at night. I miss you more every day.

Oh yes, I received our camera in good shape it was just like it was the day you sent it. I made a box for it out of wood so it wont get banged up. and I'm linning it with a towel. I'll sure be glad when I receive your picture. I'm proud of you darling. I want ever one to see your picture.

I would write to you all day if I could because I love you so much. Ruth you are wonderful. Will close for now.

Your old man, Homer
Lots of love and load of kisses

With the new camera Homer could take pictures to print and sell. Film was hard to get, so Homer tried to make each picture count—especially when he had an opportunity to go up in a plane and take aerial photos!

One of Homer's photos shows O'Hare field with military tents and huge palm trees. Most islands were bombed so severely that few trees were left, but Apamama didn't suffer pre-invasion bombs, so it still had lush vegetation and mature shade trees. Another photo shows another plane flying maneuvers that same day.

Sunday June 25
Ten P.M.

My Darling Ruthie

How's my sweetheart by now? I hope she is just as sassy as ever. I suppose its getting hot back there by now. By the time you get this it will probaly be the 4th of July.

I got a local hop in a plane this week   was up for two hours   very enjoying hop   I only wish it was to good old Missouri.

I hear we have a lot of mail in tonight   a lot of packages too   so I'm hoping for your picture more than anything.

Last night a bunch of us had a fried egg and bacon party for some of the communicatons boys that are leaving us, you should have seen the eggs we eat   a person would have thought we were a threshing crew. I got away with eight sunny side up ones   then I never went to chow this morning.

Darling I wish for you all the time but little good it does. Maby it wont be to long before this thing is all over, we can always hope for the best.

I love you always dear.
Homer

When the sun went down on Apamama, most of the men got ready to catch some shut-eye—but not Homer and his darkroom gang. At nine o'clock they geared up for their second job—printing pictures.

Friday June 30
nine p.m.

My Darling Wife;

Honey at last I received the album. It was just what I needed. Today I got some more nice souvenirs a native friend made them for me.

We had a lot of trouble today with our lines   a tree fell and broke ten lines. Well honey I've got some work to get done tonight so had better sign off. I want to thank you again for the pictures.

Darling I love you an awful lot but its nine oclock and I am going to have to close for now.

Bye, Bye, my love
Homer

P.S . I'm sending a page of Yank magazine.

The following page from YANK magazine[36] is in Ruth's scrapbook. She wrote, "My Honey! sent it to me from Apamama in the Gilberts, July 1-1944."

My Honey! sent it to me from Apamama in the Gilberts, July 1-1944

The article describes a make shift darkroom in the jungle where GIs printed "crude but clear" pictures.

After seven months on Apamama Homer concluded that he had not been properly trained for the island adventures he had encountered. The Navy trained him how to spot enemy planes, but not how to spot a pop-up island storm. He learned how to row a Navy whaleboat, but did not learn how to navigate a hand-made sailboat. He learned how to march in cadence, but not how to start a drowned-out jeep. They trained him to break down rifles; but gave no instructions on how to pack hand grenades to ship home. It was a good thing that Homer was blessed with common sense and a little bit of good luck, or his island adventures might have ended in disaster.

JULY
Sick

"We're so far behind on the map   think we've been forgotten."

—Homer's letter 7/6/44

When the month of July arrived—Homer got homesick. Back home it was time for picnics in the park, summer dances, fireworks, and the "4th of Julie"— his favorite summer holiday.

Thurs July 6
one oclock PM

My Darling Wife;
I received the congratulation card   and also two letters, honey it makes me feel so good to get a letter from you. Darling I'm sure glad you liked your birthday present.
I'm going to get some pictures taken of myself tomorrow to send home. I'm also going to send a picture taken by a cross the British built down by the mission
Every thing the natives make is by hand   they do have a few sewing machines the British gave them but very few. They didn't have any thread or cloth to sew before we came. Some of the natives speak a little English   some of them   the lucky ones   have gone to school four or five years. But its supprising how fast they catch on to English.
We arn't doing any new work just keeping our lines we have in good

working order. Our bomb disposal officer gave me two good Jap souvenirs yesterday—one tank mine and a fuse of a trench-motar shell. I had been getting some sea shells for him to give to Admiral Nimitz, head man of the Pacific fleet. The Japs are really catching hell now from all angles. I wonder when they will deside they are licked and give up   that sure will be a happy day   but the day I'm waiting for is the day I come home to you for keeps.

Its sure getting dead around this place, nothing going on. We're so far behind on the map   think we've been forgotten.

We all get so down in the dumps at times, and so tired of the same old thing over and over. I sure wish I was back there   the hell with these dam islands   the British can have them as far as I'm concerned. Well honey, I've about ran out of B.S. so will give you all my love until next time.

Good night my love.
Homer

P.S. Dammit I'm homesick.

Homer had use of the communication crew's jeep, and whenever he was out checking lines, he also looked for interesting photo opportunities—like the British cross. Ruth was shocked to learn that Homer was picking up sea shells for the famous Admiral Nimitz!

One of Homer's best memories of his days on Apamama was the friendship he forged with the natives. Homer and a few of his buddies were even allowed to attend a native wedding ceremony.

His appreciation for the native culture grew as he learned more about their customs. For example, the young native boys always sang songs while they gathered coconuts from the

Apamamese wedding couple

 tree tops. The natives were very modest and didn't have underwear, so their singing was to signal anyone passing below not to look up.

When Homer visited the native village he frequently heard native children singing songs the English speaking nuns taught them. Apamamese people lived under the most primitive conditions and still managed to sing songs of contentment.

By the middle of July Homer's homesickness waned and his mood improved because he had some exciting news to share.

Saturday July 15
nine oclock

My Darling Wife;

I have been waiting eight months to do this but I wanted to wait until I got five hundred dollars before I sent it. I drew all my back pay and its on the road to my love now. I can draw pay once every month or let it ride July 14th was the first money I had drawn since November just before we left Pearl Harbor. Honey you asked me how much I draw. I draw $96 a month state side pay. Twenty per cent over seas pay which makes it $115.20 then the $28 you get makes us draw $143.20 a month. I wanted to wait until I hit five hundred. Now my pay will start all over again. But it will count up faster now since I've gotten the raise. This will be a great help to us after this thing is all over. I have been listening to the news it sure sounds good.

Honey it looks like I'd better sign off   my knowledge has about run out. But honey I still love you oodles and oodles and I know you love me too.

I love you always.
Homer

Saturday, July 15 was a memorable day in the lives of both Ruth and Homer, but for very different reasons. Homer was writing to share his good news about sending $500 home. On the other hand Ruth spent the day in the hospital. She was so busy writing letters she hadn't written in her diary for months, but on July 15, she wrote, *"Had my tonsils out at 7:30 in the morning. Had local. Mother & Mrs. Norris were with me   came home 4:30."*

Ruth's scrapbook has a get-well card from Ma & Pa Norris.

The scrapbook also has a receipt from the hospital which shows that her tonsillectomy cost $13.25.

Ruth's recuperation included spending four days with Ma and Pa Norris, and four days with her parents. She was back at work on July 24.

The day after Ruth went back to work she received a registered letter and enclosed money order from Apamama. In her diary Ruth wrote, "<u>Tues. July 25</u>: *My Honey has saved $500.00 since November! He sent it home in a Registered Letter Cost .26 Air-Mail.*" That was the last diary entry Ruth made in 1944.

Ruth didn't want Homer to worry so she didn't tell him about her surgery until it was over. Two weeks later, news of her tonsillectomy reached the islands.

Sunday July 30

My Darling Wife

I sure hope youre feeling fine again. I know they can't keep a good person like you down very long. Honey I hope you get your strength back soon. I sure wish I was back there taking care of you instead of on this vacation as the Navy calls it.

Another month will soon be gone. Gee time flies by. Honey I have been thinking of you all day long   I miss you a terrible lot. I love you so much my darling, words can't express it. But action would I betcha.[Ha Ha]

Our chow is getting pretty common. We dont uselly get but one meal a day fit to eat. I wish this thing would come to an end soon, I'm getting so tired of this place but maby its a good thing that I dont get moved   who knows? You may think I'm home sick by the sound of this letter, the truth is by god I am. There isn't much a person can do about it out here.

Well honey this looks like the end again so I'll say again I love you lots and lots.

So long my love,
Homer

By the end of July Homer was so homesick that if it hadn't been for work in the darkroom and visiting his native friends he might have gone nuts. However, as he tore off the July calendar page he reminded himself that a lot of men in the Navy would gladly trade places with him, and resolved to make the best of his situation.

AUGUST
Tropical Heat Wave

"I went to hositipal with dengue fever Aug 6th got out Aug 10th, 1944."

—Note written in Homer's little black book

On the equator one month was just about as hot as another and the stifling August heat made Ruth feel like she was on the equator, too. She and a girlfriend even took a little time off to sun bathe.

Her friends tried to keep Ruth really busy the first part of August because they knew her third wedding anniversary was rolling around. Ruth and Homer were missing each other more than ever, and hoped this would be the only anniversary they'd have to celebrate long distance.

Ruth (left) & girlfriend sunbathing

Thursday Aug. 3

My Darling Wife;
    My love, today is our third wedding anniversary   seems only a short time since we were on our honeymoon and what a wonderful trip. Gee! I wish we were on our second honeymoon now instead of us being so very far apart but we are very close together in one way   thats our love.

How much mail means to a person cant be expressed   I hit the jack pot today sure enough. Eight letters and boy was I ever tickled   four of the nicest lettters from my darling wife   I was very glad you are getting along O.K. I wish I was there

I got a letter and a pretty anniversary card from your mother   It would have been much better if you could have shared it with me.

You told me about our bank account. I was surpprised and very, very pleased   I think we have done awful well for no longer than we have been married. I can hardly wait until we get three thousand in the bank   then we will want four I suppose. We'll sure be glad we have it when this war is over. The money we have will help a lot when we start back in business again   I wish it could be soon.

You were writing about getting ready to thrash   sure wish I was doing a little of that myself. All of those pies and big dinners   boy oh boy.

Honey I had another grass skirt but I sold it for two dollars. I thought that was a lot more than it would be worth to you. Also got twenty five for a souvenir made of sharks teeth that the natives use to fight with.

Well I'm getting mighty sleepy, I love you oodles and oodles. Honey you sure are swell, know one could possible ask for more.

Lots of kisses and hugs,
Homer

A few days after Homer wrote his anniversary letter he began running a high temperature and ended up in the hospital. Navy regulations prevented him from telling her about his illness, so Ruth wouldn't know about his four-day hospitalization with Dengue fever until after he came home.

Dengue [děn gā] fever is caused by a virus spread by mosquitoes. It thrives in the tropics in places where fresh water is stored in containers. The fever manifests as a sudden onset of a red rash, headache, and severe muscle and joint pain, hence the nick-name "break-bone fever."[37]

Homer and his buddies knew about the fever and thought they were taking the necessary precautions to prevent it, but they hadn't done enough. While he was in the hospital his tent mates added new mosquito netting to their tent and rigged up an ice box for their drinking water.

The only mention Homer made of his illness was a one-line notation he wrote in his little black book, "I went to hositipal with dengue fever Aug 6th got out Aug 10th, 1944."

When Ruth read Homer's letter of August 8, she had no idea he was writing from his hospital bed.

Tuesday, August 8
one oclock p.m.

My Darling Wife

Well hows my honey? I got a letter from Mother and Dad today saying that you had left and gone back to work. I'm sure glad you got along so well.

We have been building ourselves an ice box to keep our water cool   our water gets so hot in a tin can. We are also putting new mosquito netting on the sides of our tent   the rats eat holes in the other we had. You may have trouble reading this because I'm sitting up in bed writting   a lazy mans way of doing it.

As far as our work goes its just the same thing   shoot trouble when there is any   then take it easy. Most of the boys including myself are getting pretty tired of this rock but the longer we stay here the better the chance is of us getting state-side duty   of course thats what we all want. There sure isn't anything out here to keep a mans morale up to par.

I'll close for now, there's not a thing to write about.

Lots of love & kisses,
Homer

As far as Homer was concerned, getting caught up on his letter writing was the only good thing about being in the hospital.

One week after Homer's release from the hospital he sounded downright excited about his plans for Thursday night.

Thursday August 17
Three P.M.

My Darling Wife;

Tonight some of us are going fishing like the natives do. They take a lanatern (gas) and walk along in water about knee deep and when they see a fish they hit it with a knife   they also get lobsters   we are going to have two for supper   they are about a foot long   we dressed them last night and we got about a pound of meat from each one. We hope to catch some tonight   its white meat looks like frog legs. The way you cook them is to boil some water and put them in the water still alive and boil them for twenty minutes   then take there shell off, the tail has the most meat, just like frog legs   the body has a little meat in it but not much.

Hows every thing around Hannibal   going along smooth I hope. Just the same old thing around here ever day. Sure gets tiresome   wish I could get transferred back to good old Missouri for the duration.^{Ha Ha} *Well honey I'll close for now. So long my darling*

I love you oodles & oodles
Homer

It took the natives eight months to trust Homer and his pals enough to take them fishing—the native way. The fact that they were invited at all is a testament to the mutual trust they had developed. Homer was proud to report a successful fishing expedition. Like any true fisherman he may have exaggerated about the size of the catch, however, he sent home a picture of three native children carrying a basket filled with fish.

Tuesday August 22
Nine oclock

My Darling Wife;

We had five movie actresses to put on a show about two nights ago. How did I like it? It was rotten   I haven't heard one man say yet that he liked it.

I have got to get the truck greased tomorrow. This morning a grader cut fourteen of our telephone lines so we had to fix them the first thing.

Oh yes, I almost forgot   last week three of us went fishing with four natives and two gas lanterns and knifes about two and a half or three feet long   boy we sure had a time   we got three big baskets half full of fish   small ones, about six to eight inches and a lot of crawfish about a foot long. We got in about two oclock.

Well honey I dont know anything else to write about.

Good night my darling, I love you.

Natives carrying basket of fish

Your husband,
Homer

During the summer of '44 the Allies island-hopped their way closer to Japan, so the base on Apamama was no longer needed even as a rear base. Rumors around camp said they might be moving.

Saturday August 26
three oclock A.M.

My Darling Wife;

Boy! Yesterday was the day I got twelve letters

Every one is asleep now, very quiet around here for a change. It is now three oclock in the morning   I'm getting mighty sleepy   I'm on guard   get off at four   I went on at eleven forty five. We are pretty busy now   have been for two weeks.

We have been having plenty to do here lately. Now every morning we have to report to another outfit and help them   we have done our work   now we have to do some body elses. How's every thing going at the store and at home?

Darling I love you so much, I had the nicest dream about you   it seemed so real. Its a shame our dreams cant come true.

Good night my love, I love you darling.
Homer

It had been a long time since Homer had written anything about guard duty, and Ruth recognized his mention of it as a change in his daily routine. Homer couldn't reveal any specifics, but Ruth knew something was up when he said he reported to other outfits and helped them with their work.

Thurs August 31
eleven P.M.

My Darling Wife;

Today I received a package from you with the little red dress in it   it sure is cute. I'm anxious to see the expression on the babyies mother face. Its almost big enough for the dress now.

I had six fried eggs tonight and I'm so full yet I can't hardly breathe. Today noon we had beef steak   its so seldom we have anything fit to eat we almost founder.

Its almost September only twenty minutes of August 1944 left. I wish we could get some of that cool weather your having. Boy it sure is hot   I'm sure glad that Grandma & Grandpa are getting their house wired. I know one thing I'll never do without electric again.

Good night my darling I love you oodles and oodles.

Your old man
Ho.Ho. Homer

As Homer turned his calendar from August to September Apamama was still in the midst of a tropical heat wave. However, Homer could sense that changes were on the way—if not in the weather—at least in the Navy.

SEPTEMBER
Settling Debts

"The money I'm sending is what I saved from printing pictures."

—Homer's letter 9/4/44

Many servicemen gambled away their military pay, but Homer's goal was to accumulate a nest egg of money to draw on after the war. While he was stateside he managed to find ways make a little spending money. After landing on Apamama he couldn't imagine how to make extra money while stationed on a desolate island. Then he joined the darkroom gang and learned to print and sell pictures. In July when he sent $500 home it was military pay he had saved. The $500 he was sending now was money he earned selling pictures. On September 4 he had reason to be proud when he wrote,

Monday Sept. 4
Four oclock P.M.

My Darling Wife;
  I'm sending five hundred more dollars home   you buy xmas presents with it, as much as you need because I don't expect I'll be in a place so I can buy anything. The money I'm sending is what I saved from printing pictures. Honey by the time the war is over we should have enough money to buy us a nice little farm.
  The little dress you sent fits the baby swell. She is only three months old and wearing a year old dress, she can almost stand alone   another month she will be.

Honey you wrote and asked me to suggest something I would like to have for Christmas   there isn't a thing I need and I don't know of anything I want   maybe some hard candy. The less things a person has in a place like this the better   things are such a bother to carry around and I know we are going to be moving soon.

Darling I miss you a terrible lot. Oh yes we can tell now that we are in the Gilbert Islands now but not the Island were on   I'll bet this will be a big supprise to you.^{Ha Ha} *I think almost all the boys folks know where they are.*

Honey I'll close for now.

I love you a lot darling,
Homer

Homer would have been satisfied with the extra money he made selling pictures, but when he and Josefo came up with the idea of selling native souvenirs they really hit the jackpot. Homer sold pictures and souvenirs on an I.O.U. basis until pay day, and kept track of finances in his little black book. At the top of one page Homer wrote, "What I owe." Under that heading he wrote "Houck $60."

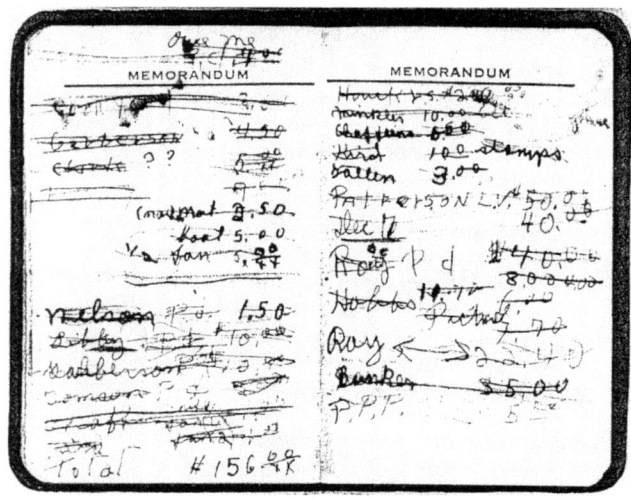

I. O. U. List

At the top of three more pages Homer wrote, "Others owe me." These pages list the name of the buyer, the souvenirs or pictures purchased, and the amount owed to Homer: Patterson = 5.00 pillow, 1.00 beads, Clark = 2.50 mat, 5.00 boat, 5.00 fan, Houck = 2.00 sheets, 2.00 beads, Hobbs = 11.00 picture, Nelson pd 1.50, Libby pd 10.00, Gabberson pd 12.00. One page totaled $156 that others owed him and the other pages had similar lists. Suffice it to say there was a lot of wheeling and dealing going on in the islands.

For months Homer was bored, then all of a sudden things started to happen and there weren't enough hours in the day to do everything. Homer and his buddies packed equipment all day and printed pictures at night. They could feel that big changes and new orders were coming soon.

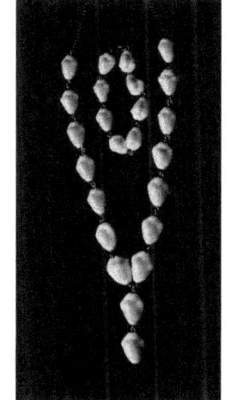

Seashell necklace

Sunday afternoon Sept. 10
Three o'clock

My Darling Wife;
We sure had a time getting into chow today   we have six hundred Marines eating with us today   thats about twice as many as we usually have.

I just finished making you a neckless out of sea shells   the next chance I have I'll make a bracelet to match it. I don't know when I can send them home because they have stopped all native souveniors being sent home so I may have to bring them home   only wish I could.

Last night Jack Benny, Carol Landis the world best harmonica player and two more girls put on a play for an hour and half it sure was good. That Jack Benny made ever one laugh until their sides hurt.

I wish I could help you with some of those watermelons   they sure make my mouth water.

I don't know yet just when we are going to leave but it won't be long. Wish I was coming home, we havn't seen each other for a year, its hell isn' it darling. I sure wish this thing would hurry up and get over so I can go home to the one I love most.

Lots of love & kisses
Your old man

Jack Benny and other entertainers

Friday Sept. 15
five o'clock

My Darling Wife;

    September is almost half gone now   my how time flies by. Today I got five letters, three from you, one each from our mothers.

    Darling your so nice to me. All I ask is for you to be waiting for me when I do get home, which I know you will be.

    My best friend's wife has taken him a roll, she has taken ever thing they have saved in seven years   property and ever thing. She was a nice looking woman and he thought the world and all of her. What a costly war in many ways to some people.

    A boy just came back from hearing the news and we have landed on some of the southern Philippines islands   that sure will be a big job because there are something like 1700 islands in the Philippines. By the news, we are really giving the Jap navy and air force the devil.

    I go on guard duty in about half an hour   its six PM now   that means that I won't go to any show tonight. Last night the show was Blonde Trouble with Mickey Rooney. That boy sure has more trouble with his girls. There were two girls twins and one liked him and the other didn't   he couldn't tell them apart   he had one hell of a time. Well honey I'll have to quit for now. Good night my darling I love you so much.

                                                   Lots of love & kisses,
                                                            Homer

Ruth knew Homer was moving and feared he would be sent to the Philippines. He tried to assure her that he wasn't going to a dangerous place and reminded her that ACORN units landed after the island was secure.

Sunday Sept. 24
2 A.M.

My Darling Wife;

Today is Sunday a day of rest in some places but not around here, we have so much work and such a short time to do in so we have to work every day.

Tonight we had a party for a bunch of ourselfs about twenty all togeather and the party hasn't entirely broke up yet   We had steak sandwiches (43) and were they good. As long as you have a cook or two at a party you cant go wrong.^{Ha Ha} *Some wondered how we got ice   we had three men that run ice boxes. Its not what a man knows in this navy   its who he knows, and thats no kidding. I always have said that and always will.*

Tonight at eleven thirty I was just getting ready to go to bed and a boy came over and said I went on guard duty in fifteen minutes and I don't get off until four   so it's going to be sort of a long night. I have a cup of good coffee. I've got so I drink coffee three times a day but would give almost anything for some good fresh milk. Its been over a year since I've had a drink of milk that wasn't powered.

Honey I think this is about all the news I know so I'll say good night my darling. Love you oodles and oodles.

Your old Man,
Homer

During the past few months Homer had moved much higher in the pecking order. By getting acquainted with the right people he managed to get better living quarters, a comfortable bed, a shower, a dog, and some ice for his coca-cola. He even found lucrative ways to make a little money on the side selling pictures and souvenirs. When Homer first landed on Apamama he ate field rations. By the end of September he was eating steak sandwiches.

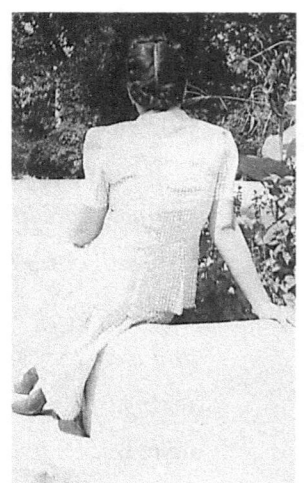

Ruth knew the best cure for anything that ailed Homer was a picture of his wife. So on a warm summer's day Ruth braided her thick black curly hair, and went to the city park to pose for a couple of photos to send to her darling husband.

The pictures did the trick and Homer wrote to show his appreciation.

Wednesday Sept. 27

My Darling Wife;

How's my beautiful wife? I sure enjoyed the pictures you sent   Honey you get better looking all the time. I like the way you have your hair fixed but expect its a lot of work keeping it looking good. Those pictures you sent look so real I just had to kiss them even your rear view.[Ha Ha]

I hope your cold is over with now and your feeling fine again. We sure have been working hard but have most of our work done   another week and we will be done with our gear   probaly will be tearing down tents then. I have been going from sixteen to eighteen hours a day   not packing gear all that time, but still working   we have been working on pictures after supper ever night. Its nine oclock now   expect to work until about twelve or one tonight. Lots of work but it's worth it.

I havn't heard any war news for about ten days   I would sure like to hear of a signed peace

Well honey I have got to go to work. I'll be dreaming of you tonight.

Lots of love, & loads of kisses

Homer

OCTOBER
Goodbyes

"I have all my things ready just waiting for the word to shove off. Things sure can happen fast."

—Homer's letter 10/9/44

One of the worst aspects of being in the military was saying goodbye to buddies. In Idaho Homer, Roscoe, and Harold survived boot camp together. Then they shipped out and didn't know if they'd ever see each other again. On Apamama he had been tent mates with Houck, Minkler, Mertz, and Patterson. Now they were all preparing to move and had no control over who would get sent where.

After ten months on Apamama their exodus would be physically easier than their arrival, but emotionally harder.

Sun Oct 1

Hello My Darling;

Here it is the first of Oct. another month started. This being Sunday I thought I'd sleep late but a truck load of boys came in and said they were going to take our telephone hut down. So that meant we had to take our switchboard out and we now have it in our tent. It was sure a lot of work to box all our phones.

We can't take a dog with us when we leave on account of diseases. The only things we can take is in our sea bags and I have so much native things that I'll have a bag of it alone.

I just got four nice letters from the most wonderful wife a man could ask for. Honey I love you so much and always will. I'm just as true as gold. And honey thats the God's truth. I really love you

Loads of love & kisses,
Homer

Once again Ruth wished Homer had used the Norris Code to tell her where he was going. What she didn't realize was that Homer had only heard the name of his next temporary home, and he didn't know how to spell it. He did know that it was a safe place, and right now that was the most important information he could share.

Thursday Oct 5
Two P.M.

My Darling Wife;

I got two swell letters from you yesterday   I'm glad the hand grenades came through   I was sure uneasy about it. They are all right having had the powder and caps taken out. I bet you almost pee'd your pants when you got to pulling things out of it.[Ha Ha]

I took our truck and turned it in to the garage yesterday morning, so we don't have any transportation now. The boy thats setting across the table from me is smoking a cigar and its about to get me down.

I got a nice mat the other day with the name of this island and Gilbert Islands on it. I had the native make it for us. I cant send it from here but will be able to send it from the next island I go to. I know where I'm going so you don't need to worry about me going to a dangerous place because its not.

Honey it looks like I've about gone my limit for this time so I'll sign off with all the love one man can furnish.

Homer

A few days before Homer left Apamama he drove the truck to the Kabangak Village to pick up the last souvenirs and visit his native friends. His dog Pattsy didn't need much encouragement to jump in the truck with him. She had no idea that it was a one-way trip. His friends in the village had agreed to take good care of Pattsy—even after Homer warned them that she liked to chase chickens.

The grass mat Josefo made for Homer was a keeper. Hand made of woven grasses, it measured 44x20 inches. Josefo used colored Ritz dye to create the delicate black border and two-inch red letters that spelled Apemama Gilbert Island.

Homer's friendship with the natives had made his stay on Apamama better. It must have been difficult to say good-bye to Josefo and his family.

Before Homer left the village Josefo gave him the most handsome wooden box Homer had ever seen. Carved from native wood, the box was approximately five inches in diameter and six inches tall. It stood on four delicately carved feet.

The two men never had any further contact, but Josefo's gift would be a prized possession for the rest of Homer's life.

A few days later Homer was packed and ready for the next leg of his journey.

Gift from Josefo

Monday Oct 9
Seven o'clock

My Darling Ruth;
I'd better make this a good long letter because it will probably be the last one for three or four weeks.
I wish you could have eaten supper with us last night   we cooked our own. We had steak cut about an inch thick and eggs all we could possibly eat. We were all so full we could hardly breathee.
I have all my things ready   just waiting for the word to shove off. Things sure can happen fast. Honey have you been able to get any more film lately   I still have some but I may want to take a lot of pictures and may run out.
Honey I can't think of anything else to write about only that I love you an awful lot, so will close for now.

Darling I love you always.
Homer

Exactly 227 days after Homer first set foot on the beaches of Apamama he watched native huts, O'Hare Field, and the British cross fade into the distance.

According to Homer's little black book, he "Left Apamama Oct 10, 44."

Part 8: Island Hopping

Kwajalein

"From the talk going around I should be home in about six or eight months."

—Homer's letter 10/15/44

Three days after Homer left Apamama, he wrote in his little black book, "arrived Kwajalein Oct 13." Back in January Homer was praying for the boys in the Marshalls, now he was in the heart of the Marshall Islands.

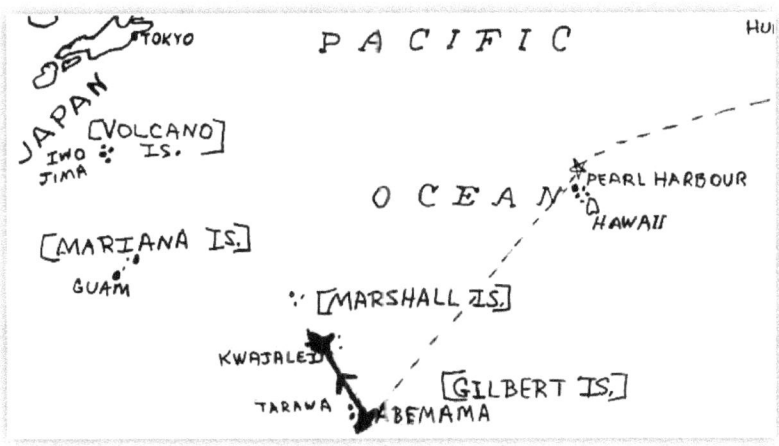

The island of Kwajalein was only 656 nautical miles from Apamama but the two islands bore little resemblance.[38] Before the war Kwajalein was lush with beautiful trees like Apamama, but sustained bombardment of Kwajalein uprooted most of the vegetation.

Homer was just one of several hundred new arrivals on Kwajalein awaiting orders. Every morning after breakfast the men mustered and were chosen for work details. When they called for volunteers to sort mail Homer's hand shot up like a flash. While working in the mail room Homer sent home souvenirs for Christmas presents including a note to his mother which read, "Mother DO NOT OPEN, Christmas present."

Homer Norris E.M. 2/C
Marshall Islands

Sun Oct. 15 eleven A.M.

My Darling Wife;

I had a nice four day voyage and very good eats. I'm in the Marshalls   I don't think so much of this place but I wont be here very long.

I don't expect to get another island as good as Abemama because the most of them have been shelled so much. The boys are sure taned around here   no shade at all. It sure is a lot different to have to live out of a sea bag again.

Yesterday we sorted mail for the hold island. Had a thousand bags   I never saw so much mail.

From the talk going around I should be home in about six or eight months. All the boys with eighteen months in a war zone gets thirty day leave and six months duty in the states   I sure hope it isn't changed before I get my time in   I have almost thirteen months in now.

Yesterday afternoon and night the wind blew so hard and so much dust flew you couldn't hardly see   reminded me of some of the Missouri dust in the summer. I bet its getting to be real fall weather back there. I expect that Hannibal is getting so its pretty cold in the mornings   I expect the wind sort of blows up your dress.^{Ha Ha}

Well honey I guess this will be all for now. I love you my darling.

Your old man,
Homer

This was the first time Homer had ever mentioned a timeline for coming home. To Ruth six or eight months meant that Homer might be home by April. Maybe then she could quit her job and go be with him.

Thurs Oct 19

My Darling Wife;

You probably have trouble reading my letters   I'm sitting in bed writting on my knee   we don't have any table. We moved yesterday. We're living in barracks now. Seems funny to live in wooden buildings again. It really is good sleeping here at nights   just as soon as the sun goes down its cool.

Honey I like for you to ask questions   sometimes I cant answer them on account of censors but I try to. Night before last I got eight letters which four was from the girl that I would reather have in my arms than anything in the world. Darling I love you so much.

You asked me what you should do about voting   you go ahead and vote the way you think best   I'm not going to vote. The Cardinals done alright in the world series. I don't play cards   lot of the boys do play. Poker mostly.

On Kwajalein October 24, 1944

We have to go about a mile to eat. It takes a lot of time. We don't have lights in our barracks yet.

There's a lot of noise here all the time. We sleep right by the air strip and the planes taking off at all hours

I saw some marines that were on Abemama and had a big talk with them yesterday. I know this is one hell of a letter   I jump subjects so much, think I'm nuts. I must be getting "rock" happy as the boys call it out here. I love you Ruth with all my heart.

Love & Kisses,
Homer

In 1944 Ruth voted for President Franklin D. Roosevelt. In the scrapbook is a sample ballot on which Ruth wrote, "I voted in the Presidential Election. My first time was 1944. A person sure does feel important."

Wed Oct 25
noon

My Darling Ruth;

I'll write this letter and I'm sure it will be the last for maby two weeks. I wrote Mother & Dad this morning. I want to pack most all my gear this after noon so I'll have it done when the time comes to take off.

Honey I checked on those part numbers, its not 11-23-1-10-1 or 12-5-9-14, its 7-21-1-13 those were the numbers of the old parts but the new one has changed. Dad said he had bought some angus cows and calves and had graveled the drive out to the road. I hope we can have a place all of our own some day and can do the work for ourselfs instead for some one else.

I'm not on a working detail today. I'm going to develope some film we took the other day.

Honey it looks like this is about all for this time. I love you with all my heart.

Lot of love, & loads of kisses
From your husband, Homer

Less than two weeks after Homer landed in the Marshalls he had relocation news to report, and he used the Norris Code to tell Ruth that his old location was: 11-23-1-10-1-12-5-9-14 (K W A J A L E I N) and his new location was 7-21-1-13 (G U A M).

On Homer's letter Ruth worked through the Norris code and on a scrap of paper she wrote:

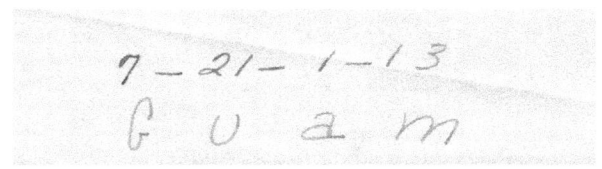

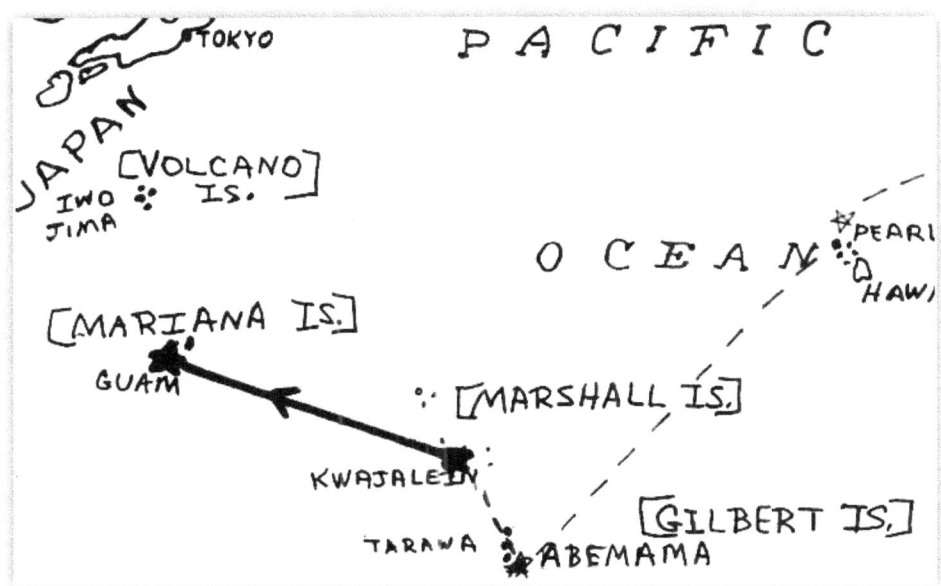

In Homer's little black book he wrote, "Left Kwa. 27 Oct." Only two weeks earlier he had traveled 656 nautical miles from Apamama to Kwajalein in the Marshalls. Now he would island hop 1570 miles from the Marshall Islands to Guam in the Marianas.

Guam

"Boy killed Jap Nov. 9, 44 outside camp."

—Note in Homer's little black book

In early August the Allies captured the Mariana Islands, including Guam. Construction battalions rebuilt five air strips to accommodate the B-24 bombers that would be used to capture Iwo Jima. In late October thousands of troops converged on Guam to prepare for the assault.

Four days after Homer left Kwajalein he wrote in his little black book, "arr. Guam Oct 31." Homer was stationed on the west side of Guam on the Orote Peninsula which reminded him of Pearl Harbor. From camp he could see the Apra Harbor with deep water for the largest battleships. The noise on Kwajalein was nothing compared to the noise of the B-24 bombers at Orote Airfield.[39]

In Homer's first letter from Guam he sounded pleased with his new temporary home. After Guam he hoped his next location would be home, sweet home. So far he had been island hopping in the **wrong** direction. Guam was only 1607 miles from Japan but 8455 miles from Missouri!

Thurs Nov 2
seven oclock

My Darling Wife;

Again I'm settled down after a very enjoyable voyage. It was far the best sea voyage I have ever had and expect it will be the best I'll ever have in this war. On board ship we had ice cream three times a day. I wish I could tell you what we came over on but can't.

We have a terrible lot of work in setting up camp but no equipment to do it with. I'm wiring our camp now. It will take several days before we can get all the tents set up with lights. We have lights in our tent   I put them in last night   the first to have lights in our tent in camp. I would like to see some of the island. But it will be some time before we can get to do that.

The mail man said today that we wouldn't get any mail for two more weeks yet. I sure would like to hear from you. Honey I have your picture over my bunk   thats about the first thing I did after getting my bunk set up. Darling I miss you so much

We only have something like five or six months more months out here and we can come back to our love ones. And then we can catch up on our loving.

Now we have about four or five fellows in here talking I'm having a hard time writting. Honey I'm going to close for now.

Lots of love & kisses,
Homer

Homer was anxious to check out more of the island, but Guam was thirty miles long (twice the size of Apamama). As one of the new men in camp, Homer hadn't yet made enough connections to even get tools for work—much less transportation.

After six days on Guam he couldn't stand it any longer and decided to take off walking and see what he could see. Homer hoped to make connections and sell souvenirs like he had done on Apamama. He soon discovered that Guam was very different from Apamama. Before the bombing Guam had actual towns, so the natives already knew how to broker their souvenirs without a middle man. At first Homer thought he would have to settle for selling the pictures and souvenirs he had brought from Apamama. Then he remembered that a while back Ruth had asked if he wanted her to send his wrist watch. He replied that there was too much salt water and he was afraid his good watch would get ruined. He was right—watches didn't last very long on the islands. So Homer and Ruth decided that if watches were such a valuable commodity, maybe she could send a few watches to Guam and he could sell them.

Nov 5 Sunday night

Hello My Dear;

How's my wife tonight? Boy would I ever like to be there in Hannibal to find out for myself. I'm all right   I looked around the island a little today but a person can't cover much of an island this size with out transportation. I'm spoiled now after having a truck & jeep for so long and could use them any time. I looked for souvenirs but didn't have any luck.

You have seen pictures of little two wheeled carts pulled with oxen   well they have a lot of them here. Their houses were right good until the bombs tore them down.

Honey if you want to and can pack them so they won't get broke you can send some wrist watches. Money dont mean a thing out here but when we start up again after this thing they call "war" it's going to come in mighty handy.

While I was on Abemama I bought a camera for thirty five dollars and film. I traded the camera to a boy for a 22 target pistol and sold him the film for fourteen dollars   tonight I was offered seventy five dollars for my pistol and I didn't sell it. Think I can get more for it.

Honey its about time for the lights to go out   Good night darling. How I'd love to kiss you good night again.

Love & kisses, Homer

For the next few weeks Homer worked as an electrician and wired three or four tents per day. By the time he finished wiring one group of tents another group had been erected. There was a steady stream of Marines converging on Guam to make final preparation for the next offensive push to take the island of Iwo Jima. Several of the boys from Perry were Marines and Homer hoped he might be able to connect up with a few of them.

Thur Nov 9
Seven P.M.

My Darling Ruth Marie;

We got a new generator yesterday a big one now we don't have any trouble with our lights. We hooked two double coffee makers up for the officers this afternoon. We sure have a lot of officers here. We get coca cola or beer ever night two bottles, thats fourteen bottles a week.

We are going to put up a new tent tomorrow ours leaks over every cot thats what we're sleeping on. I haven't had a chance to build myself a bunk yet. I have to have two by fours to make a bunk.

We have red dirt here just like Hawaii. It washes out but you sure have to wash a lot.

Jack Houck and I are still living in the same tent but the other boys I lived with for so long are living in the tent next to us. Mertz the man that lived in Kansas City isn't with us any more he is on another island. We built us a writing table and wash stand yesterday. I want to build myself a locker for my clothes but cant find the lumber and wont be able to for some time yet.

Honey be sure to find out what James Swans address is and send it to me I have to know what unit he is in to find him. I want to find out what ship Tommie Hurley is on some time. It would sure be nice to run into someone you knew before the war. St Elmer Hull finally got home he's sure been out a long time. I hope you get to see him.

Honey I'm going to have to close for now. I'm hoping to get some mail soon.

Lots of love, loads of kisses
Your old man, Homer

Later that night there was some excitement in camp and Homer learned that sleeping with one eye open was a necessary evil. He couldn't write about it in his letters, but in his little black book Homer wrote, "Boy killed Jap Nov. 9, 44 outside camp."

When the Allies recaptured Guam in August, 1944 several thousand Japanese soldiers were still hiding in the jungles. During the next few months most of the enemy holdouts were killed, or captured—but not all of them. The Japanese soldier killed on November 9 was one of the last holdouts.

* * *

While installing the new generator Homer made good connections with some officers, and managed to get a tent that didn't leak, and some two by fours to build his bed. He appreciated the creature comforts, but he was even more excited that his mail finally caught up with him.

Sun Nov 12
Nine P.M.

My Darling Ruth;

Boy was I ever tickled tonight   I got a letter from my darling wife. Honey you must have just taken your bath when you wrote it because it really smelled sweet like bath powder.

This address that I have now will be permanent. I wish I could answer some of the questions you ask that you put "important" above but I can't or I'd tell you without asking.

I'm going to take some pictures sometime soon, maby you can have some idea of what it is like here. One good thing the natives are clothed.

We never had to work today being it was Sunday. This afternoon I built myself a bunk with rubber springs   I brought the rubber with me from Abemama. I knew they wouldn't have any here.

I think I'll go get a cup of coffee   take a shower then retire and hope I dream of the most wonderful woman in the world. Good night my darling

your old man,
Homer

Sun Nov 19
eight P.M.

My Darling Wife;

I started to write last night and some boys (two) came to see me that I ran around with at Port Hueneme   I saw them in Pearl a few times   they went to Tarawa from Pearl   they had just gotten transferred into the same outfit as I am now. One of them was Fred Smith   After they left last night I had a guard from ten until two this morning. This after noon I wired three tents.

Honey I think it better to send the watches in small amounts well packed. A very good thing to remember, "don't put all your eggs in one basket." I think you can send them air mail.

Tomorrow is pay day   I think maybe I'll draw some. Honey I sure do like to hear from you. I love you sooo much.

Say I have a mustache   I'll probably have to put some shoe black on it so it will show up.^{Ha Ha} It sure is a dinger.

I think I'll go get a cup of coffee before retiring. I get a cup every night before going to bed then I can't go to sleep.^{Ha Ha} Nighty night honey

Love, Kisses & Hugs,
Homer

Captain's Mast

"Today I had to go in front of our commanding officer to Captains mast..."

—Homer's letter 11/25/44

On Thanksgiving Day Homer was feeling grateful to be on a secure island and hoped to ride out the next five months without incident. Unfortunately trouble was headed his way.

In the past fourteen months Homer had worked lots of guard duty hours, but his guard on Thanksgiving night was one he would never forget.

Sat Nov 25

My Darling Wife

Well I haven't written you for several days now its sure been three exciting days for me night before last I had a four hour camp guard from ten to two in the morning and about one oclock I went to sleep some boy fresh out of the states put me on report. Today I had to go in front of our commanding officer to Captains mast. I thought sure he would break me to EM 3/c but he didn't. He gave me fifty hours extra duty. It has to be worked after four oclock P.M. so I'm going to have some mighty busy nights ahead.^{Ha Ha}

I wasn't really asleep just dozing but that's considered sleeping on watch that boy really double crossed me. He hasn't got very many friends any way now he doesn't have nearly as many. I start to work tonight on my extra hours it won't take long. Boy! I'm sure ticked to death to not get any more than that.

> *This morning two of us was working togeather putting in a light in a tree   I was on the ground and the other man started to come down   he unfastened his safty belt and fell about twenty feet on his head and arm. He broke his arm in two places at the wrist. I had to take him to the Hospital. I got back about eleven and found out that I had to go to that Capt. Mast so I changed clothes, shaved, and got a clean hat.*
>
> *Darling I have been getting a lot of mail from you lately   something like ten or twelve letters the last three days. Honey I love you so much. I'll have to close now and go to chow.*
>
> Lots of love,
Homer

Homer was angry with the boy who reported him until he realized he didn't have anyone to blame but himself. So he decided to knuckle down and work off his extra duty.

The first night he wired tents by himself, but he couldn't wire them very efficiently without some help. He needed a job he could do solo. So he suggested that they let him put up security lights in the trees. At first they thought he would need help to do that, too. Then they saw how Homer could climb trees with his ankle spikes. After that Homer worked his extra hours installing security lights.

While Homer worked long hours, Ruth worked long hours at her job, too. Recently her salary had been increased $1 per week, so now she earned $19 a week as manager of the lingerie department. The little raise in salary meant a lot more responsibility ordering and tracking inventory. Some days she worked extra hours (off the clock) during the busy Christmas season. Actually, she didn't mind the long days because it made the time pass more quickly.

* * *

After five weeks on Guam Homer had sold all the pictures and souvenirs he brought with him from Apamama. He was amazed at the higher selling price, and made twice the amount he originally projected. When he wrote on December 3 Homer had lots of good news to report.

Sun Dec 3
eleven P.M.

My Darling Wife;

Honey I'm sorry that its been so long since I've written you a letter but I've been busyer than that old cat. I work every night until ten or eleven oclock. I have worked forty hours in eight nights starting after five oclock in the afternoon. I couldn't work tonight because I had a five hour guard duty. Two more nights and I'll have my fifty hours in.

Well I think I told you once before that the next time I sent you any money it would be a thousand dollars but I didn't think it would be this soon   you can consider this your Christmas present because it is impossible to buy anything here such as gifts.

The way I figure it will make us $4,307 in the bank. Honey you have no idea how much I plan on our future   at first I wanted enough money to start out with a tractor like we wanted to   now I have hopes of maby buying a farm all of our own   wouldn't that be swell.

I really work and try to figure how I can make and save out here. It' not hard for me to save but it's a little different to make any money.

Ruth I love you so much. I think about you all the time. Another fellow and I were talking about our wife's. I'm sure glad I have a nice wife to come home to and know she will be waiting for me.

One good thing I like about it here   we can go to the mess hall and get coffee and sandwiches any time during the night. I just came back from eating three sandwiches and two cups of coffee.

Oh yes, honey I want to congratulate you on your new raise in salary. My wife sure must be doing a wonderful job.

I'm sure having nose trouble. I'm taking cold   my nose has been running all day. Honey I'm going to have to close and go to bed   my nose is about to run off with me.[Ha Ha]

I love you oodles & oodles my darling.

I love you sweetheart,
Homer

The money order arrived several days before Homer's letter telling her about it, so the $1000 came as a complete surprise! Sending the money order made Homer anxious to get the darkroom set up—and make a little "doe-ray-me."

Sat Dec 9
eight P.M.

My Beloved Wife;

I have all my extra duty worked off now. I finished it in ten nights thats five hours a night   I couldn't work until after supper. I have a new job   I'm back into telephones now. Two of us from Apamama are working togeather. We have a board just like the one we had at Apamama only its biger has one hundred and fifty dropes   it will take two to three operators of course I'm not an operator   the two of us are going to set the board up that will probably take a month.

I'm sure glad I'm back in telephones. I didn't like the man that I was working for so I asked this officer if he couldn't use me and he was tickled to get some one that knew something about telephones.

Our mail is coming better now   the last letter I recieved from you was only eight days old   I got another package from you   was full of candy boy are we eating candy nowadays.

Darling all I do is plan on our future   if I never had a wonderful wife like you to come home to and a mother & father I love very much it sure would be a lot different. Boy my Mother & Dad sure do think your about it   they look forward from one time to another for you to go see them.

I expect you have enough watches on the road to me now but dont worry about me getting rid of them because that wont be much of a job. Think I'll sign off   I'm getting mighty sleepy. Be seeing you in my dreams.

Good night my love,
Homer

Boys From Home

"All four of us got togeather and had a swell time visiting   just like being in good old Perry but about five thousand miles away from it."

—Homer's letter 12/27/44

Guam was like Grand Central Station with troops arriving and shipping out daily. Homer frequently ran into pals from back home. It was nice to reminisce about old times with boys he had known before the war.

MARIANA'S ISLAND
Friday, Dec 15
Eight P.M.

My Darling Wife;

I went up to see James Swon about three nights ago and he wasn't at home but I did see Johnnie Bybee   they were going to pull out the next day so I won't get to see James. Johnnie gave me Rex Peer address   he is here   I want to see him the first chance I get   he's a 5 Sgt. now.

I have been working until one to three o'clock in the morning on pictures trying to get set up again. Its sure been a lot of work but I'd better make hay while the sun shines beause it wont be long until that will be all over and we will be spending a little of that money. There is one thing sure   this war cant last for ever and when that grand day comes we are going to have something of our own.

Monday I had the day off so I went to town reather what use to be a town before the war its nothing but a lot of junk now. Its Saturday now I'm sending you a few pictures we printed last night. Hope you like them. One is of the man who loves you the most.

I love you my darling
Homer

P.S. My moustache doesn't even show damit.

Homer on Guam - December 11, 1944 - Ruth in Hannibal

In Ruth's scrapbook is a photograph of Homer standing in the middle of knee-high island grasses with remnants of bomb-damaged trees in the background. On the back of the photo he wrote "Dec 11 Guam."

While Homer was having his photograph taken on a short-sleeve sort of day on Guam, Ruth was posing for a photo to send to him. However, the weather was very different back home in Missouri. Homer's mother wrote in her diary, "Dec 11 Monday Snowing and blowing all day."

Ruth loved snow, but icy sidewalks and freezing temperatures made the daily trek to work miserable. The cold and snow meant that Christmas was just around the corner.

On December 11 when the blizzard hit Hannibal, Ruth was preparing soap box packages for Homer's Christmas. She tried to include all his favorites: candy, peanuts, cheese & crackers, and a few love notes.

The weather was so awful at the Norris farm that Dad Norris had to take the team of horses to cut the cedar Christmas tree.

In preparation for holiday visitors Mom cleaned the house, washed a few windows, and mailed a card to Ruth to let her know they were looking forward to her visit.

TOTAL WAGES FOR WEEK ENDING 12-23-44

HRS. 48 AT 19.00			$ 19.00
CHRISTMAS REMEMBRANCE			$ 10.00
SUGGESTION SYSTEM AWARD			$
TOTAL			$ 29.00
DEDUCTIONS FOR			
MEALS			
FED. O. A. B. TAX		.29	
INCOME & VICT. TAX		3.10	
S.U.I. TAX			
OTHER DED.			
WAR BOND		2.00	
OTHER DED.			5.39
CASH ENCLOSED $			23.61

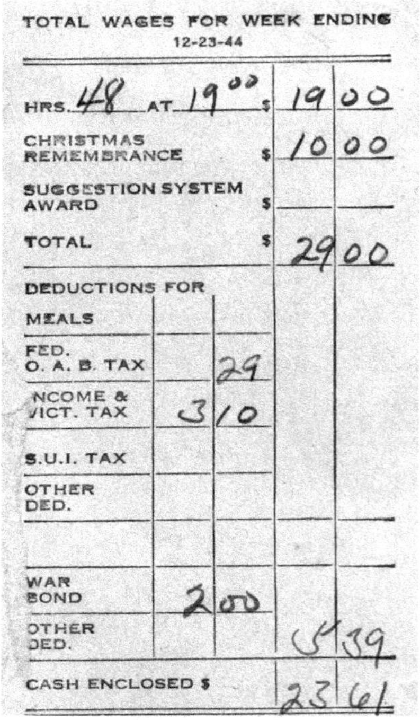

It was a hectic Christmas season at the store. When Ruth got her paycheck she was pleasantly surprised to see a $10 "Christmas Remembrance" added to her week's salary.

After work on Saturday, December 23 Ruth caught the bus to Perry and spent the night at her parents' house. She dreaded having to spend another Christmas without Homer.

Sat Dec 23
nine PM

My Darling Wife;

I know I should be spanked for not writing for severial days but believe me the way I am working now I dont have any time. I start to work at seven AM work until four, then eat supper and then print pictures until twelve one to sometimes two oclock in the morning.

Day after tomorrow will be Christmas by the calendar but just another day for me. Last year I never got off for Christmas day and this year we are going to put our switch board in operation the 25th so I'll be working harder that day than any other. It doesn't make any difference to me   if I cant be home I'd reather be working   the time will pass so much faster.

Honey I got a buildiful Christmas card from you yesterday   it had such a nice verse in it   it made tears come when I opened it. That day down at Rev. Golden's when I said I will take this woman to be my lawfully wedded wife. I meant that for ever too. Darling your the only one as far as I'm concerned. Thats all I think of day in and day out   my Ruth Marie.

Its about eleven oclock now so I'll have to sign off for now.

All my love, kisses, and everything,
Homer

P.S. I have your picture hanging about two feet from my head when I lay down in bed. I tell you nighty night ever night before I go to sleep no matter how late or how sleepy I am.

On Christmas Eve Homer's parents drove on slick country roads to pick up Ruth. She spent Christmas Day with the Norris family and caught the last bus to Hannibal that night.

Ruth was back at work on December 27 when Homer's soap box presents reached Guam.

Wed Dec 27
eight oclock

My Darling Wife;

I can never think of any other heading for my letters that suits me better because that's just what you are, my darling wife.

Today I got a package that you sent with candy, crackers, gum & cheese and everything was wrapped separate   honey your so swell to me   I remember as only it was yesterday when we use to wrap presents   I'd hold my finger on the knots when you tied them.

Well the war news sounds a little better now over on the other side, it looks like the boys have really been catching hell over there. The boys in this tent and the one next to ours dug a fox hole today   its one of the best ones in camp. I was working and couldn't help.

I just got off work   have sure been busy. I got six more men today now I have nine men and only one truck   if I could get about twelve more men and a jeep I'd be set to get some work done in a big way By the way Christmas has passed   just another day   I worked just the same but we had a good dinner. We had turkey, dressing almost ever thing a person could ask for.

Honey I'll sign off now with all my love,

your husband
Homer

P.S. I almost forgot to tell you Sunday after noon Johnnie Bybee & James Swon came down so I got the truck and we went to see Rex Peer. All four of us got togeather and had a swell time visiting   just like being in good old Perry but about five thousand miles away from it.

On New Year's Eve Ruth and Homer both went visiting. Ruth arrived in Perry on the 4:30 bus to spend the night at the Norris farm. Homer went to another tent to visit an officer he met on Apamama.

Later that night he reflected back on 1944. A year ago when Homer landed on Apamama he had no idea that he would make hundreds of dollars selling pictures and native souvenirs.

Homer was overseas for Christmas '43 and '44, and he prayed that he'd be home for Christmas '45, but with the world still at war—nothing was guaranteed. All things considered, he felt very grateful. He and Ruth were both healthy; they had a little money in the bank, and were even more in love. After reviewing the trials of 1944 they were ready to look forward and optimistically turned the calendar to January 1945.

The Countdown

"its only EIGHTY EIGHT MORE DAYS until my eighteen months..."

—Homer's letter 1/2/45

Homer ushered in the New Year with a new attitude. For months he had been afraid to think seriously about going home for fear he would jinx it. But once Christmas was over he gave himself permission to start making plans for the future—after the war.

The turning point was signing up for "relief." The Navy allowed men with eighteen months overseas duty to have a thirty-day leave and six months stateside duty. Three months before going stateside men were required to sign up for relief. The military wanted to be sure that another man was trained to take over his responsibilities and allow for a smooth transition. When Homer saw his name on the relief list, the idea of going home seemed real. He got out his 1945 calendar and counted the days until he had eighteen months overseas.

Let the countdown begin. . . .

• 88 Days •

Tues. Jan. 2, 45
eight P.M.

My Darling Wife;
Well it wont be long until I've been in this navy two years   just one more month Feb 2   its only EIGHTY EIGHT MORE DAYS until my

eighteen months then home sweet home, for me. Honey I feel in the loving mood tonight   boy I sure wish I was with you. Oh yes, I put in my name for the relief today   any one with fifteen months over seas duty or more can turn in their names, they figure it takes three months to get relief so that way you will have your relief when the eighteen months is in and that will be April 3   I should be home by my birthday   boy I'll sure be tickled to get to see you

I wonder, while I'm sitting here writting to the one I love, what she's doing at this moment so far apart but yet so close. I sure hope I'm not away from home next Christmas but a person can never tell what will happen. I have to go to print photographs in a few minutes so bye-bye honey.

Love and kisses,
Homer Lee

Back in November Ruth mailed some wrist watches that Homer could sell. She separated them into several packages per Homer's instructions. One package with three watches in it arrived the first week of January.

• 81 Days •

Sat Jan 13
ten thirty

My Darling Ruth Marie,

Honey I got the package you sent with the watches   ever thing was in perfect shape. I sold one of the watches and will sell the others as soon as we have a pay day. Today was sure a lucky day for me   I got three letters from my sweetheart   one of them really put a lump in my chest.

Honey you sure can make love by letter   Its been sort of sad around here today one of the boys that lived with me the last year got word that his father had passed away Jan 1st and the red cross never got him word until today, he's going home now for a few days probably tomorrow. So we made up money for him. I gave ten dollars   we made up around two hundred dollars. That should help out a lot.

I have lost one of my men he got drunk one night took the truck out and tried to out run a jeep fifty miles an hour but didn't succeed. He got a summary court Marshall. I dont know why a person will do a thing like that but I cant see why a person will go to sleep on watch but I did. Cant blame anyone but myself.

Honey just EIGHTY ONE MORE DAYS until my eighteen months are in boy I can hardly wait until I can get home to my darling wife and folks & friends. Darling I'll wire you so you can come to meet me probaly in Kansas City. I think its a good idea for us to spend a few days all by ourselves and let the rest of the world go by. It will be our third honeymoon.

Your husband, Homer

This was the first time Homer mentioned meeting in Kansas City. Ruth loved the idea of a third honeymoon, and immediately started to inquire about hotels in Kansas City.

Now that Homer was counting the days until he came home, she started counting days, too. One thing on her mind was having a baby. Before Homer went overseas they discussed the possibility of getting pregnant and decided to wait until he came back. Eighteen months had passed since then, and Ruth was even more anxious. She wanted to try to get pregnant while he was home on leave. In early January Ruth wrote Homer a letter to re-open the subject of "Junior." When he wrote back to her, Ruth labeled his letter "My Junior Letter" and put it in her scrapbook.

• 70 Days •

Tues Jan 23
Nine P.M.

My Darling Wife;
I have the radio turned on low every one has retired but your love writting to his better half. Honey about this subject Junior do you think

it the proper thing to do now. Have you thought over where you'd stay and how you would spend all your time if I should have to come over seas again, which is very likely. Don't get me wrong darling I want a baby just as bad as you do if not worse. But it is something that should have a lot of thinking over because its such a big undertaking for any woman by her self. Just ask any one that their husband has gone over seas. Be sure to write me what we should do. I know honey my answer has always been, lets wait, but I don't want you to think that I dont want to have any children so I'll leave it up to you this time.

I counted up today and its only SEVENTY MORE DAYS until my time is up and we're almost sure to get back home then.

Nightie night darling, I have got to turn over and you love me to sleep tonight, I loved you to sleep last night. Get up close I'm cold.^{Ha Ha}

Here's a kiss
Homer

• 66 Days •

Sat Jan 27
eight PM

My Darling Wife;

I got a letter from Lecil today. I was so tickled to get one from him   thats (I think) the first one he has witten to me, you know man to man.^{Ha Ha}

Honey I'm so proud of you for getting another raise. You'd better be careful or you'll be running that store and having Mr. Smith working for you.^{Ha Ha} *I love you so much honey.*

I got two swell letters from you today. Honey in one of your letters there was a piece of ribbon with a bow knot tied in it. I just set on the side of my bunk looking at that knot. Know matter how hard you pull it, it gets tied tighter. Thats just the way with our love darling, no matter how far this war pulls us apart the wed lock just gets pulled tighter and when the ends do get back togeather our knot will be pulled so tight it will always be tied.

I love you Ruth, (my wife).

This war cant last forever. The news tonight continued to be good. I can't see how Germany can hold out much longer   The Russians have advanced thirty eight miles in twenty four hours and Germany asking all their population thats able to get arms   it looks like the war in Europe will soon be over as far as the fighting goes.

Wouldn't it be grand if when I did get home or in the States that the war would be over and I wouldn't have to come back out here some place. I know this time what its like and I'm not kidding anyone its just plain hell.

Tomorrow is Sunday 28th, just SIXTY SIX MORE DAYS until my eighteen months are in. It can't be to soon to suit me.

Lots of love, kisses and hugs
Your husband Homer Lee

Homer and his friend Lecil had grown up together. Lecil was one of eleven children and Homer spent half his childhood at the Ulry house playing with the other boys. Three of the Ulry brothers were currently serving in the military: James and Lecil were in the Army and Robert was with the 5th Marine Division stationed on Guam in preparation for the assault on Iwo Jima.

• **59 Days** •

Wed Jan 31
nine olcock

My old lady,

You remember the time I called you that, and it made you soooo mad. ^(Ha Ha) Sweetheart I'm sending the money for the first package you sent. We shouldn't have any reason for not having a wonderful time when I get back. I would sure like to be starting up house keeping again but we can't until this thing is all over.

I just got back from work. A boy in a truck hit one of our telephone poles and broke it off and broke about twenty lines. What a mess   about ten fellows Marines, Army and Navy fixed them for tonight. In the morning we'll have to work on them some more.

This will finish my letter writting for January nineteen hundred and forty five   Tomorrow I'll be starting on my seventeenth month over seas   only have FIFTY NINE DAYS until April and then home sweet home. I hate to wish my life away but I sure wish that time would all fly by some night while I'm asleep dreaming of you Ruth Marie. Nighty night darling,

Hugs & kisses
Homer

In early February Homer was trying to amass another thousand dollars to send home. So far he had saved six hundred, and decided to send it to Ruth for a Valentine's Day surprise. He never mentioned the money in any of his letters, but Homer's ledger book says, "Money Order Feb 7 $600."

The Battle For Iwo Jima

"Out here its each man for himself."

—Homer's letter 2/9/45

Iwo Jima was one of the Pacific Volcano Islands—hilly, rocky, barren with beaches made of volcanic ash. It was a small island only five miles long and two miles wide. However, strategically this tiny island was located half way between the Marianas and Japan, only seven hundred miles from Tokyo. Allied planes could land on Iwo Jima and refuel during bombing missions against mainland Japan.[40]

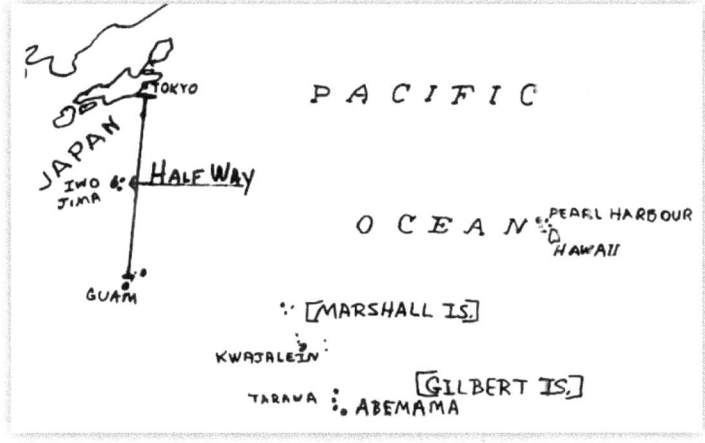

Admiral Nimitz had been preparing for the seizure of Iwo Jima for over a year. The Marine landing force would outnumber the twenty thousand Japanese defenders 3-1. Japan also had a year to plan its defense and had chosen the best strategic location on Mt. Suribachi which dominated the island at 556 feet. Inside Mt. Suribachi the Japanese built a seven-story interior structure full of weapons, ammunition, radios, fuel and sufficient rations to sustain the Japanese troops on the island. Their well-camouflaged facilities were not visible to the pre-invasion planes.[41]

Planners admitted that seizing Iwo Jima would be tough, but calculated the operation should be over in one week or less. No one predicted that this battle would be one for the record books.

D-Day for the invasion of Iwo Jima was 19 February 1945.[42]

The men on Guam knew about the planned attack on Iwo Jima, but were careful not to mention anything that might jeopardize the mission. Several of Homer's friends from home were on Guam training for the invasion. Reconnecting with them made this battle seem more personal.

Fri Feb 9
ten oclock

My Darling Wife;

Its ten thirty now   we just had a practice black out   lasted about twenty minutes. Well honey I had a right good day Sunday. I got a jeep and went up to see Bob Hodges. He was really surpprised to see me. I brought him back to our camp and fed him steaks, fried eggs and ice tea   he said that I would make a good cook for you when I got home.

After supper we went over to see Rex Peer   he looks just like he always did except he's awful poor. He's about six one and I don't expect he will weigh over a hundred and twenty pounds. But I wouldn't tell his mother that he was poor   she might worry.

I got a swell letter from you yesterday and one from my folks. I was sorry to hear about your dad getting his hand hurt but you thought maby I'd worry about it. Honey after a person is out here a while he doesn't worry about any thing like that because we see things like that every day. Men getting their arms broken and cut ever place   it just gets to be part of a days work. The only things boys worry about out here is their loved ones being there waiting for them when we come home. Out here its each man for himself.

I suppose I had just as well stop shooting the bull and get this letter on its way to my lovely wife. Ruth I love you more than anything else in the world, and the world is one hell of a big place. Bye Bye honey.

Your old man,
Homer Lee

46 Days

Even eight thousand miles apart, Ruth and Homer had a good Valentine's Day. Homer got mail call. She received a box of chocolates from Dad Norris, a scarf from Mom Norris, nine Valentines, and a $600 money order from her husband!

In order to keep his mind off the war Homer sat down and made a chart of everything they would need to buy to set up farming and housekeeping after the war. The total cost came to $4674. Today that amount would be over $46,000.

Item	$	¢	No.	Price	Total
Refrigerator	200	00	Cows	3	@ 100.	300 00
Washing Machine	70	00	Sheep	25	@ 10.	250 00
Car	1200	00	Hogs (shoats)	30	@ 5.	150 00
Tractor	1200	00	Sows	3	@ 40.	120 00
Plow	150	00	horses	2	@ 100.	200 00
disc	160	00	hens	50	@ 1.00	50 00
Cultivator	125	00	Chickens	200	@ 12.00	24 00
Harrow	60	00	Geese	50	.20	10 00
Planter	100	00	Heifers	2	50.	100 00
Wagon	125	00	Total			1204 00
rug (wool)	60	00				
Congoleum (2)	20	00				
Total	$3,470	00				

Wed Feb 14
6:50 PM

My Darling Wife;

   Today I began figuring on what we would have to buy to start farming again. I really had a lot of fun. I want to clean and grease my harness too when I'm home. I cant keep from planning, can you?

   Rex Peer was up to see me about two nights ago   we went to the movie and then I took him back. I won't get to see him any more   he's leaving and he's not coming home eather   I feel sorry for him   he's going on twenty eight months overseas   he wants to come home so bad.

   I'll sure be glad when I get to come home   its only FORTY SIX MORE DAYS until I get to see a black-haired, brown-eyed girl back in Missouri. My darling I love you so much   can hardly wait until I can hold you in my arms again. I love you oodles and oodles.

                                  Good night darling
                                  Your husband, Homer

P.S. Happy Valentines Day, Honey

Homer had a really bad feeling about Rex going to Iwo Jima. Rex was with the 3rd Marine Division and had already seen more than his share of battles. The 3rd Div. was to be held in reserve and committed one regiment at a time as needed. Homer prayed they wouldn't be needed.

During the next few days when Homer saw the big ships leaving Apra Harbor he knew his hometown friends were on some of those ships. Everyone on Guam was in a state of high alert and braced for possible retaliation attacks.

• 19-February-1945 •
D-Day on Iwo Jima

On February 19 planes flew continuously from Guam to Iwo Jima providing troop support, so Homer had frequent updates of the battles. Even though Homer wasn't physically on Iwo Jima, he was there emotionally.

The following account of the invasion of Iwo Jima is based on an article written by Lt. Col. Whitman S. Bartley, USMC. Iwo Jima: Amphibious Epic.[43]

During the early morning hours of 19 February 1945 a huge convoy of Marine Attack Forces arrived off the shore of Iwo Jima. This vast armada of 450 U.S. ships was the largest ever assembled for a Pacific operation.

At 0725 hours the launching signal was given. Ninety minutes later the first troop-carrying vehicles waddled up out of the water, lowered ramps and eight thousand Marines of the 4th and 5th Divisions swarmed out of their vehicles and sank ankle deep into the soft volcanic ash.

Jeeps and trucks became bogged down in the sand and the beach soon resembled a salvage yard. The Japanese defenders waited in well-prepared underground positions until the Marines advanced into pre-registered killing zones. Then enemy guns opened fire. As more troops and supplies arrived enemy fire intensified. The whole day was an uneven struggle in favor of the enemy. At 2400 hours D-day finally ended.

Iwo Jima proved to be one of the most impenetrable defenses encountered by the Marines in the Pacific. Thirty thousand American combat troops landed on D-Day and sustained 2,400 casualties in the process.

It didn't take long for news of the battle to reach the papers back home. Ruth knew several home-town boys in the vicious battle and her heart sank when she read the *Hannibal Courier-Post* headline: "3,650 Marines Killed Or Wounded On Iwo Jima."⁴⁴

• **40 Days** •

In mid-February Ruth moved out of the Maryland Apartments and into a house on Tenth Street. She rented by the week so she could go with Homer during his six months of stateside duty. Ruth mailed a sketch of her new place to Homer. He was glad to get her letter because it helped keep his mind off the invasion.

Wed Feb 21
18:20 P.M.

My Dearest Ruth;

Honey I got the sweetest letter from you today. It was the one you sent the drawing of your house your living in   I'm sure glad that you got such a nice place to live in and close to work too. I'm glad you have gotten moved and straighted up.

I sure wish I was there to help   darling I'm so damn home sick. I'll be on my way home in about FORTY DAYS. Do you have a phone now   If not I'll telegram you when I arrive in San Francisco.

I got a letter from Mother & Dad today. They sent me some clippings out of the Enterprise where Bill Sleyster, William Dodge, Bob Davis and John Whalen had been wounded. I know I have been mighty lucky so far. But my lucky day is ahead when I can come home to my loved ones

I'd give anything not to have to come back once I do get home. Its hell out here. Don't ever let any one tell you any different. Its a lot different than most people think. Most of the people think that it's just like you see it in the movies but that's a lot of B.S. spread around.

I'm getting some more help in the next two days about four men I think they will be my relief. Must close for now.

Lots of love, kisses & hugs
Your husband, Homer Lee

By day three the 3rd Marine Division, including Homer's friend Rex, went ashore.[45] The first good news came on day four when the Allies took Mt. Suribachi and raised the American flag atop the highest point on Iwo Jima. However, the celebration was short lived because vicious fighting resumed.

Two weeks passed and the casualty numbers continued to climb, especially among the 5th and 3rd Divisions. Homer prayed that none of his friends were on the casualty lists.

A Little Misfortune

On March 3 Homer broke his finger at work. He didn't want Ruth to know how dangerous his job was, so the story he told her about how the injury occurred differed considerably from the military version.

Mon March 5
10 oclock AM

My Darling Wife;
Day before yesterday I had a little misfortune of breaking the first finger of my right hand between the second and third knuckles. Two of us was playing around a little at noon and the other boy got my finger in a twist, he was sure sorry. I knew it was broke as soon as it poped so I set it myself and went to the sick bay   they took an x-ray of it and put the splints on it.

I never slept any the first night but it didn't hurt me much last night. I think I'll have to keep the splints on for about three weeks. It sure is the first bone I ever had broken.

I wonder about Rex Peer, Bob, James, and Johnnie Bybee. Their are sure catching hell   I know all we can do is hope for the best. I hope the war will soon end. And I can come home and love my wife and raise us some little Norrises.[Ha Ha]

Loads of love,
your old man, Homer

Following is the incident report from Homer's Navy medical records: "While repairing lines on a telephone pole the climber cut out due to a bad place in the pole, slipped and fell until his safety belt took hold. He caught his right index finger between the cable wires, and fractured it." Homer's broken finger would eventually be his ticket home.

While Homer was in pain from his broken finger, Ruth was in good spirits because her boss had taken his employees to the Mark Twain Cave for a picnic! To commemorate the outing, the Kresge girls wrote a thank-you poem to Mr. Smith:

"Boss Smith"
So to our surprise one Day
The Boss to us! Did Say,
"I'm tired of watching you slave
Let's all go down to the cave."
So hamburgers, onions, cookies, and buns
Were packed in the cars almost a ton
We played, we talked, we laughed and we ate,
Till the moon came up and it was getting late
But here's the thing we want most to say
Thank you Boss Smith in a very big way
We think if we looked the whole world round
Not a better Boss in the country could be found.
   — by S.S. Kresge Girls

• **25 Days** •

Fri March 9
3 P.M.

My Darling Wife;

Well I have only TWENTY FIVE MORE DAYS until I should be starting on my way to the girl I love so much. I'll be so glad when we can start our house keeping again, then when we can have some little dirty face Norrises running around.

My finger is getting along fine, its still plenty "fat." I'm afaired I'll have to shake hands left handed.$^{Ha\ Ha}$ I sure hope I can take the splints off before I come home.

Honey I expect I'd better sign off.

Lots of love & kisses, your old man
Homer

Post Script—Iwo Jima

"Just finished a letter . . . extending my sympathy."
—Homer's letter 3/13/45

After three weeks the battle for Iwo Jima still raged with much of the island controlled by the Japanese. Ever since D-Day Homer had not been able to shake a feeling of dread that something awful was going to happen.

On Tuesday, March 13 Homer got a letter from his mother saying that Robert Ulry had been killed on Iwo Jima. Robert was with the 5th Marine Division, 27th Regiment who stormed the beaches on D-day.

Homer had grown up with the Ulry boys, and his heart ached when he wrote to express his sympathies to Mom and Pop Ulry. He promised to come by their house as soon as he got home.

Tues March 13
two P.M.

My Darling Wife;

Just finished a letter to Mr and Mrs Ulry extending my sympathy. I was sure sorry to hear about Roberts death but its a lot better to go fast like he did than to suffer like a lot of the boys are having to do.

Have you heard anything from Rex Peer or James Swon or Bob Hodges they were all up there with Robert.

Now my relief is here and just as soon as my orders come I'll be coming home with bells on and I mean bells.[Ha Ha] *I hope I'm lucky enough to not have to come over seas again   wouldn't that be wonderful*

I sure hope I don't have to write very many more letters. But I know you like to receive mail   even if it doesn't amount to much   its a letter from the one that loves you more than anything else in the world.

Love, Kisses and Hugs,
Your husband, Homer

The invasion of Iwo Jima which was predicted to last one week or less actually lasted thirty-six days and resulted in more than 26,000 American casualties, including 6,800 dead. Of the 20,000 Japanese defenders, only 1,083 survived. Whether it was worth all the casualties is a question for the ages. However, Iwo Jima did provide a vital link in the U.S. chain of bomber bases. By war's end, 2,400 B-29 bombers carrying 27,000 crewmen made unscheduled landings on the island and were very grateful to the men who fought for it.[46]

Part 9: Homeward Bound

Last Letters

"I sit around dreaming of you and what a wonderful time we'll have togeather while I'm in the states."

—Homer's letter 3/19/45

It was typical of the Navy to keep things secretive, so Homer relied on rumors and hearsay to guesstimate when he would leave Guam. An electrician's mate with a broken finger was considered disabled for his rating, and he sensed that he might be one of the first in his group to leave. After writing over 200 letters Homer was tired of putting pen to paper. However, when he wrote the following letter he had no idea it really would be his last letter home.

Mon March 19th
Two thirty PM

My Darling Wife;

    Honey I sure got a swell letter from you yesterday telling me about your new pajamas   I know what we can do with them   one night we'll put them on the head of the bed so I can look at them and the next night we'll put them on the foot of the bed so you can look at them.^{Ha Ha}

    Well I'm still around and haven't heard of any thing for sure. I may get out of here this week if I'm lucky   I think I'll be one of the first ones to leave at least I hope so. I'm so home sick to see you. I don't even want to write at all. I sit around dreaming of you and what a wonderful time we'll have togeather while I'm in the states.

    Darling its all right with me if you don't write but every other night and you don't need to write that often if you don't want to. I know just how you feel about this letter writting   I'm the same way   I'll sure be glad when I can write you saying to not to write any more. Its nearly impossible for me to think of anything to write about   all I want is to have you in my arms.

I know now when and where ever you meet me its going to be embarassing for me because Johnnie is going to jump up and say hello Ruthie my Dear. ^{Ha Ha} *Honey I love you so much. I'm sure looking forward of seeing you. I'll sign off for now. I hope you can read this letter.*

Lots of love, hugs & kisses
Your old man, Homer

Four days later at eleven o'clock Friday night an empty seat was discovered on a plane taking one of the generals back to Hawaii. Homer got word that if he could get to the plane within the hour, he could have the empty seat. So he ran to his tent, grabbed everything he could stuff into his sea bags, and rushed to catch the plane that would take him toward home, sweet home.

A few minutes after midnight on Saturday (24 March 1945) Homer left Guam to island-hop his way across the Pacific—toward home. It was a long flight and Homer recorded the details in his little black book.

		Miles
Left Guam March 24 0045		
Arr Kwa [Kwajalein] *1100*	*Guam to Kwa*	*1570*
Left Kwa 1300	*Kwa to Johnson*	*1300*
Arrived Johnson 2300		
Left Johnson 0000	*Johnson to Pearl*	*750*
Arrived Pearl March 25 0500		
Left Pearl March 26 1700	*Pearl to States*	*2190*
Arr. San Diego April 1ˢᵗ	*Total Miles*	*5810*

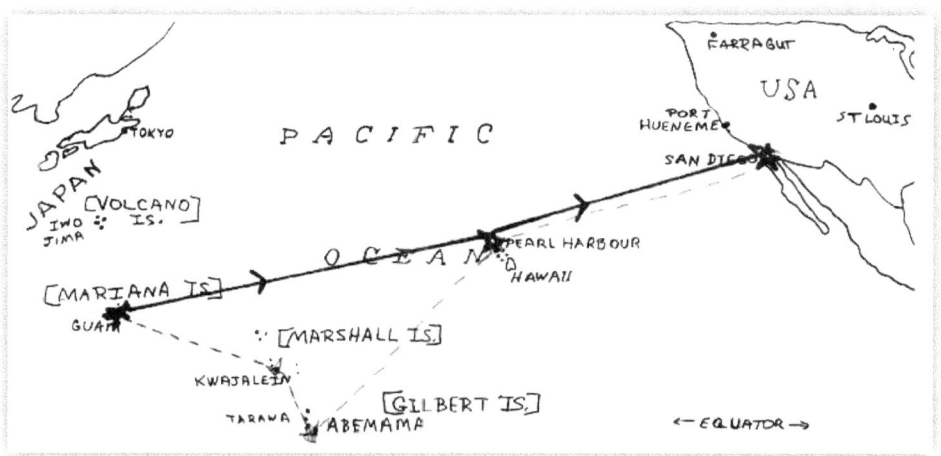

Twenty-eight hours after leaving Guam Homer landed in Pearl Harbor, Hawaii. The next day he left Pearl Harbor aboard a ship—destination San Diego, California. Six days later he set foot on U.S. soil for the first time in seventeen months, three weeks. It was Easter Sunday. The calendar said April 1, 1945, but for Homer this was no April fool's joke; it was one of the happiest days of his life.

* * *

It took Homer eight days to travel 5800 miles from Guam to San Diego. During that time several letters from the folks back home were on the way to Guam. Three letters from Mom and Dad Norris and two from Ruth were eventually returned to Perry and ended up in Ruth's trunk.

Letters From Mom and Dad Norris

"The terrible war is still going on & on. We will surely appreciate Peace when it does come."

—Letter from Mom Norris 3/13/45

While Homer was in the service his mother wrote more than one hundred letters to her only son. Her letters were conversational and she casually switched from one topic to another (weather, local gossip, farm chores, war news). Her pattern was to sit in her rocking chair with the writing tablet nestled in her lap. In the following letter we sense a mother's pride because her son had taken the time to write a sympathy letter to their closest friends.

March 13, 7:30 P.M.

Our Dear Son:

We got a letter from you today so mabe I can write with some satisfaction. We hadn't heard from you for ten days and had began to think you might be steaming across the Pacific. Since I wrote you a wk ago today—a few things have happened.

Mrs Ulry called about 3 o'clock and said they had such a nice letter from you, & were glad to get it. Said she wanted to see you, that mabe you could tell her some things she wanted to know (I suppose about Robert).

On Wed Dad & I went to Hannibal. We took some of Ruths canned stuff, some milk, & cream & eggs. Went home with her at noon. The appartment is real nice. She was so anxious for us to see it. I have been ("cleaning house") kitchen & back porch are all ready for the "prodigal son." ^{Ha Ha}

Just two wks from this Fri is Good Friday. Easter is the first Sunday in April. Hope you are here by then. But why tell you that. I know you will be if you can make it.

How is the finger? I scrubbed a brooder house today. I gathered 179 eggs today, should have found one more to make a ½ case.

We are listening to news. The terrible war is still going on & on. We will surely appreciate Peace when it does come. I'll close for now.

Love & Best Wishes, Mother

From a nearby chair Dad Norris was also writing. His letter echoed hers which is why reading their companion letters always made Homer feel like they were having an actual conversation.

Perry Mo. March 13—1945

Dear Homer:

We are well & I am hauling manure, I have hauled 39 loads to date. I hope to get 50. We had a new pair of lambs yesterday, that makes 47 living & lost 5. Last week was hot 80-85 so I pulled my long underware. I guess this darned war is going on forever, old Hitler said if he went down he would take Germany with him & the Japs is just like killing rats by the millions.

This will be my last letter before you come home. We are looking for you about the 10th of April.

I went to the ration board & asked "if you could get gasoline when you come on furlow?" They said you could get one gallon for each day your furlow called for or 30 days 30 gallon.

It is 8 oclock nite & still raining. There were a few oats sown last week.

I will close for a long time I hope

From your Dad

> **S/SGT. REX PEER WOUNDED**
>
> Staff Sergeant Rex L. Peer of the Third Marines, son of Mr. and Mrs. Rex Peer of this city, was wounded on Iwo Jima, according to a letter received from him on Tuesday morning. The family has never received any notification from the government.
>
> In speaking of his wounds in his letter which was written on March 4th, he said, "Mother, if you get one of those telegrams saying that I've been hit—well, don't go worrying about it because it's just a tiny little scratch. Please believe me. Darned if I'm not kinda ashamed to take it. I wasn't going to say anything about it but they said you'd get the word, so I don't want you worrying about it."
>
> Sgt. Peer also said he was getting his mail. He said, "Around here every morning I wake up I'd think there's going to be snow but not quite. It sure gets plenty cool here at times."
>
> The many friends of Rex are certainly glad he has not been wounded more seriously. No doubt he has been through some mighty tough going on Iwo Jima.

Mom Norris hoped Homer would be home by April 1 for Easter Sunday. Dad thought April 10 was more realistic. Time would tell who the better guesser was.

Before sealing the envelope Mom added a newspaper clipping that she knew would be of particular interest to Homer.[47]

As Mom read the article about Rex she tried to imagine how she would feel if she received word that Homer was wounded. War caused people to pull together and form close-knit communities. When one family received news all the neighbors shared the joy or the tragedy.

Compared to some war-time parents Mom and Dad Norris were fortunate; their son came home from the war. However, three years of constant worry took its toll on them, too.

While he was overseas Homer's parents hid many of their health problems from him. After he got home he was shocked at how much they had changed both physically and emotionally.

When Homer left for the service his mother was fifty-one years old and his dad was sixty-three. During the next three years their health declined dramatically. Homer's mother acquired a permanent nervousness that caused her to gain weight and her blood pressure spiked. She developed problems with her teeth and had to get dentures. A minor foot injury failed to heal properly, and she had one toe amputated.

With Homer gone, the farm work fell to Dad Norris whose back was not up to the task. The strain of trying to maintain the farm brought an onset of stomach ulcers that stayed with him for the rest of his life. Weight loss made him appear frail and old.

While Homer was on Apamama he wrote a letter which said this was a costly war in many ways to some people. He never thought this would apply to his own family. He was saddened to think that worrying about him had cost his parents their vitality.

Homer's parents (Cornelia and Harry Norris)

Letters From Ruth

"You sure are a swell husband. Gee Whiz! Any girl would be so proud to have a man like you."

—Letter from Ruth 3/13/45

When Ruth first moved to Hannibal she was scared spitless at the prospect of living on her own. A new job in a new town and her new role as a Navy wife was a lot of "new." During the next two years Ruth learned to take one day at a time. She realized that as long as she kept her thinking cap on she could take care of herself, manage a lingerie department, and still be a good sailor's wife.

Ultimately, she learned to rely on her own abilities and developed a talent for getting along with people. Her self confidence took a huge leap while she was in Idaho. There were thousands of other Navy wives living in Sandpoint and Ruth worried that she might not fit in. She was pleased to be immediately accepted by the group. It was fun to socialize with the other Navy wives; in fact, she could play pinochle with the best of them.

Upon her return to Hannibal from Idaho she easily transitioned from sales girl to department manager. Ruth even surprised herself when she sold their car for top dollar.

A lot of Ruth's belief in herself came from the support and encouragement of her family. They thought she was fearless when she traveled to Idaho by herself. Ruth and her family were members of their own mutual admiration society. With Homer gone she relied on their emotional support. They took care of her when she had her tonsils out, stored her furniture, and moved her bed and dresser several times. Ruth could always count on her family.

Likewise, she was considerate and thoughtful of her parents, grandparents, uncles, aunts, and Homer's parents, too. She sent cards and letters and called often to check on them. When she came home to visit, Ruth cheerfully milked cows, gathered eggs, dressed chickens, and helped with the canning. In everything she did Ruth exhibited a genuine enthusiasm for life.

Before Homer went overseas he mailed her a Christmas card that referred to her as his helpmate, teammate, and friend. She epitomized all of those roles and many more. Ruth was the kind of wife every man wished for. Her devotion to Homer was undeniable.

Even long distance her spirit helped to strengthen Homer's resolve. A letter from Ruth made even the worst day better because in the letters he could hear her cheerful laugh and feel her tender hugs.

While Homer was in the service she wrote every day to let him know how much she loved him and how proud she was to be his wife. Being separated for two years could have weakened their marriage. Instead, it intensified their love. After writing over 600 letters, following are excerpts from her last letter to *"My Darling Husband."*

Sunday night 8:00
March 18, 1945

My Darling Husband;

You sure are a swell husband. Gee Whiz! Any girl would be so proud to have a man like you. Got a swell letter yesterday from you and two today. Darling, I just love for you to tell me how much you love me and how proud you are of me. Because Homer I am so proud of you.

Called Grandma today to see how they were. She is feeling pretty good. Grandpa is down in his back. She said Uncle Neal & Aunt Grace was coming down tomorrow. Guess they will take our mattress & chair and things back out to Aunt Vivians. Want to get things settled before you get here.

Didn't go out home today. Seems like when Sunday comes I just relax. Sure hate to get up early and catch the bus to Perry. Will write Ma & Pa Norris a letter tonight.

Did a little sewing, ironed and cleaned up the house today. Today has been a beautiful day. Almost to warm for March. Your Dad will be in oat sowing spirits before long. Got some ice cream while we were down town.

Homer am expecting a telegram from you most any day. Am looking foreward to this third wedding trip so much. Have bought some cute things and am making some cute things. Hope you think they are alright.

Homer sweety I love you so much. Wish I could tell you some other way than with a letter, but I know you are more lonesome than me so I just hug my pillow and go on to sleep. Hoping to dream about my Husband who is so far away, but yet so close. It won't be long before we will be together.

Goodnight My Darling
I love you so much
Ruth

Western Union [STOP]

The first week of April was a very long week....

Sunday, April 1: According to Mom's diary, on Easter Sunday the Norris family had "hen & fixins and April showers." Unbeknownst to them while they speculated as to when Homer would get back to the states—he disembarked in San Diego.

Monday, April 2: At the Kresge Store on Monday morning Ruth nearly fainted when a Western Union messenger delivered the following telegram:

Ruth immediately telephoned Homer's parents. That night Mom Norris wrote in her diary, "Telegram from Homer San Diego Calif."

Ruth's prayers had been answered. After not seeing her husband for twenty months, he was only days from being in her arms again. Now it was time to reserve a hotel room in Kansas City for their next honeymoon. On a scrap of paper she scribbled a telegram to the Continental Hotel in Kansas City. Her hand-written rough draft reads,

I would like to make a reservation for a room at your Hotel. My husband is in the service and will meet me in Kansas City this week end. Would want room by Sat night. ~~If unable to~~ If you do not have a room available Please call the President, Phillips, Pickwick or Robert E. Lee and make reservation for me. Wire me as soon as possible between the hours of 8:30 to 5:30 at Kresge Dollar Store Hannibal. Thank You.

Mrs. Homer Norris

Tuesday, April 3: Ruth waited all day for a telegram from either the hotel or from Homer. But no more telegrams arrived on Tuesday.

Wednesday, April 4: Homer was still in San Diego and growing weary of all the military red tape and medical tests. The week dragged on at a snail's pace for Ruth, too as she waited for another telegram.

Thursday, April 5: *The Perry Enterprise* included an article touting Homer's return to the states.[48]

Mr. and Mrs. Harry Norris south of Perry received a telegram from their son Homer Norris, EM2c, early Monday morning which read "Arrived at San Diego Easter Sunday. Will be home in about a week." Homer has been on numerous islands in the Pacific for 18 months and his wife and parents will centainly be glad to see him. His wife, the former Ruth Yancey, resides in Hannibal.

That afternoon a messenger appeared at the store with another telegram for Ruth.

```
MRS HOMER NORRIS=
    KRESGES DOLLAR STORE HANNIBAL MO=
WILL LEAVE HERE FRIDAY (FEB 6) ABOUT NIGHT BY TRAIN SHOULD
BE IN KANSAS CITY SUNDAY NIGHT. IF UNABLE TO MEET ME THERE
ANSWER AT ONCE. LEAVE YOUR HOTEL ADDRESS AT INFORMATION
UNION STATION KANSAS CITY LOTS OF LOVE=
    HOMER NORRIS.
```

In his haste Homer accidentally wrote Friday's date as being in the month of February instead of April, but Ruth didn't even notice. Her eyes only saw the words: "Kansas City Sunday night." That evening as she packed her suitcase a messenger knocked on her apartment house door. Her eyes filled with tears when she read,

```
MRS HOMER NORRIS=
    207 SOUTH TENTH ST HANNIBAL MO=
MY ORDERS HAVE BEEN CHANGED. DONT KNOW WHEN I WILL LEAVE.
WILL WIRE WHEN I FIND OUT I LOVE YOU=
    HOMER NORRIS.
```

Friday, April 6: At the dollar store all eyes were glued to the front door hoping to see the appearance of another messenger boy. Finally, at three o'clock a telegram arrived. Ruth's hands shook as she opened the envelope. She expected the telegram to be from Homer; but it was from the Continental Hotel. As she scanned the short note, her heart sank.

```
COMPLETELY SOLD OUT SATURDAY. NOTHING AT HOTELS MENTIONED=
    HOTEL CONTINENTAL.
```

Minutes before the store closed another telegram arrived.

```
WESTERN UNION

AA9 5
A BYA456 DL PD UD=SANDIEGO CALIF 6 140    1945 APR 6  PM 4 48
MRS HOMER NORRIS=
    CARE OF KRESGES DOLLAR STORE HANNIBAL MO=

AT LAST IM ON MY WAY WILL GET IN KANSAS CITY SUNDAY NIGHT
10 PM UNION STATION LOVE=
    HOMER.
```

Panic gripped Ruth as she realized that Homer was on a train headed for Kansas City, and she didn't have a room for them! She thumbed back through the telegrams searching for a solution to her problem.

At some point Ruth remembered that in her original telegram to the Continental Hotel she had requested a hotel room for Saturday night, and they were sold out. However, Homer wasn't coming in until Sunday.

Saturday, April 7: Ruth hopped out of bed like a woman on a mission. Hers was the first telegram sent from the Hannibal Western Union that day. This time she requested a room for Sunday night, and asked them to contact other hotels if they were sold out. Then she waited for a reply.

We don't know what reply Ruth received from the hotel because her scrapbook doesn't contain any other telegrams. However, the scrapbook does have a receipt from the President Hotel in Kansas City which shows that Mr. and Mrs. Homer Norris spent Sunday and Monday nights there! After twenty months they finally had two whole days when they could be alone and let the rest of the world go by.

The room charge was $5 per night plus $1.16 for one long distance call to Perry. Coincidentally, Mom's diary reads, "Mon April 9, 1945. Homer called from K.C." We can only imagine how she felt when she heard her son's voice for the first time in almost two years!

Memo		Date	Explanation	Amt. Charged	Amt. Credited	Balance Due
	1	APR-8-45	ROOM	* 5.00		* 5.00
Perry Mo	2	APR-9-45	LDIST	* 1.16		* 6.16
	3	APR-9-45	ROOM	* 5.00		* 11.16
	4					
	5					11.39
	6					

GUEST STATEMENT
HOTEL PRESIDENT
KANSAS CITY, MO.
No. **146336**

Furlough

When Homer was still on Guam his dad wrote him a letter that ended with these words: "We are looking for you about the 10th of April." At that time no one—including Homer—knew when he would be home. Sure enough on Tuesday, April 10 Homer's parents picked up Homer and Ruth at the train station and drove them to the Norris farm. The prodigal son was home.

• A Promise Honored •

The next morning Homer went to visit Mom and Pop Ulry to express his sympathies in person.

Together they celebrated Robert's life and reminisced. They shared stories of the boyish pranks Homer and the Ulry boys had played on each other. And they wept together as they spoke of the horrible war that changed their lives forever. Homer told Mom and Pop how proud he was to have known Robert.

Marine Cemetery on Iwo Jima
"PFc ROBT R. ULRY 23 Feb 45, USMC"

When Homer left the Ulry house he promised himself that whenever someone thanked him for his service he would tell them their gratitude should go to the men who were still fighting, and to the memory of those like Robert Ulry who gave the ultimate sacrifice.

• **Homecoming** •

Homer really enjoyed his thirty-day furlough. Everyone wanted to see him and the best part was that everyone wanted to feed him. Time and again Ruth was asked the same two questions: When can you and Homer come to visit?

Homer with catch of the day

What would Homer like to eat? His favorite foods were the order of the day: fried catfish, oysters, gooseberry cobbler, chocolate pie and home-made ice cream.

While Homer ate and fished his way through the month of April, Ruth trained another Kresge girl to take over her job responsibilities. Twenty-five months ago she went to work with the understanding that when Homer came back she would leave her job to be with him. The girls at the store jokingly listed Ruth's mailing address as "wherever the ship docks." So her inevitable departure from the store was expected, but not easy.

The Kresge girls had provided emotional support during the most difficult months of Ruth's life. Even though she was excited about going with Homer, she hated saying good-bye to everyone, including her boss. Mr. Smith had given Ruth a job when others turned her down. He treated her with respect and rewarded her with raises and promotions. Ruth considered Mr. Smith "a mighty good boss," and she had done her best to be a trustworthy employee.

Homer wanted to just forget about the war, but many of his buddies were still overseas. During his furlough he kept close tabs on the news.

> **April 1** - U.S. troops landed on Okinawa.
> **April 7** - U.S. B-29s flew from Iwo Jima on their first mission against Japan.
> **April 12** - President Roosevelt died and Harry S. Truman from Missouri was sworn in as President of the United States.
> **April 30** – Hitler committed suicide. This act brought an end to the terror of the Third Reich.
> **May 8** – VE Day [Victory in Europe] the armed forces of Nazi Germany signed papers of unconditional surrender.
> This marked the end of WWII on the European front.

While military leaders signed papers in France, Homer prepared to report for six months stateside duty. He didn't want to return to active duty, but this time it was easier because Ruth was going with him!

Part 10: Stateside Duty

Atlantic Adventures

Tuesday morning, May 8 Mom and Dad Norris drove Homer and Ruth to catch the train to Norfolk, Virginia.

Three days later Homer was at the Norfolk Receiving Station working through the typical Navy red tape.

During a routine physical examination, doctors discovered that Homer's finger had not been properly set and scheduled further tests.

Ten days later Homer wrote his last entry in his little black book, "May 21, 1945 checked in hospital at NOB (Naval Operating Base) Norfolk."

After a thorough examination Homer was scheduled for reconstruction surgery. On June 1 Mom Norris's diary reads, "Homer finger operated on 10:00 A.M." Ruth documented the day by taking a photo of the Norfolk Naval Hospital.

Norfolk Naval Hospital

Apartment in Norfolk
(front view)

(back view)

The surgery was successful, and while his finger healed Homer worked in the hospital Ship's Service, and toiled at his least favorite job—cleaning window blinds. His splinted finger was perfect for cleaning every slat on gazillions of hospital blinds. After that experience, Homer's hatred for blinds was so intense that for the rest of his life he never allowed any window blinds to be hung in his house.

Homer and Ruth stayed in Virginia the whole summer of 1945. Homer worked on base during the day and every night he took the bus across town to their tiny apartment at 312 W 34th Street.

One photo shows tall wooden steps leading to a small balcony and back entrance on the second story. A couple of white cords are strung across the back of the house from one balcony to the other and on the photograph Ruth wrote, "Irma, Ruth 'our' clothesline."

Irma Combs and her husband Roby were also in Norfolk while Roby was stationed at the Naval Base. The two couples, one from Missouri, the other from North Carolina only lived next door to each other for a few months, however their friendship would last a lifetime.

With thousands of Navy wives looking for work Ruth couldn't find a job, so she took care of their apartment and window-shopped. She didn't have much money, but window-shopping was free.

Homer and Ruth didn't eat out very often. However, they were dumbfounded when some local restaurants refused to serve them. One restaurant window had a sign that read, "No dogs or sailors allowed." That sign insulted Homer and Ruth in a way that was unexplainable; they never forgot it.

Ruth also experienced Norfolk's prejudice against sailors when she tried to cash Homer's paycheck. She and Homer were miserly, but in June they ran out of money a few days before pay day. The morning after Homer got paid Ruth tried to cash his paycheck at several businesses, but the only bank that would cash a Navy paycheck was twenty blocks away in downtown Norfolk. With no money for a cab or bus, Ruth walked all the way to the bank in the stifling heat, cashed the check, and returned home hours later.

That night they ate at a restaurant that welcomed sailors. They hadn't eaten much for a couple of days and ordered so much food that the waitress brought an extra plate because she assumed a third person was joining them. It took them a while, but the two of them ate every crumb.

Homer at restaurant in Norfolk

One good thing about their Atlantic adventure was the Chesapeake Bay Ferry. For only fifty cents per person they enjoyed a four-hour ferry boat ride.

On the front page of the ferry schedule Ruth wrote,

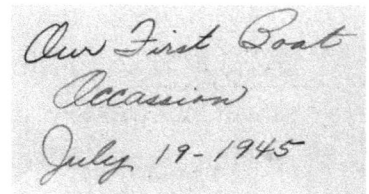

From the deck of the ferry they took a photograph of Ruth's first close-up view of a battleship. The long canon barrel made the ship's purpose very obvious.

One of Homer and Ruth's favorite activities was playing miniature golf at the Ocean View Amusement Park. They had lots of fun, in spite of terrible golf scores. Par for the course was 44. Score cards in her scrapbook show that Homer shot a 74 and Ruth shot 108.

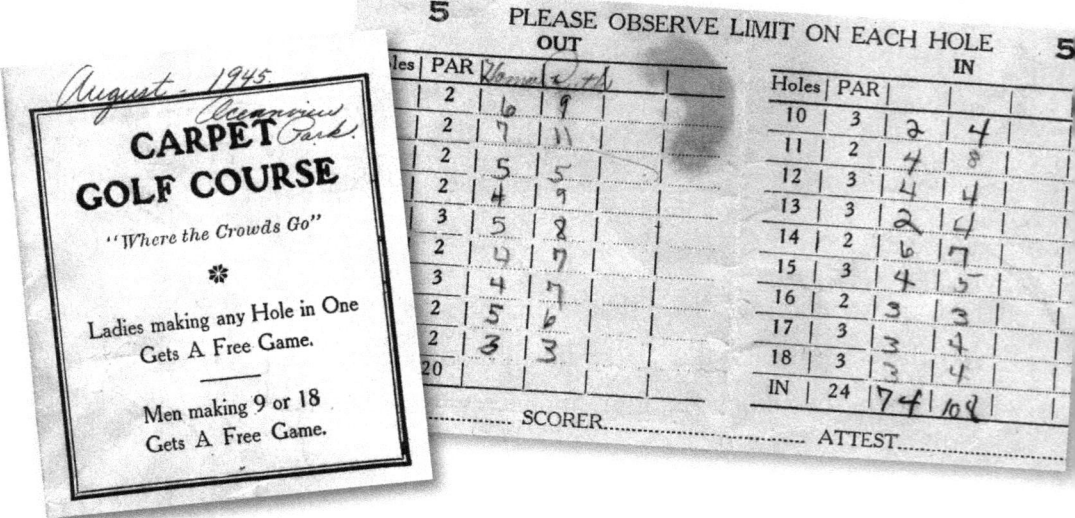

While they were in Norfolk Homer and Ruth saw the Atlantic Ocean for the first time. Ruth couldn't get over the big ocean waves. After spending months surrounded by the Pacific Ocean, Homer was grateful to be looking at the Atlantic, rather than sailing across it.

* * *

In late July tensions continued to build in the Pacific Campaign as the U.S. and Japan prepared for a final showdown. For twenty months the American forces had island-hopped their way across the Pacific and were now within striking distance of the homeland of Japan. On August 6 the U.S. dropped atomic bombs on Hiroshima, Japan. Homer and Ruth vigilantly followed the news, and prayed that this action would bring an end to the war.

However, Japan remained defiant, so on August 9 President Truman authorized the U.S. to drop atomic bombs on Nagasaki. The next day Japan announced its readiness to negotiate for peace. It was three years and eight months after the Japanese attack on Pearl Harbor.

Back in Missouri the Norris family cheered the prospect of peace. Mom's diary reads,

"Aug 14 Tue   WAR OFFICIALLY OVER Listened to radio all aft noon."

On Saturday, September 1, the attention of the nation was on Tokyo Bay for the formal surrender of Japan aboard the battleship USS *Missouri*. Mom Norris wrote in her diary,

"Sept 1 Sat. Listened to signing by MacArthur. Sept 2 Sun. VJ Day." [Victory over Japan Day]

When President Truman announced the peace, a unanimous sigh of relief spread across the U.S.

* * *

Homer and Ruth celebrated by going out for the day to have a little fun. Her exuberant smile is evidence of how happy they were.

Rumors around the base were rampant, and each day more sailors got discharge orders. In anticipation that Homer might soon be discharged, they mailed some of their things home, and moved two blocks down the street to an apartment that rented for eight dollars per week.

Homer's six months of stateside duty was due to end November 3, and the longer he waited for new orders, the more he feared getting sea duty. The war was officially over, but some sailors were shipping out on overseas missions to clean up, rebuild, or maintain the peace.

Homer knew that being in the military meant things can happen fast. On September 13 Homer and Ruth were shopping at the Commissary Store in Norfolk, Virginia. A week later they were 265 miles north in Asbury Park, New Jersey—enroute to the New Jersey Convalescent Hospital. Homer joked that he was going there because the New Jersey Hospital had a lot of blinds that required cleaning. In reality he was being sent there for rehabilitation therapy on his finger. The nature of Homer's injury was listed as "Union Fracture, Faulty Proximal Phlanx Rt. Index Finger."

Three weeks later the Navy released Homer from the hospital with the following notes on his medical record: "Rt index finger has approximately 75% normal flexion—extension is full. Grip good. Good functional hand. Anxious to go to duty. Discharged to duty 10-5-45."

With his therapy complete Homer and Ruth returned to Norfolk and he resumed work in Ship's Service at the Norfolk Hospital. He hoped a crooked index finger might render him too useless for the Navy.

New Orders!

On Monday morning, October 15 Homer showed up for work as usual, but was told to report to his commanding officer. As he stood at attention and waited to hear his fate, Homer tried to appear composed, but his heart pounded in his throat. Homer's new orders were delivered the Navy way—straight forward and to the point. His commanding officer thanked Homer for his service, handed him a piece of paper followed by a heal-clicking salute, and it was over. With his head still spinning, the bus ride back to their apartment was a blur. Reality didn't set in until he saw Ruth's reaction when she read his orders. Tears streamed down her face and her voice cracked as she spoke the words they had dreamed of saying, "discharge orders . . . now we can go home to stay."

The rest of the day Homer and Ruth ran around in a frenzy. They packed, paid bills, and sent a telegram to Homer's folks saying they were **coming home.**

The next morning Ruth kissed her sailor-husband good-bye for the last time, because she knew when they saw each other again Homer would be a civilian.

Homer boarded a train heading to the 9th Naval District Headquarters in Great Lakes, Illinois to begin the demobilization process.

    A friend drove Ruth to the train station in a luxurious Packard. She was leaving Norfolk in style!

    On the train ride home Ruth's mind flipped between remembering events of the past three years and looking to the future. When Homer joined the Navy, Ruth never dreamed that she would get to travel to Idaho, Virginia, and New Jersey. Living in Sandpoint had felt like home because the community welcomed sailors and their families.

    While they were stationed on the east coast, it was thrilling to have boating occasions on the Chesapeake Bay and see the Atlantic Ocean. However, some people in Virginia and New Jersey were disrespectful to sailors. Dealing with their negative attitude made Ruth homesick.

    Both Homer and Ruth were ready to put the war behind them and start a new life. Ruth was especially excited about getting their furniture out of storage and setting up housekeeping. She was a little nervous about the prospect of living with family members until they could find a place of their own.

Her heavy suitcase filled with souvenirs from Norfolk reminded Ruth of the many boxes of souvenirs from the islands. Each item Homer mailed home helped her see the war through his eyes. Some wives were disgusted when they received pictures of topless natives, but not Ruth. She saved every picture of island natives, tropical scenery, Navy buddies, even Bob Hope. But Ruth didn't just save photographs; she documented their whole war experience in photo albums and scrapbooks to safeguard their memories. Unknowingly, she created a legacy for future generations.

Ruth and Homer had matured while he was in the Navy, and would start the next phase of their lives with much more self-assurance and determination. As the train rolled along Ruth sat with her fingers habitually touching the beautiful gold locket Homer had sent to her before he went overseas.

Now that they had survived World War II, she felt like they could live through anything as long as they were together. She was right.

After three days on the train Ruth deboarded in St. Louis, and took the bus to Mexico. That night Mom Norris wrote in her diary, "<u>Oct 19 Fri</u> Ruth come @ 2 P.M. We to church."

Demobilization

• Saturday, October 20 •

At the Great Lakes Naval Headquarters Homer tediously filled out stacks of paperwork. It was almost as much trouble to get out of the Navy as it had been to get in. Finally Homer dotted all the i's and crossed all the t's to the satisfaction of the U.S. Navy.

• Sunday, October 21 •

Homer mailed his duffle bag home—at the Navy's expense. On the line for 'Date' he wrote "demobilization." As he filled out the shipping tag he remembered the many pictures and souvenirs he had shipped from Apamama. The mail really had been his lifeline to home.

Unlike many families who grew apart during the war, his family was more close-knit now than when he left. As Homer had written to Ruth in his letter of January 27, 1945: "no matter how far this war pulls us apart the wed lock just gets pulled tighter . . ."

• Monday, October 22 •

Monday night Homer boarded the train for his last ride as a sailor. On his way to St. Louis Homer reflected on the past three years. His journey began in February of 1943 when he boarded the train at Union Station in St. Louis to go to boot camp. Since then the Navy had moved him sixteen times: Missouri — > Idaho — > Missouri — > Idaho — > California — > Hawaii — > Apamama — > Kwajalein — > Guam — > Hawaii — > California — > Missouri — > Virginia — > New Jersey — > Virginia — > Illinois — > Missouri. Homer crisscrossed the United States and several Pacific Islands and finally came full circle back to Union Station in St. Louis where his World War II journey would end.

• Tuesday, October 23 •

On Tuesday Homer deboarded in St. Louis.

• Wednesday, October 24 •

Wednesday night while he sat in his room anticipating his discharge ceremony the next day, Homer struggled to make peace with his personal war experience. For the first time in years he allowed himself to believe that he might finally be able to go back to civilian life. He thought about Roscoe Gibbs, Harold Rhodes, Elmer Hull, Rex Peer, Bob Hodges, James Swon, Johnnie Bybee, Robert Ulry, and all the other boys from Perry who grew up together and went to the same war but had such different experiences. Try as he might he simply could not explain why some died and others survived.

He finally decided that a large part of surviving war is just plain luck. He was one of the lucky ones because at the end of the war **he came home**.

• D-DAY (Discharge Day) •
Thursday, October 25, 1945

Thursday afternoon Electrician's Mate 2/C Homer Lee Norris stood at attention on Lambert Field in St. Louis and was honorably discharged from the United States Navy. It was two years, eight months and twenty-three days since he had taken the Oath of Enlistment.

As far as Homer was concerned, World War II ended when he walked off Lambert Field with his discharge papers in hand. From that day forward Homer never talked about the war. He never spoke of the Farragut Naval Training Station and his boot camp experience. He never mentioned his training in California, or the things he saw in Pearl Harbor. He never talked about the Pacific Islands or mentioned Josefo or even his tent mates: Houck, Patterson, Mertz, or Minkler. He felt that talking about his war experience was somehow disrespectful to the memory of Robert Ulry and thousands like him who would never come home.

In the life story of Homer Norris the chapter titled "World War II Navy Years" was finished.

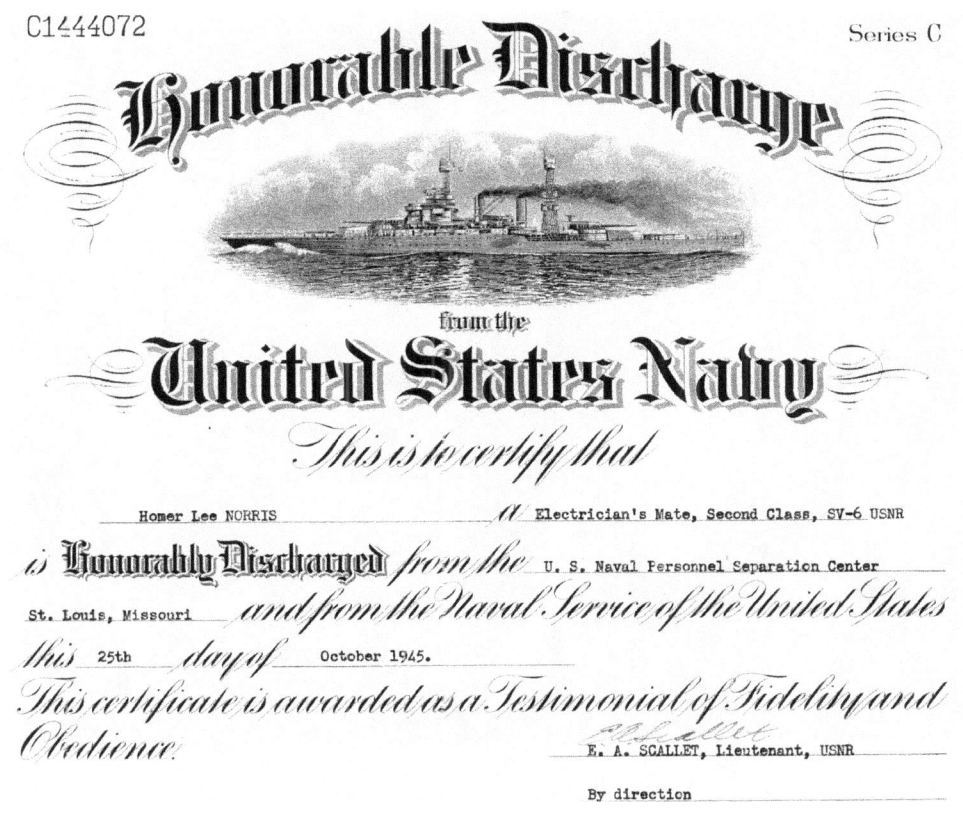

The November 15, 1945 edition of *The Perry Enterprise* had an article about Homer under the section "Servicemen Are Coming Home From Overseas." According to the article: Homer Norris EM2c, son of Mr. and Mrs. Harry Norris arrived home October 25th with his discharge, received at Lambert Field, St. Louis. . . .

Homer spent 20 months overseas. He left the States in October, 1943 and went to Pearl Harbor for six weeks. He spent 11 months in the Gilbert Islands, just 27 miles off the equator . . . Homer was in a communications outfit which set up telephone lines and switchboards . . . He was at Kwajalein in the Marshalls for six weeks and then headed for Guam . . . He had been stationed at Norfolk, Va. since May. His wife, the former Ruth Yancey, was with him at Norfolk.[49]

Part 11: Home, Sweet Home

Coming Home

"Moved to our new home at Laddonia."

—Ruth's diary 12/26/45

History books would record several significant events in World War II:
December 7, 1941—Japanese attack on Pearl Harbor
May 8, 1945—Victory in Europe Day
September 2, 1945—Victory over Japan Day

However, the most important day for the Norris family was October 25, 1945 when Homer came home from the war.

This homecoming was different; there was no picnic in the park, no big to-do. Homer's attitude was different, too. From the minute he arrived home all he wanted to do was slip quietly back into civilian life and begin the next chapter of his life with Ruth.

Homer had only been home for two days when they started looking for a farm to rent. Homer and Ruth had hoped to buy a small farm of their own after the war. Unfortunately, while they were saving money the price of land escalated. For the time being they would have to be content to rent and not own.

Four weeks later the Norris family celebrated Thanksgiving while gathered around a table filled with turkey and all the trimmings. They gave thanks for Homer's safe return, and remembered those who did not come home from the war. Homer and Ruth also prayed that they would find a nice farm to rent.

They truly believed their prayers would be answered, but didn't expect the answer to come so soon. Two days after Thanksgiving they rented a farm—five miles from Homer's parents—which made it conveniently close, but not too close.

The next morning Homer woke at dawn, went to the barn, and began cleaning his harness. To Homer, oiling his harness was symbolic of being ready to farm—and that was his dream. Only thirty days after his discharge he had packed away his Navy uniform, rented farm land, and oiled the harness. Homer Norris—son, husband, and farmer—was back home, and ready to farm.

* * *

The month of December was a blur of activity as Homer and Ruth prepared to set up housekeeping. Homer and his dad attended local auctions and bought cows, calves, sheep, and farm equipment. Each day when he and Ruth went to feed and water the livestock they moved furniture and supplies into their farm

house. They painted several rooms, raked the yard, burned trash, and didn't even notice that the temperatures were below zero. Without their own car or truck, they had to rely on others for transportation so it took longer than either of them would have wished.

After spending two Christmases apart, they savored every part of the holiday season. They wrapped presents, decorated the Christmas tree at Mom and Dad

Norris's house, and looked forward to having a tree in their own house the next year.

On Christmas Day Ruth's family came to the Norris home for turkey dinner and spent the day. It truly was a Christmas to remember.

The day after Christmas Ruth's diary reads, "*26 Dec 1945 Moved to our new home at Laddonia.*" It was three years—to the day—since Homer got his notice to report for military service. The whirlwind of war had picked up Homer and Ruth, spun them around for three years, and dropped them back down just miles from where they started.

Physically Homer and Ruth were relatively unchanged, but there were long-lasting emotional changes brought about by the war. After rationing for several years, they continued to save every scrap of paper, every tiny piece of aluminum foil, every empty plastic container or milk jug. Ruth found the most creative uses for silk stockings because they were too valuable to ever throw away. Homer utilized his Navy electrician's training to install lights in his farm buildings. He attended welding school on the G.I. Bill and used his welding skills to build farm wagons and keep his machinery in good repair.

The Final Chapter

It was five years before Homer and Ruth had any little Norris babies. In 1950 Marsha Lee was born; Howard Russel arrived in 1955.

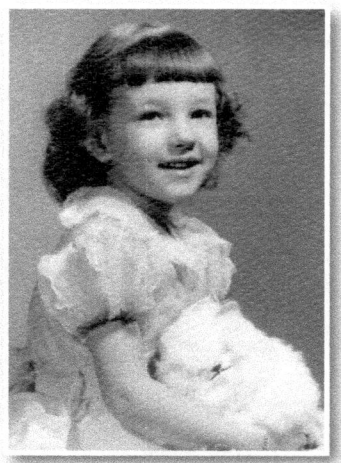
Marsha Lee Norris

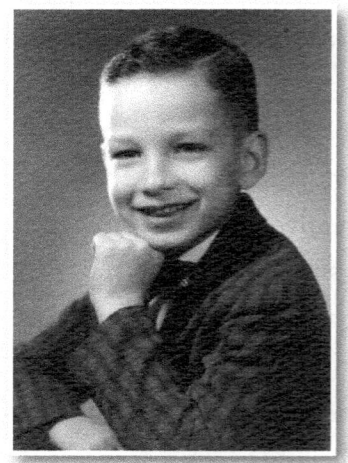
Howard Russel Norris

Oil painting of Norris farm.

Twelve years after the war Homer and Ruth finally realized their dream of owning a farm. In 1957 they bought a 160-acre farm with a farmhouse, garage, big red barn, hen house, and storage shed. They lived on their farm for the rest of their lives.

In 1991 Homer and Ruth celebrated their Golden Wedding Anniversary commemorating fifty years of marriage. Later that fall the whole family posed for a photograph.

Norris family in 1991.
(Left to right) Kevin Norris (grandson of Homer and Ruth, son of Howard and Kathy), Marsha Norris Knudsen (daughter), Ron Knudsen (husband of Marsha), Ruth and Homer, Howard Norris (son), Kathy Norris (wife of Howard), Rob Norris (grandson of Homer and Ruth, son of Howard and Kathy).

In May of 2004 Homer was honored at the grand opening of the Ralls County Historical Society Museum. The local newspaper pictured him standing next to his Navy uniform which is part of the museum's World War II exhibit. It was a privilege for Homer's family to see him recognized for his service. Even Homer was moved by the tribute.

Homer and Ruth Norris, former residents of the Perry area, pose with window display of their life which had been in Ralls County Historical Society Library/Museum window.

Homer and Ruth's World War II experience caused them to appreciate the simple things in life and cherish each day they were together. The war also instilled in them an unwavering patriotism and respect for the American flag. For the remainder of their lives they endeavored to be good citizens, helpful neighbors, and first-class parents—and they were!

Homer Lee Norris (1920-2005)   Ruth Marie Yancey Norris (1922-2008)

Once upon a time in Ralls County, Missouri "a most attractive and charming young lady" named Ruth Marie Yancey met Homer Lee Norris, "an industrious and likeable young man." They fell in love, married, survived World War II, raised two children on their family farm . . . and lived happily ever after.

Their love story lasted through sixty-three years of marriage. Homer left this earthly life in 2005 at the age of eighty-four. Three years later Ruth passed away at the age of eighty-five.

* * *

Epilogue

Everyday Heroes

My parents never thought of themselves as heroes, but they were. They were everyday heroes who spent their lives trying to do the right thing.

In some respects their World War II experience is personal, but in many ways their story is representative of a whole generation of Americans who selflessly did their part to help the cause.

- These everyday heroes patriotically rose to the occasion—because it was the right thing to do.
- Homer volunteered for the service and Ruth went to work at the store—because it was the right thing to do.
- They used ration coupons, bought war bonds, and donated blood to the Red Cross—because it was the right thing to do.
- There were thousands of Americans just like them who planted victory gardens and donated food and supplies to the USO, who met troop trains at trackside canteens and held homecoming picnics to honor returning veterans—because it was the right thing to do.

I am the keeper of my parents' war-time memories. Every day I remember my mother and father who are **my** heroes.

If you are the keeper of your family memories, treasure them, and share the stories so future generations will know about the ancestors they will never meet.

Why? **Because it's the right thing to do**.

Endnotes

[1] Lewis, Jone Johnson. "Women and World War II-Women at Work. Women's History-Comprehensive Women's History Research Guide. 15 April 2009 http://www.womenshistory.about.com/od/warwwii/a/women_work.htm.

[2] "Popular Young Couple Married." *The Perry Enterprise* 7 Aug. 1941: 1. Print.

[3] "Popular Young Couple Married."

[4] "Pearl Harbor, Day of Infamy." Web. 29 Nov. 2013 http://www.military.com/Resources/HistorySubmittedFileView?file=history_pearlharbor.htm.

[5] Glans, Roger E. *Farragut Naval Training Station*. Athol, Idaho: Farragut State Park. 1992: 5-6. Print.

[6] Glans, Roger E. 1992: 8.

[7] Glans, Roger E. 1992: 14.

[8] *The Bluejackets' Manual*. Eleventh Ed. Annapolis, Maryland: U. S. Naval Institute, 1943: 21. Print.

[9] "The Origins of Navy Terminology." [Mobile Riverine Force Association] Web. 22 Mar. 2013 http://mrfa.org/navyterms.htm.

[10] "WORLD WAR II USO." Web. 17 Sep. 2009 http://www.beau.org/~velmer/local/uso.html

[11] "At the Movies." *SANDPOINT SHOPPING BULLETIN* 10 June 1943: 3. Print.

[12] "Navy Wives Meet." *SANDPOINT SHOPPING BULLETIN* 29 July 1943: 4. Print.

[13] "Expect Farragut to Really Come to Town Sunday." *SANDPOINT SHOPPING BULLETIN* 1 July 1943: 1. Print.

[14]"Fifty Couples Dance to Navy Orchestra." *SANDPOINT SHOPPING BULLETIN* 6 May 1943: 4. Print.

[15]"100's of New Reduced Prices at Safeway." *SANDPOINT SHOPPING BULLETIN* 12 Aug. 1943:1. Print.

[16]"World's Busiest Highway." [Brochure Advertisement]. Association of American Railroads Time Schedule, 1945. Print.

[17]United States. Department of the Navy NAVFAC Historical Program. *Declassified Naval Documents.* 2005. Print.

[18]"V-Mail, The Wonder of WWII." Web. 8 Dec. 2013 http://www.postalmuseum.si.edu/exhibits/2d2a_vmail.html

[19]Furlong, USN Rear Admiral William R. "Your Navy in Action: Pearl Harbor." *PICTORIAL HISTORY of the SECOND WORLD WAR* 1946: Davies, Al E., ed. Vol. 6. New York: Wm. H. Wise, 1946. 64. Print.

[20]"Operation Galvanic: The Battle for Tarawa November 1943." Web. 29 Nov. 2013. http://www.historyofwar.org/articles/battles_tarawa.html

[21]"Attack on the Gilbert and Marshall islands." Web. 17 Mar. 2004 http://www.us.reocities.com/Pentagon/3758/gilbert.htm

[22]Davies, Al E., ed. *PICTORIAL HISTORY of the SECOND WORLD WAR.* Vol. 3. New York: Wm. H. Wise. 1944. 1089. Print.

[23]Photo of SS *Robin Wentley.* Web photo. 29 Nov. 2013 http://www.photoship.co.uk/JAlbum%20Ships/Old%20Ships%20R/index18.html

[24]"Harney, Will. "Battel of Tarawa Facts." Web. 8 Dec. 2013 http://www.worldwar2facts.org/battle-of-tarawa.html

[25]Davies, Al E., ed. 1944. 1031.

[26]Tolbert, Sgt. Frank X. "APAMAMA, A model operation in miniature." [Special issue newspaper distributed to troops in Pacific Campaign]. 1945. Print.

[27]United States. Department of the Navy NAVFAC Historical Program. *Declassified Naval Documents.* 2005. Print.

[28]"Building the Navy's Bases Online: Apamama in the Gilberts." Web. 29 Nov. 2013 http://www.microworks.net/pacific/bases/html

[29]"Building the Navy's Bases in World War II." Web. 26 Jan. 2009 http://www.ibiblio.org/hyperwar/USN/Building_Bases/bases-27.html

[30] "Building the Navy's Bases Online: Apamama in the Gilberts."

[31] Hickman, Kennedy. "World War II: Battle of Kwajalein." Web. 22 Mar. 2013 http://militaryhistory.about.com/od/worldwarii/p/kwajalein.htm

[32] Hickman, Kennedy.

[33] "Building the Navy's Bases Online: Bases in the Central Pacific." Web. 25 Feb. 2010 http://microworks.net/pacific/bases

[34] Davies, Al E., ed. 1944. 1037.

[35] Hickman, Kennedy.

[36] CPA Variety Show "YANK LOOKS OVER THE GILBERTS." *YANK* [Newspaper distributed to troops in Pacific Campaign]. 1944. Print.

[37] Cunha, John P. "What Is Dengue Fever?" Web. 8 Dec. 2013 http://www.medicinenet.com/dengue_fever

[38] Building the Navy's Bases Online: Bases in the Central Pacific."

[39] "War In The Pacific—Guam." [National Park Service, U. S. Department of the Interior] Web. 29 Nov. 2013 http://www.pacificwrecks.com/airfields/marianas/orote/index.html

[40] Schmidt, USMC Lieutenant General Harry. "Your Navy in Action: The Battle for Iwo Jima." *PICTORIAL HISTORY of the SECOND WORLD WAR* 1946. Davies, Al E., ed. Vol. 6. New York: Wm. H. Wise, 1946. 323. Print.

[41] "Battle for Iwo Jima, 1945." [The Navy Department Library]. Web. 24 May 2012: http://www.history.navy.mil/library/online/battleiwojima.htm

[42] Alexander, Colonel Joseph. "Battle of Iwo Jima." Web. 6 Dec. 2013 http://www.ibiblio.org/hyperwar/USMC/USMC-C-Iwo/index.html

[43] Bartley, Lt. Col. Whitman S. (1945). "Iwo Jima: Amphibious Epic." *USMC Historical Monograph.* [Historical Section Division of Public Information]. Web. 24 May 2012 http://www.ibiblio.org/hyperwar/USMC/USMC-M-IwoJima.html

[44] Dopking, Al. U. S. Pacific Fleet Headquarters, Guam. "3,650 Marines Killed Or Wounded On Iwo Jima." *Hannibal Courier-Post.* 21 Feb. 1945: 1. Print.

[45] "Battle for Iwo Jima, 1945."

[46] "Battle for Iwo Jima, 1945."

[47] "S/SGT. REX PEER WOUNDED." *The Perry Enterprise* 15 Mar. 1945. Print.

[48] "Our Men in The Service." *The Perry Enterprise* 5 Apr. 1945. Print.

[49] "Our Men Are Coming Home from Overseas." *The Perry Enterprise* 15 Nov. 1945. Print.

Works Cited

Alexander, Colonel Joseph. "Battle of Iwo Jima." Web. 6 Dec. 2013
http://www.ibiblio.org/hyperwar/USMC/USMC-C-Iwo/index.html

"Attack on the Gilbert and Marshall islands." Web. 17 Mar. 2004
http://www.us.reocities.com/Pentagon/3758/gilbert.htm

Bartley, Lt. Col. Whitman S. (1945). "Iwo Jima: Amphibious Epic." *USMC Historical Monograph*. [Historical Section Division of Public Information]. Web. 24 May 2012 http://www.ibiblio.org/hyperwar/USMC/USMC-M-IwoJima.html

"Battle for Iwo Jima, 1945." [The Navy Department Library]. Web. 24 May 2012 http://www.history.navy.mil/library/online/battleiwojima.htm

The Bluejackets' Manual. Eleventh Ed. Annapolis, Maryland: U. S. Naval Institute, 1943. Print.

"Building the Navy's Bases in World War II." Web. 26 Jan. 2009
http://www.ibiblio.org/hyperwar/USN/Building_Bases/bases-27.html

"Building the Navy's Bases Online: Apamama in the Gilberts." Web. 29 Nov. 2013 http://www.microworks.net/pacific/bases/html

"Building the Navy's Bases Online: Bases in the Central Pacific." Web. 25 Feb. 2010 http://microworks.net/pacific/bases

CPA Variety Show "YANK LOOKS OVER THE GILBERTS." *YANK* [Newspaper distributed to troops in Pacific Campaign]. 1944. Print.

Cunha, John P. "What Is Dengue Fever?" Web. 8 Dec. 2013
http://www.medicinenet.com/dengue_fever

Davies, Al E., ed. *PICTORIAL HISTORY of the SECOND WORLD WAR*. New York: Wm. H. Wise. 1944. Print.

Dopking, Al. U. S. Pacific Fleet Headquarters, Guam. "3,650 Marines Killed Or Wounded On Iwo Jima." *Hannibal Courier-Post.* 21 Feb. 1945: 1. Print.

Furlong, USN Rear Admiral William R. "Your Navy in Action: Pearl Harbor." *PICTORIAL HISTORY of the SECOND WORLD WAR* 1946: Davies, Al E., ed. Vol. 6. New York: Wm. H. Wise, 1946. 64. Print.

Glans, Roger E. *Farragut Naval Training Station.* Athol, Idaho: Farragut State Park. 1992. 5-14. Print.

Harney, Will. "Battle of Tarawa Facts." Web. 8 Dec. 2013 http://www.worldwar2facts.org/battle-of-tarawa.html

Hickman, Kennedy. "World War II: Battle of Kwajalein." Web. 22 Mar. 2013 http://militaryhistory.about.com/od/worldwarii/p/kwajalein.htm

Lewis, Jone Johnson. "Women and World War II-Women at Work. Women's History-Comprehensive Women's History Research Guide. 15 April 2009 http://www.womenshistory.about.com/od/warwwii/a/women_work.htm

"Operation Galvanic: The Battle for Tarawa November 1943." Web. 29 Nov. 2013 http://www.historyofwar.org/articles/battles_tarawa.html

"The Origins of Navy Terminology." [Mobile Riverine Force Association] Web. 22 Mar. 2013 http://mrfa.org/navyterms.htm.

"Pearl Harbor, Day of Infamy." Web. 29 Nov. 2013 http://www.military.com/Resources/HistorySubmittedFileView?file=history_pearlharbor.htm.

The Perry Enterprise 7 Aug. 1941, 11 Feb. 1943, 1 July 1943, 19 Aug. 1943, 15 Mar. 1945, 5 Apr. 1945, 15 Nov. 1945, Print.

Photo of SS *Robin Wentley.* Web photo. 29 Nov. 2013 http://www.photoship.co.uk/JAlbum%20Ships/Old%20Ships%20R/index18.html

SANDPOINT SHOPPING BULLETIN. 6 May 1943, 10 June 1943, 12 Aug. 1943, 1 July 1943, 29 July 1943, Print.

Schmidt, USMC Lieutenant General Harry. "Your Navy in Action: The Battle for Iwo Jima." *PICTORIAL HISTORY of the SECOND WORLD WAR 1946.* Davies, Al E., ed. Vol. 6. New York: Wm. H. Wise, 1946. 323. Print.

"Somebody Blabbed/Button Your Lip!" [Brochure Advertisement]. Northern Pacific Passenger Train Schedule. 20 June 1943. 43. Print.

Tolbert, Sgt. Frank X. "APAMAMA, A model operation in miniature." [Special issue newspaper distributed to troops in Pacific Campaign]. 1945. Print.

United States. Department of the Navy NAVFAC Historical Program. *Declassified Naval Documents.* 2005. Print.

"V-Mail, The Wonder of WWII." Web. 8 Dec. 2013 http://www.postalmuseum.si.edu/exhibits/2d2a_vmail.html

"War In The Pacific—Guam." [National Park Service, U. S. Department of the Interior] Web. 29 Nov. 2013 http://www.pacificwrecks.com/airfields/marianas/orote/index.html

"World's Busiest Highway." [Brochure Advertisement]. Association of American Railroads Time Schedule, 1945. Print.

"WORLD WAR II USO." Web. 17 Sep. 2009 http://www.beau.org/~velmer/local/uso.html

**Links cited were valid at the time this information was compiled, however, due to the changing nature of the Internet some links may have changed. Use your Internet search engine if link is no longer valid.

About the Author

Marsha Norris Knudsen (daughter of Homer and Ruth) is an educator, historian, and public speaker. She holds a Bachelor's Degree in Education and a Master's Degree in Speech and Dramatic Art from the University of Missouri. During her career Marsha taught English, creative writing, public speaking and acting. For twenty-five years she and her husband worked together in their portrait studio business.

Marsha's passion for history has inspired her to create and present numerous programs for schools, civic organizations, and conferences. Dressed in costume she has brought history to life in presentations about women of the past including Susan B. Anthony--"The Woman Who Dared."

Marsha now hopes to encourage others to create a legacy for future generations by preserving their own family histories.

Please visit her website: www.sailorsmail.net

www.ingramcontent.com/pod-product-compliance
Lightning Source LLC
Chambersburg PA
CBHW081125170426
43197CB00017B/2759